The Fantastic Fifties
COOKBOOK

1,000 CLASSIC RECIPES BY
MARY MARGARET McBRIDE

TO STELLA
whose book this is,
with love

The Fantastic Fifties Cookbook
1,000 Classic Recipes by Mary Margaret McBride

Mary Margaret McBride
Revised and Updated by Steve Chadde

ISBN: 979-8869031624

Recipes from *The Fantastic Fifties Cookbook* originally appeared in *Mary Margaret McBride's Harvest of American Cooking*, published in 1956 by G. P. Putnam's Son, New York. The original book is now in the public domain.

Foreword

THE FANTASTIC FIFTIES COOKBOOK is a complete collection of well-tested recipes compiled by Mary Margaret McBride during the course of her long career as a journalist and radio personality. The recipes capture the essence of the 50's decade in America, with women (primarily) being charged with buying, and sometimes growing, food for their family, and preparing daily meals and hosting get-togethers with relatives and friends. Included in the book are a wide-ranging variety of recipes, using readily available ingredients, each provided with succinct yet detailed instructions to follow. From appetizers to drinks, main courses, vegetables, and desserts, you will find them here. We hope that you enjoy making and eating these creations as much as we have!

Mary Margaret McBride was a successful radio commentator and journalist, reaching the height of her popularity in the twenty year period between 1935 to 1955. During the course of her daily radio program, she interviewed over 1,200 people, ranging from fan dancer Sally Rand to President Harry Truman. She refined a unique, unscripted interview style noted for its folksy ease and informality which enabled her to skillfully draw out spontaneous, revealing responses from her guests.

Copies of her recordings are now archived in the Mary Margaret McBride Collection at the Library of Congress. The recordings contain hundreds of interviews with leading public and political figures of her time: entertainers, other radio personalities, authors, educators, doctors, adventurers, restaurateurs, and average folks who had interesting stories to tell.

Her subjects provide a highly personal perspective on American life during the dramatic and quickly changing years from the Great Depression through World War II, its aftermath, and the beginning of the Cold War. A brief list of her interview personalities include Eleanor Roosevelt, Governor Thomas E. Dewey, Frank Lloyd Wright, Bob Hope, Carl Sandburg, Margaret Bourke-White, Zora Neale Hurston, Tennessee Williams, and Joe DiMaggio. Her program offered an alternative to afternoon soap operas and demonstrated that women's interests were broader than household cleaning tips and food recipes. McBride maintained complete editorial and commercial control over her program and in doing so made lasting changes in the style of radio talk shows.

Mary Margaret McBride graduated from the University of Missouri School of Journalism in 1919, and began broadcasting for WOR in New York in 1934. Her show attracted millions of listeners, mostly women, with her personal confessions and interviews with noted personalities of the day. She also wrote for such magazines as *Cosmopolitan*, *The Saturday Evening Post*, and *Good Housekeeping*, authored a newspaper column for The Associated Press, and wrote numerous books including *How Dear To My Heart* in 1940. She authored two cookbooks including *Harvest of American Cooking* (1956, and the basis for this book) and *Encyclopedia of Cooking* (1960). McBride passed away on April 7, 1976.

Contents

Mary Margaret McBride (1899-1976)

Introduction

WHEN I was a young, green Middle Westerner newly come to New York and scared of my shadow, my intrepid friend Estella Karn —lately come, too, but from California—taught me to eat in twenty-eight languages. The woman actually knew restaurants in the city that served authentic food of that many countries.

I had plenty of misgivings at first but, almost before I knew it, began to take a reporter's interest if not unbounded eating pleasure in such unfamiliar items as sharkfin soup, grape leaves stuffed with pine nuts and currants, fried bean flour bread, sour cream soup, snails, broiled eels and tamales.

Since then, I've eaten my way appreciatively across America, collecting recipes discriminately and pounds rather less so. I treasure hundreds of ancient "receipts," mostly in spidery handwriting on yellowed bits of paper: Cousin Belle's Unfailing Rule for Green Tomato Ketchup handed down by her English greatgrandmother; Mrs. Meredith's Moonshine (a dessert not a drink) that has descended from Welsh ancestors; Aunt Jacynthia's Dutch Flansjes.

Estella Karn kept insisting through the years that I ought to do a cookbook which would show the role of food in our history. I kept protesting, contending that I would rather show my appreciation of American food by eating it than writing about it. But because I have a weakness for trying anything once— even such atrocities as chicken fried in egg batter, and com bread with sugar in it—I finally did begin the well-nigh impossible task of writing the history of America in its foods.

Four years later I realize that to do justice to the subject would consume not alone my lifetime but the lifetimes of a staff of researchers as well. The experience has also caused me to feel impassioned about the admirable men and women who came to this country to start life over again, bringing with them among their dearest possessions the recipes for the dishes of their homelands. And now, though I know some may scold me because of omissions they consider important, I am glad I have attempted to tell the story of America through its foods. However, I am not promising to teach how to cook in fifty or sixty languages. There are plenty of descriptions of odd, even outlandish dishes and gargantuan banquets that are fun to read about, but which Im sure no cook in her right mind would want to reproduce in this diet-conscious, vitamin-aware age. Yet here I have tried to tell about those marvels of delight that each group has created out of a faraway past in the new, magnificent America that surrounded them.

When I did a television show from the 1956 Kitchen of Tomorrow, I found myself dialing for a recipe that was promptly flashed on a small screen in front of my eyes, drying dishes by sound waves, measuring ingredients by a "magic eye," viewing a push-button refrigerator which obligingly turned one side of itself outdoors so as to be convenient for the delivery boy. Later I saw an electric oven that bakes a layer cake in three minutes and cooks a five-pound roast of beef in thirty. And we are all bombarded constantly with news of dehydrated steaks, faster mixes, even food squeezed from tubes for the nurture of helmeted adventurers rocketing into outer space.

So you may ask: Why a cookbook at all in such times?

Well, I recently came on a consumer survey which reported that in the midst of this mad whirl of no-hands cooking, the sale of baking powder has increased substantially! Which proves what I have always believed—that nothing will ever surpass light-as-air biscuits made from scratch, served hot from the oven with butter melting in their tender little hearts, just as no satisfaction will ever equal the joy a woman finds in setting those biscuits and other delicious products of her own skill before her family.

So in the twenty-first century I predict that women will still be swapping recipes and pridefully bringing to their tables magnificent pies or cakes, at sight of which families and guests will gasp, "And to think you made it all yourself!"

ACKNOWLEDGMENTS

Many have helped with this book, but I want to mention especially Estella Karn, Janice Devine, Helen Josephy Robison, and Gloria Marshall, whose wonderful efforts were far beyond the call of duty. Bless them.

Appetizers

HORS D'OEUVRES

NUTTY HORS D'OEUVRE

1 cup shelled pecans
1 cup shelled almonds
1 cup shelled filberts
2 tablespoons olive oil
2 drops garlic extract

Arrange nuts in shallow baking pan. Combine oil and garlic extract; let stand 20 minutes. Combine nuts and oil mixture; mix lightly. Bake in moderate oven (325° F.) 10 minutes. Makes 2 cups.

SALMON-CHEESE CANAPES

1 7-ounce can salmon
1 8-ounce package cream cheese
3 tablespoons mayonnaise
½ cup chopped celery
¼ teaspoon salt
½ teaspoon prepared mustard
2 tablespoons chopped parsley
16 slices bread
Parsley

Drain fish and flake. Blend cheese and mayonnaise. Stir in fish, celery and seasonings. Remove crusts from bread. Cut each slice into 3 strips and toast. Spread salmon on toast strips. Garnish with parsley. Makes 48.

BOLOGNA CANAPES

½ pound bologna
2 hard-cooked eggs, chopped
1 tablespoon chopped pimiento
2 tablespoons minced green pepper
Salad dressing
Toast rounds

Chop bologna; add eggs, pimiento, green pepper and enough salad dressing to moisten. Spread on toast rounds. Makes about 24.

MARINATED CAULIFLOWER

½ cup French dressing
2 tablespoons lemon juice
1 tablespoon grated onion
2 cups raw cauliflowerets

Combine dressing, lemon juice and onion. Add cauliflowerets and chill thoroughly. Drain. Makes about 18.

STUFFED EGG SPECIAL

6 hard-cooked eggs
2 tablespoons sour cream
¼ cup chopped liverwurst
1/8 teaspoon salt

Cut eggs in half, lengthwise, and remove yolks. Mash egg yolks with sour cream, liverwurst and salt. Fill whites with yolk mixture. Serve as appetizers. Makes 12.

BROILED CHEESE APPETIZERS

1 cup grated American cheese
1 tablespoon chopped chives
2 tablespoons mayonnaise
Crackers

Combine cheese, chives and mayonnaise. Spread on crackers. Broil 3 or 4 inches from source of heat 3–5 minutes. Makes about 24.

GULF SHRIMP BALLS

2 cups sifted all-purpose flour
3 teaspoons baking powder
¼ teaspoon salt
1/8 teaspoon paprika
1 egg, beaten
1 cup milk
1½ cups cooked chopped shrimp

Sift flour with baking powder, salt and paprika. Combine egg and milk; add to sifted ingredients and mix until blended. Add shrimp and mix lightly. Drop by tablespoonfuls in deep hot fat (375° F.) and cook until browned on all sides. Drain on absorbent paper. Makes about 24.

BAKED ROLL-UPS

1 recipe plain pastry
1 cup grated sharp cheese
2 tablespoons chopped chives
1/8 teaspoon paprika
1/8 teaspoon salt

Roll pastry out on lightly floured surface to 1/8" thickness. Cut into strips 1x4 inches. Combine cheese, chives, paprika and salt. Sprinkle cheese mixture over pastry and roll up jelly-roll fashion. Seal edges. Place on greased baking sheet. Bake in hot oven (400° F.) 10-12 minutes, or until slightly browned. Makes about 42.

HOT TUNA STICKS

1 cup flaked, cooked tuna
1 tablespoon grated onion
1 teaspoon Worcestershire sauce
Mayonnaise
4 slices buttered bread
1/4 cup grated Swiss cheese

Combine tuna, onion, Worcestershire sauce and enough mayonnaise to moisten. Spread tuna mixture on bread slices. Top with cheese. Cut bread slices into 4 strips. Broil 3 or 4 inches below source of heat about 3 minutes, or until cheese is melted. Makes 16.

CHEESE AND PARSLEY BALLS

1/2 cup American cheese spread
2 tablespoons crumbled blue cheese
1 teaspoon grated onion
2 tablespoons chopped nuts
Mayonnaise
Chopped parsley

Combine cheeses, onion, nuts and enough mayonnaise to moisten. Shape into small balls and roll in parsley. Makes about 12.

HOT SWISS CANAPES

1 tablespoon all-purpose flour
1¼ cups grated Swiss cheese
1¼ teaspoon paprika
1/8 teaspoon salt
1 tablespoon chopped stuffed olives
2 tablespoons chopped walnuts
1 egg white

Combine flour, cheese, paprika, salt, olives and walnuts. Beat egg white until stiff and fold into cheese mixture. Shape into small balls. Fry in deep hot fat (370° F.) about 1-2 minutes, or until lightly browned on all sides. Drain on absorbent paper. Makes about 12.

ANCHOVY CANAPES

1/4 cup cream cheese
1 tablespoon chopped parsley
Crackers
2 hard-cooked eggs, sliced
1 can anchovy fillets

Combine cheese and parsley. Spread cheese mixture on crackers. Top with egg slices and anchovies. Makes about 12.

TOMATO-OLIVE APPETIZERS

4 small tomatoes
1/4 cup chopped stuffed olives
1 tablespoon salad oil
2 tablespoons vinegar
1 tablespoon chopped parsley
1/2 teaspoon salt

Remove stem ends from tomatoes. Scoop out pulp leaving shell about 5i" thick. Combine tomato pulp, olives, oil, vinegar, parsley and salt. Fill tomato shells with olive mixture. Makes 4 servings.

STUFFED CELERY

1 8-ounce package cream cheese
1 tablespoon chili sauce
1 tablespoon sour cream
8 celery stalks (approx.)

Combine cream cheese, chili sauce and sour cream. Beat until light and fluffy. Fill celery stalks with cheese mixture. Chill. Cut into 2" pieces if desired. Makes about 8 stalks.

STUFFED WALNUTS

¼ cup cream cheese
1 tablespoon chopped parsley
1 cup walnut halves

Combine cheese and parsley. Spread cheese mixture over half of walnuts. Top with remaining walnuts. Makes about 12.

SAUSAGE WITH OLIVES

1 can cocktail sausages
1 cup large stuffed olives (approx.)

Broil sausages 3 or 4 inches from source of heat for about 5 minutes, or until browned on all sides. Arrange sausages with olives on toothpicks. Makes about 12.

PICKLED HERRING

2 medium-sized salt herring
1 cup vinegar
½ teaspoon pepper
2 tablespoons sugar
6 peppercorns, crushed
¼ cup minced onion

Soak herring several hours. Drain and remove skin and bones. Add remaining ingredients and chill several hours. Makes 6 servings.

SWISS CHEESE CUBES

1 cup Swiss cheese cubes (½-inch cubes)
¼ cup salad dressing (approx.)
2 tablespoons chopped chives

Dip cheese cubes in dressing and roll in chives. Place on toothpicks. Makes about 18.

COCKTAIL OLIVES

1 cup stuffed olives
1 cup ripe olives
½ cup French dressing
1 clove garlic, peeled

Combine all ingredients. Cover and chill several hours. Drain and serve. Makes 2 cups.

ANCHOVY APPETIZERS

2 hard-cooked egg yokes, sieved
12 boneless anchovy fillets

Sprinkle egg yolks over anchovy fillets. Serve with shredded lettuce, as desired. Makes 4 servings.

PROSCIUTTO AND MELON

1 medium-sized cantaloupe
¼ pound thinly sliced prosciutto

Peel cantaloupe. Cut into slices ¼" thick. Remove seeds. Arrange cantaloupe slices and prosciutto on serving plates. Makes 4 servings.

BOLOGNA CORNUCOPIAS

12 slices bologna
12 sweet gherkins

Roll bologna slices into cornucopias and fasten with toothpicks. Fill cornucopias with pickles. Makes 12.

SYRIAN SALAMI KABOBS

1 cup salami cubes (½-inch cubes)
¼ cup small stuffed olives
¼ cup pickled onions

Alternate salami, olives and onions on toothpicks. Makes about 12.

GARLIC RIPE OLIVES

1 can ripe olives
2 cloves garlic, peeled
¼ teaspoon salt

Combine olives, olive liquid, garlic and salt. Cover and chill several hours; drain.

SPREADS

LOX AND EGG SPREAD

½ pound smoked salmon, ground
2 hard-cooked eggs, chopped
1 tablespoon chopped chives
Salad dressing

Combine salmon, eggs and chives. Add enough salad dressing to moisten. Makes about 1½ cups.

LIVER AND MUSHROOM SPREAD

1 cup cooked chicken livers, chopped
½ cup cooked mushrooms, chopped
1 hard-cooked egg, chopped
2 tablespoons chopped parsley
Salad dressing

Combine livers, mushrooms, egg, parsley and enough salad dressing to moisten. Makes about 1½ cups.

MEXICAN CHEESE SPREAD

1 cup yellow cheese, grated
1 cup sour cream
¼ cup milk
2 tablespoons grated onion
1 tablespoon chopped parsley

Combine all ingredients and mix well. Makes about 2½ cups.

ONION AND EGG SPREAD

¼ cup chopped onion
4 hard-cooked eggs, chopped
¼ teaspoon salt
2 tablespoons chopped parsley
Mayonnaise

Combine onion, eggs, salt and parsley. Add enough mayonnaise to moisten. Makes about 1 cup.

ALMOND CHEESE SPREAD

1 8-ounce package cream cheese
¼ cup chopped toasted almonds
2 tablespoons salad dressing
¼ teaspoon salt

Combine all ingredients and mix well. Makes about 1¼ cups.

BLUE CHEESE-ONION SPREAD

1 cup crumbled blue cheese
2 tablespoons grated onion
2 tablespoons mayonnaise or sour cream

Combine all ingredients and mix well. Makes about 1¼ cups.

SARDINE-OLIVE SPREAD

1 4-ounce can sardines, drained and mashed
¼ teaspoon Worcestershire sauce
1 tablespoon lemon juice
2 tablespoon chili sauce
¼ cup chopped stuffed olives

Combine all ingredients and mix well. Makes about ¾ cup.

STUFFED OLIVE SPREAD

½ cup chopped stuffed olives
1 cup softened butter
1/8 teaspoon pepper
1 tablespoon grated onion
1 teaspoon vinegar
1 tablespoon chopped parsley

Combine all ingredients and mix well. Spread on hot French bread for appetizers, as desired. Makes about 1¼ cups.

PECAN APPETIZERS

1/3 cup cottage cheese
1 tablespoon mayonnaise
½ cup chopped pecans
1/8 teaspoon salt
1/8 teaspoon Tabasco
1/8 teaspoon onion salt

Combine all ingredients. Serve on crackers, as desired. Makes about 2/3 cup.

SALMON-PICKLE SPREAD

1 cup cooked, flaked salmon
2 tablespoons chopped parsley
¼ cup chopped mustard pickles
Mayonnaise

Combine salmon, parsley, pickles and enough mayonnaise to moisten. Makes about 1¼ cups.

AVOCADO-OLIVE SPREAD

1 cup mashed avocado
2 tablespoons lemon juice
½ teaspoon grated lemon rind
½ cup chopped stuffed olives

Combine all ingredients and mix well. Makes about 1½ cups.

CHEDDAR CHEESE SPREAD

1 jar Cheddar cheese spread
1 tablespoon grated onion
2 tablespoons mayonnaise
1 tablespoon chopped parsley

Combine all ingredients and mix well. Makes about ¾ cups.

TURKEY SPREAD

1 cup cooked ground turkey
¼ cup chopped celery
¼ cup chopped cucumber
French dressing

Combine turkey, celery, cucumber and enough dressing to moisten. Makes about 1½cups.

WATER CRESS SPREAD

1 8-ounce package cream cheese
¼ cup chopped water cress
1 teaspoon grated onion
2 tablespoons mayonnaise

Combine all ingredients and mix well. Makes about ¾ cup.

DIPS AND DUNKS

AVOCADO DIP

1 medium-sized avocado
¼ cup chili sauce
1 tablespoon grated onion
1 tablespoon lemon juice

Cut avocado in half lengthwise. Remove pulp; reserve shells. Mash pulp and add chili sauce, onion and lemon juice. Fill shells with pulp mixture. Serve with crackers, as desired. Makes about 1 cup.

CHEESE AND CARROT DUNK

2 cups cottage cheese
¼ cup salad dressing
1 teaspoon Worcestershire sauce
½ cup grated carrots
2 tablespoons chopped green pepper
¼ cup grated radishes
¼ teaspoon salt

Combine all ingredients and chill. Makes about 2¾ cups.

CHIVE AND PARSLEY DUNK

1½ cups sour cream
½ cup chopped chives
¼ cup chopped parsley
½ cup chopped green pepper
2 tablespoons prepared horseradish
¼ teaspoon salt

Combine all ingredients and chill. Makes about 2¼ cups.

CLAM DIP

1 cup cottage cheese
1 7-ounce can minced clams, drained
2 tablespoons chopped chives
½ teaspoon paprika

Combine all ingredients and mix well. Serve with crackers and potato chips, as desired. Makes about 1½ cups.

CURRY CHEESE DIP

1 cup cottage cheese
½ cup grated cucumber, drained
1/3 cup salad dressing
2 tablespoons light cream
1 teaspoon curry powder
½ teaspoon salt

Combine all ingredients and chill. Makes about 1½ cups.

ROQUEFORT DIP

1 cup cottage cheese
½ cup Roquefort cheese
2 tablespoons grated onion
¼ cup sour cream

Combine all ingredients and mix well. Makes about 1¾ cups.

Beverages

COLD DRINKS

GINGER GRAPE JUICE

2 whole cloves
½ small stick cinnamon
3 tablespoons lemon [uice
3 tablespoons sugar
1 quart grape juice
2 cups ginger ale

Tie spices in cheesecloth. Add lemon juice, sugar and grape juice and cook over low heat 15 minutes. Chill thoroughly. Just before serving, add ginger ale. Serve with ice. Makes 6–8 servings.

NECTAR PUNCH

½ cup sugar
¾ cup light corn syrup
1 cup water
1/8 teaspoon cinnamon
4 thin lemon slices
½ cup currant jelly
3 cups apricot nectar
2/3 cup lime juice

Boil sugar, syrup, water, cinnamon and lemon slices together 5 minutes. Remove from heat and remove lemon slices. Beat in jelly with rotary beater. Add nectar and lime juice, blending well. Chill. Serve in chilled glasses. Makes 4–6 servings.

ORANGE NOG

4 eggs, beaten
¼ cup sugar
1 1/3 cups orange juice
2 cups milk
Nutmeg

Combine eggs, sugar and juice. Beat until well blended. Pour into 4 glasses. Fill glasses with milk. Sprinkle with nutmeg. Makes 4 servings.

GRAPEFRUIT-ORANGE SHAKE

2 cups orange juice
2 cups grapefruit juice
2 cups milk
¼ teaspoon salt
¼ teaspoon vanilla
¼ cup sugar
1 cup cracked ice

Combine all ingredients and shake until thoroughly blended. Serve immediately. Makes 6–8 servings.

SPICY BANANA MILK SHAKE

4 cups milk
4 bananas, mashed
2 tablespoons lemon juice
¾ teaspoon cinnamon
¼ teaspoon nutmeg
3 tablespoons sugar
1 pint vanilla ice cream

Combine ingredients; beat well. Pour into glasses and serve immediately. Makes 6–8 servings.

GOLDEN NECTAR

4 eggs, separated
3 cups grapefruit juice
1 cup orange juice
¼ cup honey
1/8 teaspoon salt

Beat egg yolks until thick. Gradually add fruit juices, beating constantly. Add honey and salt; beat well. Beat egg whites until stiff. Fold into grapefruit-juice mixture. Pour into chilled glasses. Makes 4–6 servings.

CONCORD GRAPE PUNCH

2 **cups grape juice**
2 **cups water**
1/3 **cup lemon juice**
½ **cup orange juice**
½ **cup sugar**

Mix ingredients. Allow to stand until sugar is dissolved. Serve over ice. Makes 6-8 servings.

RASPBERRY REFRESHER

2 **cups sugar**
3 **cups boiling water**
1½ **cups red raspberries**
2 **cups orange juice**

Dissolve sugar in water. Mash berries. Combine all ingredients and chill 2 hours. Strain and pour over ice. Makes 6-8 servings.

CHERRY BING

2 **cups juice from canned Bing cherries**
1½ **cups water**
½ **cup orange juice**

Mix ingredients. Pour over cracked ice in glasses. Makes 6 servings.

FRESNO APRICOT COOLER

2 **cups apricot nectar**
¾ **cup orange juice**
3 **tablespoons lemon juice**
2 **tablespoons granulated sugar**
2 **cups ginger ale**

Stir nectar, fruit juices and sugar together until sugar is dissolved. Chill. Just before serving, add ginger ale. Makes 6 servings.

ORANGE MILK SHAKE

1½ **cups chilled orange juice**
1 **tablespoon lemon juice**
¼ **cup sugar**
2 **cups cold milk**

Mix orange juice, lemon juice and sugar. Stir fruit-juice mixture slowly into milk. Shake and serve at once. Makes 4 servings.

HOT DRINKS

VERMONT MAPLE NOG

1/3 **cup maple syrup**
1/8 **teaspoon salt**
3 **egg yolks, well beaten**
2 **cups milk**
½ **cup heavy cream, whipped**
1/8 **teaspoon ginger**

Combine syrup, salt, egg yolks and milk. Beat until blended with rotary beater. Pour into glasses. Combine cream and ginger. Top each serving with cream. Makes 4 servings.

SAMARKAND HOT TEA PUNCH

½ **cup sugar**
½ **cup water**
1 **2-inch stick cinnamon**
2 **teaspoons grated lemon rind**
¼ **cup orange juice**
2 **tablespoons lime juice**
¼ **cup pineapple juice**
3 **cups boiling water**
3 **tablespoons tea leaves**

Combine sugar, water, cinnamon and lemon rind. Simmer 5 minutes. Remove cinnamon. Add fruit juices. Meanwhile pour boiling water over tea leaves; let stand 3 minutes. Strain tea into hot fruit-juice mixture. Serve hot. Makes 6-8 servings.

CAFÉ BRULOT

1-inch **stick cinnamon**
8 **whole cloves**
3 **lumps sugar**
3 **jiggers brandy**
3 **cups strong coffee**

Place cinnamon, cloves and sugar in chafing dish. Place brandy in large ladle; ignite brandy and pour over sugar mixture. Ladle until sugar is dissolved. Gradually add coffee, ladling until flames fade. Serve immediately. Makes 6-8 servings.

FIRESIDE CIDER CUP

1 **quart cider**
1/3 **cup sugar**
2 **3-inch cinnamon sticks**
12 **whole cloves**

Combine all ingredients. Heat to boiling point. Chill several hours. Remove spices. Heat and serve. Makes 6-8 servings.

DRINKS FOR A CROWD

GALA APPLE PUNCH

1½ quarts apple juice
2 quarts ginger ale
Lemon slices
Green and red maraschino cherries

Chill apple juice and ginger ale. Combine. Pour into punch bowl over ice cubes. Garnish with lemon slices and cherries. Makes 24 servings.

BOG CRANBERRY PUNCH

2½ cups fresh cranberries
2 cups water
1 cup sugar
2 cups apple juice, chilled
1 cup cranberry juice
½ cup lemon juice, chilled
1 cup canned pineapple cubes
1 quart ginger ale

Combine cranberries, water and sugar. Cook over low heat until tender. Strain and chill. Add cranberry mixture to remaining ingredients. Chill. Makes 25 servings.

EGG NOG

1 dozen eggs
2 1/3 cups super fine sugar
2 cups brandy
1 cup Jamaica rum
1 cup peach brandy
1 quart milk
1 quart heavy cream

Separate eggs. Beat sugar into egg yolks. Slowly stir in liquors. Add milk. Beat heavy cream and fold in. Beat egg whites and fold in. Makes about 30 servings.

FESTIVAL PUNCH

2 quarts ginger ale
1 quart hulled strawberries
1 cup sliced bananas
2 cups pineapple juice
1 cup orange juice

Combine all ingredients. Serve over ice. Makes 18–20 servings.

FISHHOUSE PUNCH

1¾ cups sugar
2 quarts water
1 quart lemon juice
2 quarts rum
1 quart brandy
½ cup peach brandy

Combine sugar and 2 cups water. Stir until sugar is dissolved. Add remaining ingredients and mix well. Pour punch over ice. About 42 servings.

PIE PLANT PUNCH

4½ cups diced rhubarb
1 quart water
¾ cup sugar
¼ cup orange juice
3 cups pineapple juice
12 fresh orange slices

Combine rhubarb and water. Simmer 20 minutes; strain. Add sugar and stir until sugar is dissolved. Add orange juice and pineapple juice. Chill thoroughly. Garnish with orange slices to serve. Makes 12 servings.

PINEAPPLE PUNCH

2 cups sugar
1 cup water
1 cup strong tea
2 cups pineapple syrup
¾ cup lemon juice
2 cups orange juice
2 cups pineapple juice
Ice water
½ cup pineapple chunks
½ cup maraschino cherries
1 quart ginger ale

Boil sugar and water 5 minutes; add tea, pineapple syrup and fruit juices. Let stand 30 minutes and add enough ice water to make 1½ gallons. Add pineapple, cherries and ginger ale. Serve in punch bowl Makes 44 servings.

Soups

HOT SOUPS

ARIZONA BEAN SOUP

1 cup garbanzas (pinto beans)
1 quart cold water
2 green onions, chopped
1 clove garlic, chopped
2 teaspoons chili powder
1 teaspoon oregano
1 teaspoon salt
Dash cayenne pepper
1½ cups beef broth or bouillon

Soak garbanzas in water overnight. Drain and add cold water. Simmer 4–6 hours, adding water as needed, until garbanzas are tender. Add onions, garlic, chili powder, oregano, salt and cayenne pepper; cook until onions are tender. Rub through colander. Add broth or bouillon. Heat to serving temperature. Serves 6.

MANHATTAN CLAM CHOWDER

¼ pound salt pork, diced
2 medium-sized onions, chopped
2 carrots, diced
1 green pepper, chopped
2 large potatoes, diced
½ cup chopped celery
½ cup chopped parsley
1 10-ounce can minced clams
2½ cups tomatoes
2 cups water
2 teaspoons salt
½ teaspoon black pepper
½ teaspoon paprika

Fry salt pork in large kettle until crisp. Remove pork from kettle. Add onions, carrots, green pepper, potatoes, celery and parsley to pork drippings and cook until onions are tender. Add clams, saving the liquor. Add tomatoes, water and seasonings. Simmer 1 hour. Add clam liquor and heat to serving temperature. Serves 6.

STOCKYARD CHOWDER

¼ pound salt pork
½ pound veal, ground
½ pound beef, ground
2 carrots, chopped
½ cup diced celery
1 medium-sized onion, chopped
1½ cups tomato paste
1 teaspoon salt
⅛ teaspoon pepper
¼ cup rice
1½ quarts boiling water
2 cups cubed potatoes

Cook salt pork until browned. Remove pork. Brown veal and beef in pork fat. Add carrots, celery, onion, tomato paste, salt, pepper, rice, salt pork and water. Heat to boiling point. Simmer, covered, 1 hour. Add potatoes and cook, covered, 15–20 minutes or until potatoes are tender. Serves 6–8.

HARVEST GOLD SQUASH SOUP

1 cup light cream
4 cups milk
1 tablespoon chopped chives
1 bay leaf
2 cups cooked sieved squash
1 cup diced cooked celery
3 tablespoons butter or margarine
3 tablespoons all-purpose flour
1 teaspoon salt

Combine cream, milk, chives and bay leaf; heat to boiling point. Add squash and celery and mix well. Melt butter or margarine and blend in flour and salt. Gradually add milk mixture and cook over low heat, stirring constantly, until thickened. Remove bay leaf. Serves 6.

QUICK TOMATO BOUILLON

2½ cups tomato juice
1 tablespoon orange juice
1 teaspoon grated orange rind
½ teaspoon salt
1/8 teaspoon pepper
1 teaspoon grated onion
1 teaspoon chopped chives
¼ teaspoon Worcestershire sauce

Combine all ingredients and heat to serving temperature. Serves 4-6.

CHICKEN HAM CHOWDER

3 cups cooked, diced chicken
2 cups cooked, diced ham
1 large onion, chopped
3 tablespoons butter, melted
1/8 teaspoon thyme
2 tablespoons chopped parsley
1 quart water
2 quarts chicken stock
1 bay leaf, crushed
1 red pepper, chopped
2 teaspoons salt
2 cups cooked shrimp
1 tablespoon chili powder
1 cup cooked rice

Cook chicken, ham and onion in butter until onion is tender. Add thyme, parsley, water, chicken stock, bay leaf, red pepper and salt. Simmer, covered, for 1 hour. Add shrimp, chili powder and rice. Heat to serving temperature. Serves 8-10.

MONTANA BARLEY BROTH

½ cup barley
1 quart boiling water
2 quarts chicken broth
½ cup finely diced turnip
½ cup peas
½ cup diced celery
½ cup diced onions
½ cup diced carrots
2 teaspoons salt

Combine barley and water. Cover and cook over low heat until barley is tender. Drain. Add remaining ingredients. Cover and cook over low heat until vegetables are tender. Serves 8.

JERSEY CREAM OF TOMATO SOUP

2 tablespoons butter
2 tablespoons all-purpose flour
2 cups milk
1 teaspoon celery seed
2 tablespoons chopped onion
2 cups tomato juice
1 teaspoon salt Sour cream

Melt butter and blend in flour. Gradually add milk, and cook, stirring constantly, until thickened. Combine celery seed, onion and tomato juice. Heat to boiling point and strain. Gradually add tomato mixture to white sauce, stirring constantly. Add salt. Heat to serving temperature, stirring constantly. Pour into serving dishes. Top with sour cream. Serves 6-8.

TURTLE SOUP

1 medium-sized turtle
1 tablespoon butter
1 onion, chopped
2 cloves garlic
2 tablespoons all-purpose flour
1 No. 2 can tomatoes, drained
1 bay leaf
2 quarts boiling water
¼ teaspoon salt
¼ teaspoon black pepper
1/8 teaspoon cayenne pepper
3 sprigs parsley
1 tablespoon chopped dill
2 slices lemon
2 hard-cooked eggs

Clean turtle and cut in small pieces. Melt butter; add onion and garlic; brown. Add flour, stirring constandy. Add turtle meat, tomatoes and bay leaf. Stir constantly 10 minutes. Add boiling water, salt, black pepper and cayenne pepper. Cook over low heat about 2½ hours or until turtle meat is very tender. Add parsley, dill and lemon; continue cooking 10 minutes. Chop hard-cooked eggs in soup bowls, pour soup over eggs. Serves 8.

OLD NORTH OYSTER CHOWDER

1 quart oysters
2 cups diced cooked potatoes
1 cup diced cooked carrots
1 tablespoon grated onion
1 tablespoon butter or margarine

1 teaspoon celery salt
1/8 teaspoon pepper
3 cups milk
1 cup light cream
Pilot crackers

Cook oysters in oyster liquor until edges curl. Add potatoes, carrots, onion, butter or margarine, celery salt, pepper, milk and light cream. Heat to serving temperature, stirring occasionally. Pour into serving bowls. Top with crackers. Serves 6.

OYSTER PEPPER CHOWDER

1 pint oysters and liquor
1 cup tomato sauce
1 cup water
2 tablespoons catsup
2 tablespoons lime juice
2 tablespoons butter
1/2 green pepper, minced
Salt
Cayenne pepper

Heat oysters slowly in liquor. Heat tomato sauce, water, catsup, lime juice, butter and green pepper. Add oysters and liquor. Season with salt and cayenne pepper. Simmer only until oysters are plump. Serves 4.

NEW ENGLAND CLAM CHOWDER

1 quart clams, shelled or 3 cans minced clams
   (10 to 10 1/2 ounces each)
Water
1/4 pound salt pork or bacon, diced
1 medium onion, chopped
3 cups diced potatoes
1/2 teaspoon salt
1/8 teaspoon pepper
6 coarsely crushed soda crackers
3 cups milk
Paprika

Drain clams, measure liquid and add water to make two cups; chop clams. In large pan cook salt pork or bacon until lightly browned; add onion and cook until tender. Add clams, clam liquid, potatoes, salt and pepper; cover and cook about 15 minutes or until potatoes are tender. Combine crackers and milk, soak 5 minutes; add to potato mixture. Heat thoroughly. Pour into serving bowls; sprinkle with paprika. Serves about 6.

BAR HARBOR LOBSTER CHOWDER

2 small lobsters, cooked
1 cup cold water
3 cups milk
1 cup light cream
1 carrot, sliced thin
1 cup diced cooked potatoes
1/3 cup butter
2 crisp salted crackers, crumbled fine
1 teaspoon salt
1/4 teaspoon black pepper
1/4 teaspoon paprika
1 tablespoon minced chives

Remove lobster meat from shell and cut in cubes; cover shell with cold water, bring to boil, reduce heat and simmer 10 minutes; strain and reserve stock. Scald milk and cream with carrot and potatoes; strain. Cream butter and mix well with cracker crumbs; add scalded milk and cream gradually, stirring until smooth. Add lobster and stock, salt, pepper, paprika and chives; heat thoroughly. Serves 4.

ROMANO EEL SOUP

2 tablespoons butter or oil
4 small leeks, sliced
2 small onions, sliced
5 cups boiling water
2 pounds small eels, skinned and cut into 1½
   inch pieces
2 cups chopped spinach
2/3 cup soft bread crumbs
3 egg yolks, beaten
2/3 cup light cream
1 teaspoon salt
1/4 teaspoon pepper

Heat butter or oil; add leeks and onions and cook 3 minutes. Add water and eels. Boil 2 minutes. Reduce heat and cook 20 minutes. Remove eels and take out bones. Return eels to stock. Add spinach and cook 10 minutes over low heat. Stir in bread crumbs and remove from heat. Mix egg yolks and cream. Add salt and pepper. Blend well and stir gradually into eel mixture. Serve hot. Serves 4–6.

MARBLEHEAD FISH CHOWDER

1 4-pound haddock
2 cups water
4 slices salt pork, diced
1 medium-sized onion, sliced
4 cups diced potatoes
1 cup diced carrots
2 cups boiling water
2 teaspoons salt
1/8 teaspoon pepper
3 tablespoons butter
3 cups milk
1 cup light cream

Skin fish. Cut head and tail from fish. Remove fish from backbone and cut into 2" pieces. Break backbone in pieces. Place backbone, head and tail in 2 cups water. Heat to boiling point and cook 5 minutes. Brown salt pork lightly. Add onion and cook until onion is tender. Remove pork and onion. Add potatoes and carrots to pork drippings. Add boiling water and cook, covered, 5 minutes. Drain liquid from fish head and tail and add to potato mixture. Cook, covered, 15 minutes. Add pork, onion, salt, pepper, butter, milk and cream. Heat to serving temperature. Pour into serving bowls and top with crackers, as desired. Serves 8.

GASPÉ LEEK SOUP

2 bunches leeks
3 tablespoons butter or margarine
3 tablespoons all-purpose flour
2 quarts water
1/4 teaspoon black pepper
1/4 teaspoon salt

Wash and cut leeks in 1" pieces. Melt butter or margarine; add leeks and cook until tender and lightly browned. Stir in flour. Gradually add water, pepper and salt; simmer 1 hour. Serves 4.

REAL OLD-FASHIONED LENTIL SOUP

1 pound lentils
4 cups cold water
1 large onion, diced
1 large tomato, diced
2 carrots, diced
2 potatoes, diced
1/2 bay leaf
1 tablespoon chili sauce
1 tablespoon salt
Ham shank

Soak lentils several hours. Drain. Combine lentils, cold water and remaining ingredients. Simmer, covered, 2 hours. Remove ham shank. Dice ham and return to lentil mixture. Heat to serving temperature, stirring occasionally. Serves 6–8.

CAROLINA LIMA CHOWDER

2 slices bacon, diced
3 small onions, minced
4 potatoes, pared and diced
1 white turnip, diced
2 carrots, diced
2 cups cooked lima beans
1 teaspoon salt
1/4 teaspoon pepper
Boiling water
2 cups medium white sauce

Cook bacon with onions until onions are tender. Add potatoes, turnip, carrots, lima beans, salt and pepper. Add enough boiling water to cover. Cover and cook until vegetables are tender. Add white sauce. Heat to serving temperature, stirring occasionally. Serves 6.

PROVENÇAL PEA SOUP

1 pound dried yellow peas
2 large onions chopped
1/2 pound salt pork
1 cup chopped frankfurters
1/4 teaspoon salt
1/4 teaspoon pepper

Soak peas several hours, drain. Cover peas, onions and salt pork with water. Simmer, covered, until peas are tender. Add frankfurters and heat to serving temperature. Season with salt and pepper. Garnish with parsley, if desired. Serves 8.

ALASKA SALMON BISQUE

1/4 cup butter or margarine
1/2 cup chopped celery
1/4 cup all-purpose flour
1 teaspoon salt
1/4 teaspoon pepper
1 quart milk, scalded
1 cup diced cooked salmon
1/2 teaspoon onion salt
1 cup cooked corn

Melt butter or margarine; add celery and cook until tender. Blend in flour, salt and pepper.

Gradually add milk and cook over low heat, stirring constantly, until thickened. Add remaining ingredients and heat to serving temperature, stirring occasionally. Serves 4-6.

FISHERMEN'S SCALLOP SOUP

1 pint scallops, chopped
1 tablespoon lime juice
1 cup cold water
4 cups milk
1 tablespoon butter
1 teaspoon salt
1/8 teaspoon pepper
2 tablespoons sherry

Sprinkle scallops with lime juice. Let stand 15 minutes. Add water and heat to boiling point. Add milk, butter and seasonings. Heat to serving temperature. Serves 4.

SEAFOOD CHOWDER

1 pound lean fish, cubed
4 large potatoes, sliced
2 large onions, sliced
6 cups hot water
1/3 cup rice
2 green peppers, diced
1/4 cup diced bacon or salt pork
3 tablespoons minced parsley
1 cup diced carrots
1 cup diced tomato
Salt and pepper

Combine fish, potatoes, onions, water, rice, green peppers, bacon or salt pork, parsley, carrots and tomato. Simmer, covered, about 30 minutes or until vegetables are tender. Season to taste with salt and pepper. Heat to serving temperature. Serves 6-8.

CHARLESTON SHRIMP CHOWDER

1/4 cup chopped onion
1/4 cup melted bacon drippings
2 tablespoons butter
2 tablespoons all-purpose flour
1 quart milk
1 teaspoon salt
1/4 teaspoon paprika
2 cups cooked, chopped shrimp
1 cup light cream

Cook onion in bacon drippings until tender. Melt butter and blend in flour. Gradually add milk and cook, stirring constantly, until thickened. Add onion, salt, paprika, shrimp and cream. Heat to serving temperature over low heat, stirring occasionally. Serves 4.

VEGETABLE SOUP PAYSAN

1/2 pound wax beans
1 small head cabbage
6 carrots
1 turnip
1 cup fresh lima beans
2 teaspoons salt
1/4 teaspoon pepper
2 quarts water
6 link sausages
5 medium-sized potatoes, peeled and sliced

Cut beans into 1" pieces. Shred cabbage. Slice carrots. Cut turnip in quarters. Combine vegetables, salt, pepper and water. Heat to boiling and simmer, covered, 1½ hours. Add sausages and potatoes. Cook, covered, 30 minutes. Serves 6.

BAKED-BEAN SOUP PLYMOUTH

3 cups baked beans
4 cups water
2 tablespoons chopped onion
1/4 cup chopped celery
1/2 cup diced salt pork
2 tablespoons all-purpose flour
2 cups chopped tomatoes
1 teaspoon salt
1/8 teaspoon pepper

Combine beans, water, onion and celery; cook over low heat 30 minutes. Force through a sieve. Brown salt pork and blend in flour. Add tomatoes, salt and pepper. Cook, stirring constantly, until slightly thickened. Combine bean mixture and tomato mixture. Cook over low heat 1 hour, stirring occasionally. Serves 8-10.

BLACK BEAN SOUP

2 cups black beans
2 quarts water
1/2 pound salt pork
2 cups beef stock
4 frankfurters, thinly sliced
1/8 teaspoon freshly ground pepper
1 tablespoon lemon juice
1 tablespoon sherry wine

Soak beans several hours; drain. Add water and salt pork. Cook, covered, until beans are tender. Force through a sieve. Add beef stock, frankfurters, pepper, lemon juice and wine. Heat to serving temperature, stirring occasionally. Pour soup into serving dishes. Serves 8–10.

ACROSS THE BORDER SOUP

2 tablespoons butter
1 cup chicken livers
1/3 cup chopped onions
1 tablespoon chopped chives
1 bay leaf
1 cup light cream
3 cups chicken broth
1/8 teaspoon salt
1/8 teaspoon black pepper

Melt butter; add chicken livers and onions. Cook over low heat until onions are tender. Force through a sieve. Add remaining ingredients and heat to serving temperature, stirring occasionally. Serves 6–8.

MATZOTH BALL SOUP

2 tablespoons chicken fat
2 eggs, well beaten
½ teaspoon salt
1 cup matzoth meal
1 quart boiling chicken broth

Soften fat. Add eggs, salt and enough matzoth meal to make a soft dough. Chill several hours. Shape into small balls. Drop into broth. Cook, covered, about 15 minutes. Serves 4.

MONTEREY MUSSEL SOUP

6 medium-sized onions, chopped
¼ cup butter, melted
3 cups cold water
1 tablespoon butter, melted
¼ cup all-purpose flour
2 cups scalded milk
1 quart mussel meat
1 teaspoon salt
Dash cayenne pepper

Cook onions in the ¼ cup butter until tender. Add water. Cover and cook over low heat 30 minutes. Press through a sieve. Melt the 1 tablespoon butter, stir in flour. Gradually add milk, stirring constantly. Add mussel meat and seasonings. Cook over low heat 5 minutes,

stirring constantly. Add sieved onion stock. Heat to serving temperature. Serves 6–8.

CREAM OF POTATO SOUP

2 medium-sized onions, minced
2 tablespoons melted butter or margarine
6 cups cooked, sieved potatoes
1 teaspoon salt
¼ teaspoon pepper
3 cups potato water
1 cup heavy cream
Paprika

Cook onions in butter or margarine until tender. Add potatoes, salt, pepper, potato water and cream. Heat to serving temperature, stirring frequently. Pour into bowls. Sprinkle with paprika. Serves 6.

DAIRYLAND POTATO SOUP

3 medium-sized potatoes
2 cups boiling salted water
Milk
3 tablespoons butter
½ small onion, chopped
2 tablespoons all-purpose flour
1 teaspoon salt
1/8 teaspoon paprika
1/8 teaspoon cayenne pepper
2 cups grated American cheese
1 tablespoon chopped chives

Cook potatoes, covered, in boiling salted water until tender. Rub through a sieve. Measure the liquid and add enough milk to make 4 cups. Melt butter, add onion and cook until tender. Stir in flour and seasonings. Add potato milk. Cook 3 minutes and strain, if desired. Add cheese and beat until smooth. Add chives and serve hot. Serves 6.

RICE DUMPLING SOUP

2/3 cup cooked rice, mashed
2½ tablespoons all-purpose flour
1 teaspoon onion juice
1 teaspoon chopped parsley
1 egg
¼ teaspoon salt
¼ teaspoon Worcestershire sauce
1/8 teaspoon pepper
1 can beef consommé

Combine rice, flour, onion juice, parsley, egg, salt, Worcestershire sauce and pepper; mix well. Prepare consommé according to label directions. Heat to boiling point. Drop rice mixture by teaspoonfuls into consommé. Cover and cook 5 minutes. Serves 4.

QUEEN MARIE VEAL SOUP

1 medium-sized breast of veal
Water
¼ teaspoon paprika
2 tablespoons melted butter
½ cup chopped onions
1 cup diced carrots
2 cups diced potatoes
½ cup diced celery
½ cup dry white wine
2 teaspoons salt
1 cup sour cream

Cover breast of veal with water. Cover and cook over low heat until tender, about 1¼, hours. Combine paprika, butter, onions, carrots, potatoes, celery, wine and salt. Add to veal. Cover and cook over low heat about 20 minutes or until vegetables are tender. Serve topped with sour cream. Serves 6-8.

DUTCH PEA SOUP

1 pound dried peas
½ cup chopped onions
1 cup chopped celery
3 pounds pork shoulder
2 teaspoons salt
¼ teaspoon pepper
Water

Soak peas several hours; drain. Combine peas, onions, celery, pork, salt and pepper. Add enough water to cover. Cover and cook over low heat 3-4 hours, or until pork is tender. Serves 10-12.

KALAMAZOO CELERY CHOWDER

5 cups cooked diced celery
2 tablespoons chopped chives
2 tablespoons butter or margarine
½ teaspoon onion salt
1 teaspoon salt
1 cup diced cooked potatoes
3 cups milk
2 egg yolks, well beaten

Put celery through sieve. Combine celery, chives, butter or margarine, onion salt, salt, potatoes and milk. Heat to boiling point over low heat. Add a little of milk mixture to egg yolks and mix well. Cook over low heat, stirring constantly, 3 minutes. Serves 6.

CHICKEN ALMOND SOUP

1 cup chopped celery
½ cup shredded carrots
4 cups chicken bouillon
1 egg, beaten
1 cup light cream
1/8 teaspoon salt
½ cup ground almonds
Paprika

Cook celery and carrots, covered, in bouillon until tender. Combine egg and cream; mix well. Gradually add to celery mixture. Cook, over low heat, stirring constantly until thickened. Add salt and almonds. Heat to serving temperature. Pour into serving bowls and sprinkle with paprika. Serves 6.

CREAM OF CHICKEN SOUP

3 tablespoons rice
2/3 cup diced celery
3 cups hot chicken stock
2 tablespoons lemon juice
2 cups hot milk
Salt and pepper
8 slices lemon
Chopped chives

Boil rice and celery until tender, drain and rub through sieve. Combine with stock, lemon juice and milk; season to taste. Serve hot with lemon slices covered with chives. Serves 4.

VERMONT CORN CHOWDER

1/3 cup diced salt pork
1 small onion, thinly sliced
3 cups boiling water
3½ cups diced potatoes
2½ cups milk
2¼ cups corn, cooked or canned
1 teaspoon salt
1/8 teaspoon pepper
2 tablespoons chopped parsley

Brown salt pork. Remove pork from pan. Add onion to pork drippings and cook until tender.

Add water and potatoes. Cook, covered, 15 minutes. Add pork, milk, corn, salt and pepper. Heat to serving temperature. Top with parsley. Serve with split pilot crackers, as desired. Serves 6.

CRAB SOUP CORTEZ

2 tablespoons butter
2 tablespoons all-purpose flour
3 cups milk
1 tablespoon Worcestershire sauce
1 teaspoon salt
1/8 teaspoon pepper
2 cups cooked, chopped crab meat
1/4 cup sherry
Thin lemon slices

Melt butter and blend in flour. Gradually add milk and cook, stirring constantly, until thickened. Add Worcestershire sauce, salt, pepper, crab meat and sherry. Heat to serving temperature, stirring occasionally. Pour into serving bowls and garnish with lemon slices. Serves 4.

COUNTRY CABBAGE SOUP

1 3-pound soupbone
2 quarts cold water
2 teaspoons salt
1/4 teaspoon pepper
1 bay leaf
1 medium-sized head cabbage, quartered
2 medium-sized onions, sliced
1 cup chopped celery
1 tablespoon butter

Cover bone with water. Add salt, pepper and bay leaf. Heat to boiling point. Cover and cook 1½ hours. Add remaining ingredients. Cover and simmer 1 hour. Remove meat from bone and return to cabbage mixture. Serves 8.

FRENCH CANADIAN CHOWDER

¾ cup chopped onions
¼ cup melted butter
3 cups flaked halibut
1½ cups cooked celery
1½ cups cooked carrots
2½ cups condensed tomato soup
2½ cups milk
1 teaspoon salt
½ teaspoon pepper

Brown onions slightly in butter. Combine halibut, vegetables, soup, milk and seasonings. Heat slowly to serving temperature. Serves 8.

NORWEGIAN HOLIDAY SOUP

2 tablespoons butter or margarine
2 tablespoons all-purpose flour
2 quarts bouillon
2 carrots, cubed
1 cup diced cooked potatoes
Dash cayenne pepper
2½ tablespoons sherry
1 tablespoon chopped parsley
½ teaspoon salt
12 small cooked meat balls

Melt butter. Stir in flour. Add bouillon slowly. Stir until slightly thickened. Add carrots and simmer until carrots are tender. Add potatoes, cayenne pepper, sherry, parsley, salt and meat balls. Heat to serving temperature. Serves 6.

VICKSBURG OKRA SOUP

1 ham bone
6 cups okra, cut in small pieces
2½ cups tomatoes
1 cup chopped green pepper
Salt to taste

Boil ham bone for 1 hour in enough water to cover. Add okra, tomatoes and green pepper. Simmer, covered, 3 hours. Season with salt. Serves 4.

CARIBBEAN ONION SOUP

1 cup shelled almonds
6 cups beef bouillon
1 cup sliced onions
1 cup croutons
½ cup grated Parmesan cheese
1 teaspoon lemon juice

Grind almonds; add bouillon and onions. Cook, covered, over low heat, 1 hour. Arrange croutons in serving bowls. Add soup. Top with cheese and lemon juice. Serves 4.

PARMESAN ONION SOUP

¼ cup butter
2 cups thinly sliced onions
2 quarts chicken stock or bouillon
1 teaspoon salt
1/8 teaspoon white pepper
Grated Parmesan cheese
Chopped parsley

Melt butter; add onions and cook until tender. Add stock or bouillon, salt and pepper. Cover and cook over low heat 1 hour. Pour into serving bowls. Top with cheese and parsley. Serves 8.

GEORGIA PEANUT BUTTER SOUP

½ cup butter
2 tablespoons minced onion
1 tablespoon all-purpose flour
1 cup peanut butter
1 quart chicken consommé
¼ teaspoon paprika
¼ teaspoon pepper
1 teaspoon salt
1 cup light cream
1 4-ounce can mushrooms, drained

Melt butter. Add onion and cook until tender. Blend in flour and peanut butter. Gradually add consommé and cook over low heat, stirring constantly, until thickened. Add remaining ingredients. Heat to serving temperature, stirring occasionally. Serves 8-10.

PHILADELPHIA PEPPERPOT

2 pounds fresh tripe
1 veal knuckle with meat
2 teaspoons salt
2 bay leaves
1 sweet red pepper, chopped
1 green pepper, chopped
4 medium-sized potatoes, diced
1/8 teaspoon cayenne pepper
½ cup chopped parsley

Clean and wash tripe. Simmer 4-5 hours in water to cover. Cook veal knuckle in water to cover until meat falls off bone. Cut tripe and veal into small pieces. Strain veal stock and add water to make 3 quarts. Add bay leaves, red pepper and green pepper. Simmer ½ hour. Add potatoes, cayenne pepper, parsley, veal and tripe. Simmer, covered, until potatoes are tender. Dumplings may be added, if desired. Serves 8.

CLASSIC OYSTER BISQUE

1 quart oysters
1 green pepper
¾ cup chopped celery
1 tablespoon butter
1 tablespoon all-purpose flour
1 quart milk
1 teaspoon Worcestershire sauce
1 teaspoon salt
1/8 teaspoon pepper
2 tablespoons chopped pimiento

Grind oysters, green pepper and celery. Melt butter and blend in flour. Gradually add milk, and cook, stirring constantly, until thickened. Add Worcestershire sauce, salt, pepper, oysters, green pepper, celery and pimiento. Heat to serving temperature. Serves 4-6.

OYSTER STEW CHABLIS

1 pint oysters
¼ cup butter, melted
3 cups chicken bouillon
1 cup Chablis wine
½ teaspoon salt
Parsley

Cook oysters in butter until oyster edges curl. Add chicken bouillon, wine and salt. Heat to serving temperature. Pour into serving bowls and garnish with parsley. Serves 6.

NUT CREAM SAN JUAN

½ pound almonds or cashews, ground
3 tablespoons all-purpose flour
3 tablespoons butter
2 cups milk
1 cup light cream
1 teaspoon salt

Combine all ingredients and cook over low heat, stirring constantly, until thickened. Serves 4.

OYSTER STEW U.S.A.

¼ cup butter
1 quart oysters
1 teaspoon salt
1/8 teaspoon pepper
¼ teaspoon celery salt
Dash cayenne pepper
4 cups light cream

Melt butter, add oysters and cook over low heat until edges curl. Add seasonings and cream. Heat to serving temperature. Serve at once. Serves 8.

SALT PORK PARSNIP CHOWDER

1/3 cup diced salt pork
4 medium-sized onions, sliced
2 cups pared, sliced parsnips
1 can tomato paste
2 cups boiling water
4 cups hot milk
3 tablespoons butter
Salt and pepper
½ cup cracker crumbs

Fry salt pork. Add onions and cook until brown. Add parsnips and tomato paste. Add water and cook, covered, until the vegetables are tender. Add milk, butter and seasonings. Add cracker crumbs. Heat to serving temperature. Serves 8.

TOMATO WHIP

2 tablespoons butter
1 teaspoon sugar
1 small onion, sliced
½ cup chopped celery
1 quart quartered tomatoes
1 tablespoon lemon juice
1 teaspoon pickling spices
1 teaspoon salt
¾ cup heavy cream, whipped
Croutons

Melt butter. Add sugar, onion and celery. Cook until tender. Add tomatoes, lemon juice and seasonings. Simmer 5 minutes. Rub through sieve. Heat to serving temperature. Add cream. Beat until frothy. Serve with croutons. Serves 6.

SOYBEAN SOUP

2 cups soybeans
1 cup diced celery
2 quarts cold water
2 small onions, thinly sliced
2 tablespoons melted butter
2 tablespoons all-purpose flour
1 teaspoon salt
1/8 teaspoon pepper
1 cup diced cooked carrots
2 hard-cooked eggs, sliced
1 lemon, cut into thin slices

Soak beans several hours. Drain. Add celery and cold water. Cook, covered, over low heat about 4 hours or until tender. Rub through sieve. Brown onion slightly in butter. Add flour, seasonings, bean stock and carrots. Heat to serving temperature, stirring occasionally; pour over eggs and lemon slices. Serves 6-8.

CRAB SOUP PIMLICO

1 pound crab meat, flaked
3 cups water
1 No. 2½ can tomatoes
2 cups okra, diced
2 stalks celery, diced
2 carrots, diced
2 onions, diced
2 teaspoons salt
½ teaspoon pepper
3 drops Tabasco
1 teaspoon Worcestershire sauce
1 bay leaf
½ teaspoon gumbo filê
2 tablespoons butter

Combine all ingredients and simmer 2 hours. Serves 8-10.

MICHIGAN NAVY BEAN SOUP

3 pounds navy beans
4 quarts water
1½ pounds ham hocks
½ cup chopped onions
2 tablespoons butter or margarine
2 teaspoons salt
¼ teaspoon pepper

Wash beans thoroughly. Add water, ham hocks and onions. Cover and cook over low heat about 3 hours. Add remaining ingredients and mix well. Serves 12.

CELESTIAL WATER CRESS SOUP

2 cups water
1 tablespoon salt
1 teaspoon diced leek
¼ cup bamboo shoots
¼ cup butter
2 cups chicken stock or bouillon
1 cup chopped water cress
1 egg, beaten

Simmer water, salt, leek, bamboo shoots and butter 20 minutes. Add stock or bouillon and simmer 20 minutes. Add water cress. Heat to boiling. Add egg and heat, stirring constantly, to serving temperature. Serves 6.

SHOKAN OXTAIL SOUP

1 oxtail
2 tablespoons butter
¼ cup chopped onion
6 cups beef broth or bouillon
½ cup carrot slices
½ cup chopped celery
1 bay leaf
1 cup chopped tomatoes
1 can tomato soup
1 tablespoon Worcestershire sauce
2 teaspoons salt
½ teaspoon pepper

Split oxtail into small joints. Melt butter and add oxtail and onion. Cook until onion is tender. Add remaining ingredients. Cook, covered, over low heat for 3-4 hours, or until meat is tender. Stir occasionally. Serves 6-8.

COLD SOUPS

SPICY SUMMER FRUIT SOUP

3 tablespoons quick-cooking tapioca
1½ cups boiling water
2 cups pineapple juice
2 cups orange juice
½ cup sugar
2 teaspoons lemon rind, grated
1 2"-stick cinnamon
1 cup strawberries, sliced
¼ cup white wine

Stir tapioca into water. Cook, until tapioca is clear, stirring constantly. Add pineapple and orange juices. Bring to boil. Add sugar, lemon rind and cinnamon. Cook, over low heat, 10 minutes. Remove from heat. Add strawberries and wine. Chill. Serves 6.

CHILLED SHRIMP BISQUE

1 quart buttermilk
1 teaspoon prepared mustard
1/8 teaspoon pepper
1 teaspoon salt
½ teaspoon paprika
1 tablespoon chopped chives
¼ cup grated cucumber
½ pound shrimp, cooked and chopped

Combine all ingredients. Chill thoroughly. Serves 6-8.

FARMERS' DILL SOUP

12 small potatoes
3 cups boiling water
2 tablespoons all-purpose flour
¼ cup cold water
1 cup sour cream
1 large bunch dill
1 bay leaf
2 egg yolks, slightly beaten
1/3 teaspoon salt

Cut potatoes into quarters. Cover with boiling water. Cook, covered, 20 minutes or until tender. Drain potatoes, saving them for another meal. Measure 2 cups of the potato water. Blend flour with cold water to make a smooth paste and add, with sour cream, to potato water. Chop dill. Add dill and bay leaf to cream mixture and cook, stirring constantly, until thickened. Stir a small amount of hot soup into egg yolks. Add to soup mixture, mixing well. Add salt. Chill. Serves 4.

NORWEGIAN FRUIT SOUP

1½ quarts blueberries
3 quarts water
¼ cup cornstarch
Cold water
½ cup sugar
1 teaspoon grated orange rind

Combine berries and water. Cover and cook over low heat until berries are soft. Put through sieve. Heat berries and juice to simmering point. Moisten cornstarch with water. Add to berry mixture and cook, stirring constantly, until thickened. Add orange rind. Chill thoroughly. Serves 6-8.

SCANDINAVIAN FRUIT SOUP

¾ pound dried peaches
1 3-inch stick cinnamon
1 cup sugar
3 quarts water
3 tablespoons tapioca

Cook peaches according to package directions. To cooked, drained peaches, add remaining ingredients and cook until tapioca is clear. Serve chilled. Serves 6–8.

VICHYSSOISE

4 leeks
1/3 cup chopped onions
3 tablespoons melted butter or margarine
5 medium-sized potatoes, pared and thinly sliced
4 cups chicken bouillon or stock
2 cups milk
1 cup light cream
Salt and pepper
Chopped chives

Cut leeks in thin slices. Brown leeks and onions lightly in butter or margarine. Add potatoes and bouillon or stock. Heat to boiling point. Cover and simmer 30 minutes or until potatoes are tender. Press through a sieve. Add milk and cream. Cook 10 minutes. Season to taste with salt and pepper. Chill thoroughly. Garnish with chopped chives. Serves 6–8.

JELLIED CHICKEN CONSOMMÉ

1 envelope unflavored gelatin
¼ cup cold water
3 cups chicken bouillon
2 tablespoons sherry
1 teaspoon lemon juice
¼ teaspoon nutmeg
Salt and pepper to taste

Soften gelatin in water. Heat chicken bouillon to boiling point; add gelatin and stir until dissolved. Add remaining ingredients and mix well. Chill thoroughly. Serves 6–8.

GOLDEN SUMMER SOUP

2 cups orange juice
1 teaspoon cornstarch
2 tablespoons cold water
½ cup sugar
1 teaspoons grated orange rind
½ cup shredded coconut

Heat orange juice. Combine cornstarch and water. Stir into juice. Cook over low heat, stirring constantly, until thickened. Add sugar, orange rind and coconut. Chill. Serves 4.

Breads, Rolls, Pancakes and Waffles

BISCUITS

CAMPER'S BREAD TWISTS

1 cup all-purpose flour
1 teaspoon baking powder
1/8 teaspoon salt
1 tablespoon shortening
1/2 cup milk (approx.)
Green stick, 3/4-inch thick, peeled part-way
Flour

Combine the 1 cup flour, baking powder and salt; cut in shortening. Add enough milk to make stiff dough. Heat stick and sprinkle with flour. Place 1/4 of dough on stick in a spiral fashion. Hold about 6 inches away from coals to bake inside. Hold about 4 inches from coals until lightly browned. Turn continually. Remove from stick. Repeat with remaining dough. Makes 4 twists.

SOUR MILK BISCUITS

2 cups sifted all-purpose flour
2½ teaspoons baking powder
1/4 teaspoon salt
1/4 teaspoon baking soda
3 tablespoons shortening
1 cup sour milk

Sift dry ingredients together. Cut in shortening. Add milk and mix lightly. Turn out on lightly floured surface and knead lightly. Cut with floured cutter. Arrange on lightly greased baking sheet. Bake in hot oven (450° F.) 12-15 minutes. Makes about 12.

TOMATO CHEESE BISCUITS

2 cups sifted all-purpose flour
3 teaspoons baking powder
1/2 teaspoon salt
1/4 cup shortening
2/3 cup tomato juice
1/2 cup grated American cheese

Sift flour, baking powder and salt together. Cut in shortening. Add tomato juice and cheese; mix lightly. Turn out on lightly floured surface and knead 30 seconds. Pat out to 1/2-inch thickness. Cut with floured 2" cutter. Place on greased baking sheet. Bake in hot oven (450° F.) 12-15 minutes. Makes about 18.

WHOLE WHEAT BISCUITS

1 cup sifted all-purpose flour
3 teaspoons baking powder
1/2 teaspoon salt
1 cup whole wheat flour
1/4 cup shortening
2/3 cup milk

Sift all-purpose flour, baking powder and salt together. Add whole wheat flour and mix lightly. Cut in shortening. Add milk and mix lightly. Turn out on lightly floured surface. Roll out to 1/2-inch thickness. Cut with floured 2" cutter. Place on greased baking sheet. Bake in hot oven (400° F.) about 15 minutes. Makes about 18.

CHEESE BISCUITS

2 cups sifted all-purpose flour
3 teaspoons baking powder
1/2 teaspoon salt
1/3 cup shortening
2/3 cup milk
1 cup small Swiss cheese cubes

Sift flour, baking powder and salt together. Cut in shortening. Add milk and mix lightly. Turn out on lightly floured surface. Roll out to 1/2-inch thickness. Cut into diamond shapes and place on greased baking sheet. Press cheese cube lightly into center of each biscuit. Bake in hot oven (450° F.) 12-15 minutes. Makes about 18.

SOUTHERN YAM BISCUITS

2 cups sifted all-purpose flour
3 teaspoons baking powder
1 teaspoon salt
1 teaspoon brown sugar
¼ cup shortening
½ cup milk
1 cup mashed cooked yams

Sift together flour, baking powder, salt and sugar. Cut in shortening. Add milk and yams. Roll out on lighdy floured surface. Cut with floured cutter. Bake in hot oven (450° F.) 12–15 minutes. Makes about 18.

MUFFINS

CHEESE MUFFINS

2 cups sifted all-purpose flour
3 teaspoons baking powder
½ teaspoon salt
¾ cup grated Cheddar cheese
1 egg, well beaten
1 cup milk
2 tablespoons melted shortening

Sift flour, baking powder and salt together. Add cheese and mix lighdy. Combine remaining ingredients. Add milk mixture to dry ingredients and mix only until ingredients are blended. Turn into greased muffin pans. Bake in hot oven (400° F.) 20–30 minutes, or until done. Makes about 12 medium-sized muffins.

SCOTCH OATMEAL MUFFINS

1 cup sifted all-purpose flour
1 teaspoon baking powder
½ teaspoon salt
½ teaspoon baking soda
1 cup sour milk
1 cup quick-cooking oats
1 egg, well beaten
1/3 cup firmly packed brown sugar
1/3 cup melted shortening

Sift flour, baking powder, salt and baking soda together. Pour milk over oats; add egg and brown sugar. Stir in sifted ingredients and shortening.

Mix until ingredients are just blended. Fill greased muffin pans 2/3 full. Bake in hot oven (400° F.) 20–25 minutes. Makes about 12 medium-sized muffins.

SPICY BUTTERSCOTCH MUFFINS

3 tablespoons butter
2/3 cup brown sugar, firmly packed
2 cups sifted all-purpose flour
3 teaspoons baking powder
½ teaspoon salt
¼ teaspoon nutmeg
½ teaspoon cinnamon
¼ teaspoon ginger
1 egg
1 cup milk
2 tablespoons melted shortening

Grease 18 2½" muffin cups and place ½ teaspoon butter and 1 teaspoon brown sugar in each cup. Sift flour, baking powder, salt and spices together. Beat egg; add milk, shortening and remaining brown sugar. Add to sifted dry ingredients, stirring only enough to dampen all the flour. Fill muffin pan ¾ full. Bake in hot oven (425° F.) 20 minutes. Makes 18.

DATE AND NUT MUFFINS

2 cups sifted all-purpose flour
3 teaspoons baking powder
¼ teaspoon salt
1 tablespoon sugar
½ cup chopped dates
½ cup chopped walnuts
1 egg, slightly beaten
1 cup milk
1/3 cup melted shortening

Sift flour, baking powder, salt and sugar together. Add dates and walnuts; mix lightly. Combine remaining ingredients and add to date mixture. Mix only until ingredients are blended. Fill greased muffin pans 2/3 full. Bake in hot oven (400° F.) 20–25 minutes. Makes 12 medium-sized muffins.

CARROT-RAISIN MUFFINS

1 cup sifted all-purpose flour
3 teaspoons baking powder
2 tablespoons sugar
¼ teaspoon salt
1 cup whole wheat flour
1/3 cup raisins
1 egg, well beaten
1 cup carrot juice
¼ cup melted shortening

Sift flour, baking powder, sugar and salt together. Add whole wheat flour and raisins; mix lightly. Combine egg, carrot juice and shortening. Add to dry ingredients and mix until ingredients are just blended. Fill greased muffin pans 2/3 full. Bake in hot oven (400° F.) 20–25 minutes. Makes about 12 medium-sized muffins,

BANANA MUFFINS

1¾ cups sifted all-purpose flour
2 teaspoons baking powder
¼ teaspoon baking soda
¼ teaspoon salt
½ cup sugar
1 egg, well beaten
¼ cup melted shortening
1 cup mashed bananas

Sift flour, baking powder, baking soda, salt and sugar together. Combine egg, shortening and bananas; add to sifted ingredients and mix until just blended. Turn into greased muffin pans. Bake in hot oven (400° F.) 20–25 minutes. Makes 12 medium-sized muffins.

RAISIN BRAN MUFFINS

¾ cup sifted all-purpose flour
2 teaspoons baking powder
½ teaspoon salt
1 cup bran
½ cup raisins
2 tablespoons molasses
1 tablespoon melted shortening
½ cup milk
1 egg, well beaten

Sift together flour, baking powder and salt. Add bran and raisins. Combine molasses, shortening, milk and egg. Add to dry ingredients and stir just until flour is moistened. Bake in greased muffin pans in hot oven (400° F.) 20–25 minutes. Makes 12 medium-sized muffins.

HOLIDAY MINCE MUFFINS

2½ cups sifted all-purpose flour
¼ teaspoon salt
½ cup sugar
3 teaspoons baking powder
2 cups bran
2 eggs
1½ cups milk
1/3 cup melted shortening
½ cup chopped dates
½ cup mincemeat

Sift first 4 ingredients together and add bran. Beat eggs well; add milk, shortening, dates and mincemeat. Add to dry ingredients and stir until just blended. Fill greased muffin pans about 2/3 full. Bake in hot oven (400° F.) about 25 minutes. Makes 18 medium-sized muffins.

CORN MUFFINS

2 cups cornmeal
2 teaspoons baking powder
½ teaspoon baking soda
½ teaspoon salt
½ teaspoon sugar (optional)
2 cups buttermilk
2 eggs
¼ cup melted butter

Sift meal with dry ingredients. Add buttermilk, eggs and butter. Beat with rotary egg beater. Pour batter into greased muffin pans. Bake in hot oven (400° F.) about 25 minutes. Makes about 12 medium-sized muffins.

HONEY MUFFINS

¼ cup honey
2 cups sifted all-purpose flour
3 teaspoons baking powder
¼ teaspoon salt
1 teaspoon nutmeg
¼ cup melted shortening
1 egg, well beaten
1 cup milk

Grease 12 2½" muffin cups; place 1 teaspoon honey in each cup. Sift flour, baking powder, salt and nutmeg together. Add shortening, egg and milk. Mix until ingredients are just blended. Fill muffin cups 2/3 full. Bake in hot oven (400° F.) 20–25 minutes. Makes 12.

PEANUT BUTTER MUFFINS

½ cup peanut butter
3 tablespoons shortening
½ teaspoon salt
3 tablespoons sugar
1 egg, well beaten
1½ cups milk
2 cups sifted all-purpose flour
3 teaspoons baking powder

Cream peanut butter, shortening, salt and sugar until light and fluffy. Combine egg and milk. Sift flour with baking powder. Add milk mixture and sifted ingredients alternately to creamed mixture. Fill greased muffin pans 2/3 full. Bake in hot oven (400° F.) 20–25 minutes. Makes 12 medium-sized muffins.

BLUEBERRY MUFFINS KENNEBEC

2 cups sifted all-purpose flour
3 teaspoons baking powder
2 tablespoons sugar
¼ teaspoon salt
2 eggs, well beaten
1 cup milk
3 tablespoons melted shortening
¾ cup blueberries

Sift flour, baking powder, sugar and salt together. Combine eggs, milk and shortening. Add to sifted ingredients and mix until ingredients are just blended. Add blueberries; mix lightly. Fill greased muffin pans 2/3 full. Bake in hot oven (425° F.) 25–30 minutes. Makes about 18 small muffins.

POPOVERS, SCONES, OLD-FASHIONED DOUGHNUTS

SCOTCH CREAM SCONES

2 cups sifted all-purpose flour
3 teaspoons baking powder
½ teaspoon salt
1/3 cup butter
½ cup light cream

Sift flour, baking powder and salt. Cut in butter and add cream. Knead 5 minutes on lightly floured surface and roll out to ½-inch thickness. Cut into small triangles. Place on lightly greased baking sheet. Bake in hot oven (450° F.) 10–15 minutes or until light brown. Makes about 12.

POPOVERS

1 cup milk
¼ teaspoon salt
1 tablespoon melted butter or margarine
3 eggs, slightly beaten
1 cup sifted all-purpose flour

Combine milk, salt, butter or margarine and eggs. Add flour and beat until smooth. Fill greased baking cups ½ full. Bake in hot oven (425° F.) 40–45 minutes. Makes 6 large popovers.

OLD-FASHIONED DOUGHNUTS

2 cups sifted all-purpose flour
½ teaspoon baking soda
¼ teaspoon nutmeg
¼ teaspoon salt
2 tablespoons shortening
½ cup sugar
1 egg
½ teaspoon vanilla
½ cup sour milk

Sift flour, baking soda, nutmeg, salt together. Cream shortening and sugar until light and fluffy. Add egg and beat welL Blend in vanilla. Add sour milk and sifted ingredients alternately. Stir only until ingredients are blended. Roll dough out on a lightly floured surface 1/3-inch thick. Cut dough with floured 2½" cutter and let stand 10 minutes. Fry in deep hot fat (365° F.) until lightly browned on all sides. Drain on absorbent paper. Makes 18.

COCONUT SCONES

2 cups sifted cake flour
3 teaspoons baking powder
¼ teaspoon salt
1 tablespoon sugar
¼ cup shortening
2 egg yolks
1 egg white
1 teaspoon grated orange rind
¼ cup shredded coconut
1/3 cup light cream

Sift flour, baking powder, salt and sugar together. Cut in shortening. Combine egg yolks, egg white, orange rind, coconut and cream. Beat well. Stir into flour mixture and mix lightly. Roll out on lightly floured surface to ½-inch thickness. Cut into triangles. Place on greased baking sheet. Bake in hot oven (450° F.) about 15minutes. Makes about 18.

CORN BREADS

HARVEST CORN SQUARES

¾ cup sifted all-purpose flour
¾ cup cornmeal
3 teaspoons baking powder
¼ teaspoon salt
1 tablespoon sugar
1 egg, slightly beaten
¾ cup milk
¾ cup diced apples
3 tablespoons melted shortening

Sift together flour, cornmeal, baking powder, salt and sugar. Add egg and milk. Stir well. Add apples and shortening. Mix thoroughly. Pour into greased 8" x 8" baking pan. Bake in hot oven (425° F.) 25–30 minutes. Cool and cut into squares. Makes 8 servings.

CORN BREAD STICKS

1 2/3 cups sifted all-purpose flour
¾ cup yellow cornmeal
3 teaspoons baking powder
2 tablespoons sugar
¼ teaspoon salt
1 egg, well beaten
1 cup milk
¼ cup melted shortening

Sift flour, cornmeal, baking powder, sugar and salt together. Combine egg, milk and shortening. Add to dry ingredients and mix until ingredients are just blended. Turn into greased cornstick pans. Bake in hot oven (425° F.) 20–25 minutes. Makes about 18.

BUTTERMILK SPOON BREAD

1 cup yellow cornmeal
2 cups boiling water
1 teaspoon salt
2 tablespoons salt pork drippings
2 eggs, separated
1 cup buttermilk
½ teaspoon baking soda
2 teaspoons baking powder

Gradually add cornmeal to water; cook over hot water 15 minutes. Cool. Add salt, drippings, egg yolks, buttermilk, baking soda and baking powder; mix thoroughly. Beat egg whites until stiff and fold into cornmeal mixture. Turn into greased 2-quart baking dish. Bake in moderate oven (350° F.) about 40 minutes. Serves 6.

CRACKLIN' BREAD

1½ cups cornmeal, white or yellow
2 tablespoons all-purpose flour
2 teaspoons sugar (optional)
½ teaspoon salt
3 teaspoons baking powder
1 egg, well beaten
1¼ cups milk
1 1/3 cups cracklin's

Combine cornmeal, flour, sugar, salt, baking powder, egg and milk. Add cracklin's and beat thoroughly. Turn into well-greased 12" x 9" pan. Bake in hot oven (450° F.) about 20 minutes. Makes 12 servings.

TEXAS CORN BREAD

1 cup sifted all-purpose flour
½ teaspoon salt
1 teaspoon baking soda
¾ cup yellow cornmeal
2 eggs, well beaten
1 cup sour milk
¼ cup melted shortening

Sift flour, salt and baking soda together; add cornmeal and mix lightly. Combine remaining ingredients and add to dry ingredients. Beat until smooth. Turn into greased 8" x 8" pan. Bake in hot oven (425° F.) 30–35 minutes. Makes 8 pieces.

JONNY-CAKE

1 cup yellow cornmeal
1 teaspoon salt
¼ teaspoon baking soda
1 cup boiling water
½ cup light cream
2 tablespoons molasses

Combine cornmeal, salt and baking soda. Gradually add water and mix well. Add remaining ingredients and mix well. Shape into cakes and bake on greased griddle until well browned on both sides. Serves 6.

HUSH-PUPPIES

2 cups white cornmeal
½ teaspoon baking soda
1 teaspoon baking powder
1 tablespoon salt
1 egg
1½ cups buttermilk (about)

Mix dry ingredients. Add egg and milk to make a thick batter. Drop from spoon into deep hot fat (375° F.) and cook until golden brown. Drain on absorbent paper. Serve hot. Makes about 24 small hush-puppies.

BAKING POWDER AND SODA BREADS

SOUTHERN ORANGE BREAD

2 cups sifted all-purpose flour
½ teaspoon salt
3 teaspoons baking powder
½ cup sugar
2 teaspoons grated orange rind
¾ cup orange juice
2 eggs, beaten
1 teaspoon almond extract
¼ cup melted shortening
2 tablespoons grated orange rind
½ cup sugar
1 teaspoon cinnamon
1 tablespoon butter or margarine

Sift flour, salt, baking powder and ½ cup sugar together. Add 2 teaspoons orange rind, orange juice, eggs, almond extract and shortening. Mix only until dry ingredients are moistened. Pour into waxed paper-lined 8" x 8" pan. Combine remaining ingredients; sprinkle over batter. Bake in hot oven (400° F.) 30 minutes. Cut into squares. Serve hot Makes 6–8 servings.

PECAN ROLLS

2 cups sifted all-purpose flour
2½ teaspoons baking powder
2 tablespoons sugar
½ teaspoon salt
1/3 cup shortening
¾ cup milk
¼ cup butter or margarine
¾ cup firmly packed brown sugar
½ cup pecans

Sift flour, baking powder, sugar and salt together. Cut in shortening. Add milk and mix lightly. Place 1 teaspoon butter or margarine, 1 tablespoon brown sugar and about 4 pecans in bottom of each greased muffin cup. Drop biscuit mixture into muffin pans. Bake in moderate oven (375° F.) 20–25 minutes. Turn out of cups immediately. Makes 12.

FRUIT SALLY LUNN

2 cups sifted all-purpose flour
3 teaspoons baking powder
¼ cup sugar
½ teaspoon salt
¼ cup shortening
1/3 cup chopped candied cherries
½ cup raisins
1 egg, beaten
¾ cup milk

Sift together flour, baking powder, sugar and salt. Cut in shortening. Add cherries and raisins; mix lightly. Combine egg and milk; add to shortening mixture and mix well until ingredients are just blended. Spread in greased 8" x 8" pan. Bake in moderate oven (350° F.) 25–30 minutes. Makes 6 servings.

ALMOND BREAD

3 cups sifted all-purpose flour
½ cup sugar
½ teaspoon salt
3 teaspoons baking powder
¾ cup chopped almonds
1½ cups milk
1 egg, well beaten
3 tablespoons melted shortening

Sift flour, sugar, salt and baking powder together; add almonds and mix lightly. Combine remaining ingredients and add to almond mixture. Mix until ingredients are blended. Turn into greased 9" x 5" x 3" pan. Bake in moderate oven (375° F.) 60 minutes. Makes 1 loaf.

DATE AND NUT BREAD

¾ cup boiling water
1 cup pitted dates, cut in half
1¾ cups sifted all-purpose flour
1 teaspoon baking powder
½ teaspoon baking soda
¼ teaspoon salt
½ cup chopped pecans
1 tablespoon melted shortening
½ cup sugar
1 egg

Add water to dates and let stand 20 minutes. Sift flour, baking powder, baking soda and salt together; add pecans and mix lightly. Combine shortening, sugar and egg; beat well. Add dry ingredients alternately with date mixture to sugar mixture, beating well after each addition. Pour into greased 9" x 5" x 3" pan. Bake in moderate oven (350° F.) 45–50 minutes. Makes 1 loaf.

APRICOT-PECAN LOAF

1 cup dried apricots
3 cups sifted all-purpose flour
¾ cup granulated sugar
4 teaspoons baking powder
1½ teaspoons salt
1 cup chopped pecans
1 egg, beaten
1½ cups milk
¼ cup melted shortening
2 tablespoons grated orange rind

Cover apricots with water and boil 15 minutes, or until tender. Cool, drain and chop. Sift together flour, sugar, baking powder and salt. Add pecans.

Combine egg, milk, shortening and rind. Stir liquid mixture and apricots into dry mixture. Turn into greased 9" x 5" x 3" loaf pan. Let stand 15 minutes. Bake in moderate oven (350° F.) 1–1¼ hours. Makes 1 loaf.

APPLESAUCE-ALMOND BREAD

2 cups sifted all-purpose flour
¾ cup sugar
3 teaspoons baking powder
1 teaspoon salt
½ teaspoon baking soda
½ teaspoon cinnamon
½ teaspoon nutmeg
1 cup coarsely chopped blanched almonds
1 egg
1 cup applesauce
2 tablespoons melted shortening

Sift dry ingredients together. Add almonds. Beat egg; add applesauce and melted shortening. Add dry ingredients and stir until just blended. Pour into greased 9" x 5" x 3" loaf pan. Bake in moderate oven (350° F.) 1 hour. Makes 1 loaf.

BANANA BREAD

1¾ cups sifted all-purpose flour
2 teaspoons baking powder
¼ teaspoon baking soda
¼ teaspoon salt
1/3 cup shortening
2/3 cup sugar
2 eggs, well beaten
1 cup mashed bananas

Sift flour, baking powder, baking soda and salt together. Cream shortening and sugar until light and fluffy; add eggs and beat well. Add sifted ingredients and bananas alternately to creamed mixture, beating well after each addition. Turn into greased 9" x 5" x 3" pan. Bake in moderate oven (350° F.) about 60 minutes. Makes 1 loaf.

BOSTON BROWN BREAD

½ cup cornmeal
½ cup whole wheat flour
½ cup rye flour or white flour
½ teaspoon salt
1 teaspoon baking soda
½ cup raisins
2/3 cup molasses
1 cup buttermilk

Blend together cornmeal, flours, salt and baking soda. Mix in raisins. Add molasses and buttermilk. Mix well. Turn into greased 5-cup mold. Cover tightly. Place mold on a rack in kettle. Pour boiling water into kettle to a depth of about 1 inch. Cover kettle tightly. Steam 4 hours. Add water as needed. Makes 1 large loaf.

PANCAKES AND WAFFLES

SOURDOUGH PANCAKES

2 potatoes, cubed
1 cup water
½ package active dry yeast
½ cup warm, not hot, water
2 tablespoons sugar
1 cup all-purpose flour
1 egg, beaten
2 tablespoons butter or margarine
½ teaspoon baking soda
1 tablespoon hot water

Cook potatoes in the 1 cup water 25 minutes. Mash potatoes without draining. Cool to lukewarm. Dissolve yeast in the warm, not hot, water. Combine with lukewarm potato mixture. Add sugar and stir. Cover. Let stand 24 hours. Add flour, stir, cover, and let stand 24 hours. Add egg, butter or margarine. Dissolve soda in hot water. Add and stir well. Pour lightly on greased griddle. Brown on both sides. Serve with syrup, as desired. Serves 4–6.

VERMONT THINS

1 cup sifted all-purpose flour
1½ teaspoons baking powder
¼ teaspoon nutmeg
¼ teaspoon salt
1 tablespoon maple syrup
¼ teaspoon vanilla
1 egg, beaten
1 cup milk
3 tablespoons melted shortening

Sift flour, baking powder, nutmeg and salt together. Combine syrup, vanilla, egg and milk; add gradually to flour, mixing only until smooth. Add shortening. Bake on hot greased griddle. Makes about 10.

DUTCH BUCKWHEAT CAKES

1½ cups buckwheat flour
½ cup all-purpose flour
3 teaspoons baking powder
¼ teaspoon salt
2 tablespoons dark molasses
1 tablespoon melted butter or margarine
1½ cups light cream

Mix together buckwheat flour, all-purpose flour, baking powder and salt. Combine molasses, butter or margarine and light cream. Gradually add cream mixture to flour mixture; mix well. Drop by spoonfuls on greased griddle until browned on both sides. Serve with melted butter and shaved maple sugar, as desired. Serves 6.

CORN HOT CAKES

1¼ cups sifted all-purpose flour
1 teaspoon baking powder
1½ tablespoons sugar
¼ teaspoon salt
1 egg, well beaten
¾ cup milk
3 tablespoons melted shortening
1¼ cups whole kernel corn

Sift flour, baking powder, sugar and salt together. Combine egg, milk and shortening; add sifted ingredients and beat until smooth. Add corn and mix lightly. Drop by spoonfuls on hot greased griddle and brown on both sides. Makes about 12 4" hot cakes.

HUCKLEBERRY GRIDDLECAKES

2 cups sifted all-purpose flour
3 teaspoons baking powder
¼ teaspoon salt
2 teaspoons sugar
1 egg, well beaten
1½ cups milk
1 cup huckleberries or blueberries

Sift flour, baking powder, salt and sugar together. Combine remaining ingredients and add to sifted ingredients. Mix until ingredients are blended. Drop by tablespoonfuls on hot greased griddle. Brown on both sides. Makes about 18 4" pancakes.

SOUR MILK WAFFLES

2 cups sifted all-purpose flour
1 teaspoon baking soda
1 tablespoon sugar
¼ teaspoon salt
2 eggs, separated
2 cups sour milk
1/3 cup melted shortening

Sift flour, baking soda, sugar and salt together. Beat egg yolks and milk together; add sifted ingredients and shortening. Stir until smooth. Beat egg whites until stiff and fold into batter. Bake in heated waffle iron 3–4 minutes. Makes 6.

ALMOND PANCAKE

½ cup sifted all-purpose flour
¼ teaspoon salt
4 eggs, well beaten
½ cup light cream
1 teaspoon almond extract
2 tablespoons confectioners' sugar

Sift flour and salt together. Add eggs and cream alternately to flour mixture. Mix until smooth. Add almond extract. Turn into greased 10" skillet. Bake in moderate oven (350° F.) about 25 minutes. Sprinkle with sugar. Serves 4.

BROWN SUGAR PANCAKES

1¼ cups sifted all-purpose flour
1 ¾ teaspoons baking powder
¼ teaspoon salt
1½ tablespoons brown sugar
1/8 teaspoon ginger
1/8 teaspoon nutmeg

1 egg, separated
¾ cup light cream
2 tablespoons butter

Sift flour, baking powder, salt, sugar and spices together. Beat egg yolk; add cream and mix well. Stir egg mixture into sifted ingredients. Beat egg white until stiff. Fold into flour mixture. Melt butter. Drop batter by tablespoonfuls onto buttered hot griddle. Cook over low heat until browned on both sides. Makes 6–8.

FLANNEL CAKES

2 cups sifted all-purpose flour
½ teaspoon salt
1 teaspoon baking soda
2 eggs
2 cups buttermilk
3 tablespoons melted butter

Sift flour with salt and baking soda. Beat eggs until light, add buttermilk and butter. Add to dry ingredients. Beat well. Drop from spoon on hot griddle and brown on both sides. Serve as dessert with melted butter, as desired. Makes about 20.

YEAST BREADS

ANADAMA BREAD

2 cups water
½ cup yellow cornmeal
2 tablespoons shortening
½ cup molasses
1½ teaspoons salt
1 package active dry yeast, or
1 cake compressed yeast
½ cup warm, not hot water (lukewarm for
  compressed yeast)
5 cups sifted enriched flour (about)

Boil water. Stir the cornmeal very slowly into the boiling water. When thoroughly mixed add the shortening, molasses and salt. Pour mixture into a large mixing bowl and cool to lukewarm. Sprinkle or crumble yeast into water (warm, not hot, water for active dry yeast; lukewarm water for compressed yeast). Stir until dissolved. When cornmeal-molasses mixture is lukewarm, stir in dissolved yeast and enough flour to make a stiff dough. Turn dough out on a lightly floured board and knead until smooth and elastic, about 8-10 minutes. Place in a greased bowl; cover with a cloth and let rise in a warm place, free from draft, until doubled in bulk, about 1 hour. Turn out on a lightly floured board. Cut dough in half and form each half into a loaf. Place loaves in greased bread pans, 7 ½" x 3 ½" x 2¾". Cover with a cloth. Let rise in a warm place, free from draft, until doubled in bulk, about 1 hour. Bake in a hot oven (400° F.) 50-60 minutes. Makes 2 loaves.

WHITE BREAD

1 **package active dry yeast, or 1 cake**
   compressed yeast
¼ **cup warm, not hot, water (lukewarm for**
   compressed yeast)
2 **cups milk, scalded**
2 **tablespoons sugar**
1½ **teaspoons salt**
1 **tablespoon shortening**
6 **cups sifted all-purpose flour (approx.)**

Dissolve yeast in water (active dry yeast in warm, not hot, water; compressed yeast in lukewarm water). Combine milk, sugar, salt and shortening; cool to lukewarm. Add yeast and 2 cups flour; mix well. Add enough of 4 cups flour to make stiff dough. Turn out on lightly floured surface and knead until smooth. Turn dough into greased bowl. Cover and let rise in warm place until doubled in bulk. Punch down. Cover and let rise until doubled in bulk. Divide dough in half and let stand 10 minutes. Shape into 2 loaves and place in 2 greased 9" x 5" x 3" pans. Cover and let rise until doubled in bulk. Bake in hot oven (400° F.) 50-60 minutes. Makes 2 loaves.

FASTNACHTS

3 **medium potatoes**
¾ **cup sugar**
1 **teaspoon salt**
5 **cups sifted all-purpose flour**
1 **package active dry yeast, or 1 cake**
   compressed yeast
¼ **cup warm, not hot, water (lukewarm for**
   compressed yeast)
½ **cup soft butter or margarine**
2 **eggs**
½ **teaspoon nutmeg**

Peel potatoes and cook in 2 cups boiling salted water until tender. Drain off water reserving 1 cup. Pour water into a large mixing bowl. Stir in sugar, salt and 1 cup of the flour. Beat until smooth. Sprinkle or crumble yeast into the ¼ cup water (warm, not hot, water for active dry yeast; lukewarm water for compressed yeast). Stir until dissolved, then beat into batter. Cover with a cloth and let rise in a warm place, free from draft, until bubbly. Meanwhile, mash hot potatoes in pan in which they were cooked; measure 1 cup. Place in mixing bowl. Beat in margarine or butter, eggs, and nutmeg. When batter is full of bubbles, stir in potato mixture and remaining flour or enough to make a stiff dough. Turn dough out on a floured board and knead 8 to 10 minutes or until dough is smooth and elastic. Place in a greased bowl, and brush top of dough with soft or melted shortening. Let rise in a warm place, free from draft, until doubled in bulk. Punch down dough. Cut in half. Roll each half 1/3 of an inch thick on floured board. Cut with a doughnut cutter or into 2" squares with a sharp knife. Place doughnuts on a floured board, cover with a cloth and let rise in a warm place until light and doubled in bulk. Slip doughnuts into deep fat heated to 365° F. As soon as they rise to the top, turn with a long-handled fork to brown on other side. Drain on absorbent paper toweling. Coat doughnuts with granulated sugar by shaking a few at a time in a paper bag containing about ½ cup sugar. Makes about 48.

CRULLERS

2 **teaspoons sugar**
½ **cup warm, not hot, water (lukewarm for**
   compressed yeast)
2 **packages active dry yeast, or 2 cakes**
   compressed yeast
½ **cup milk**
1 **teaspoon salt**
½ **cup sugar**
¼ **cup shortening**
2 **eggs**
4¼ **cups sifted all-purpose flour**
½ **teaspoon mace**
Fat for frying

Mix the 2 teaspoons sugar and water (warm, not hot, water for active dry yeast; lukewarm water for compressed yeast). Sprinkle or crumble in yeast and stir until dissolved. Scald milk. Stir in salt, the ½ cup sugar and the shortening. Cool to lukewarm. Add dissolved yeast to lukewarm milk mixture. Add eggs and mix thoroughly. Add half the flour and mace and beat until smooth. Add remaining flour and stir to mix thoroughly. Turn out on floured board and knead until smooth and elastic, about 8 minutes. Place in greased bowl. Cover and let rise in warm place until double in bulk (about 1 hour). Without punching down, turn out onto lightly floured board. Roll very thin. Cut dough into strips ½" wide and 9" long. Fold in half, twist and fasten ends. Place on lightly floured baking sheet; let rise uncovered in warm place until very light (about 1 hour). Fry in deep hot fat (350° F.) until golden, turning only once. Drain on absorbent paper, cool and roll in sugar. Makes about 48.

GUGELHOPH

½ cup milk
½ cup sugar
½ teaspoon salt
¼ cup butter or margarine
¼ cup warm, not hot, water (lukewarm for compressed yeast)
1 package active dry yeast, or 1 cake compressed yeast
2 eggs, beaten
2½ cups sifted all-purpose flour
14-16 whole blanched almonds
½ cup seedless raisins
½ teaspoon grated lemon rind

Scald milk. Stir in sugar, salt and butter or margarine. Cool to lukewarm. Measure water into a large mixing bowl (warm, not hot, water for active dry yeast; lukewarm water for compressed yeast). Sprinkle or crumble in yeast. Stir until dissolved. Stir in lukewarm milk mixture. Add eggs and flour. Beat vigorously, about 5 minutes. Cover. Let rise in a warm place, free from draft, until doubled in bulk, about 1 hour and 30 minutes. Sprinkle fine bread crumbs over sides and bottom of well-greased 1½-quart casserole or fancy mold. Arrange almonds on bottom of casserole or mold. Stir batter down. Beat thoroughly. Stir in raisins and lemon rind. Turn into prepared casserole or mold. Let rise in warm place, free from draft until doubled in bulk, about 1 hour. Bake in moderate oven (350° F.) about 50 minutes. Makes 1 cake.

CHEESE BREAD

1 cup milk
¼ cup sugar
1 tablespoon salt
2 packages active dry yeast, or 2 cakes compressed yeast
½ cup warm, not hot, water (lukewarm for compressed yeast)
5 cups sifted all-purpose flour (about)
2 cups grated sharp cheese

Scald milk. Add sugar and salt and stir in. Cool to lukewarm. Sprinkle or crumble yeast into water (warm, not hot, water for active dry yeast; lukewarm for compressed yeast). Stir until dissolved. Add lukewarm milk mixture. Add 2½ cups flour and beat until smooth. Add cheese and stir in. Add enough remaining flour to make a stiff dough. Turn dough out on lightly floured board and knead quickly and lightly 8 to 10 minutes or until smooth and elastic. Place in greased bowl; brush lightly with soft or melted shortening. Cover with cloth; let rise in a warm place, free from draft, until doubled in bulk, about 1 hour and 20 minutes. Punch down, pull sides into center and turn out on board. Divide into 2 equal portions. Shape into loaves. Place in greased bread pans (9" x 5" x 3"). Cover with cloth. Let rise in warm place, free from draft, until doubled in bulk, about 1 hour. Bake in a moderate oven (350° F.) about 35 minutes or until loaf sounds hollow when tapped. Turn out on cooling rack. Makes 2 loaves.

PARKERHOUSE ROLLS

½ cup milk
½ cup butter or margarine
1/3 cup sugar
½ teaspoon salt
¼ cup warm, not hot, water (lukewarm for compressed yeast)
1 package active dry yeast, or 1 cake compressed yeast
4 eggs
3½-4 cups sifted all-purpose flour
1 tablespoon sugar

Scald milk. Cool to lukewarm. Cream butter or margarine thoroughly. Gradually cream in sugar and salt. Measure water into a large mixing bowl (warm, not hot, water for active dry yeast; lukewarm water for compressed yeast). Sprinkle or crumble in yeast; stir until dissolved. Stir in lukewarm milk and creamed mixture. Separate one of the eggs, adding yolk to yeast mixture and putting egg white into a small bowl for use later. Add remaining 3 whole eggs and enough of the sifted flour to make a very soft dough. Beat 10 minutes. Cover. Let rise in a warm place, free from draft, about 2 hours or until more than doubled in bulk. Stir down. Beat thoroughly. Cover tighdy with waxed paper or aluminum foil. Store in refrigerator overnight. Stir down and turn out soft dough on floured board. Roll out with floured rolling pin. Cut into rounds with 2½" cookie cutter. Crease with dull edge of knife to one side of center. Brush lightly with melted butter or margarine. Fold larger side over smaller so edges just meet. Seal. Place on greased baking sheet about 1 inch apart. Cover. Let rise in warm place, free from draft, until doubled in bulk. Brush lightly with melted butter or margarine. Bake in hot oven (400° F.) about 15 minutes. Makes about 24.

HOT CROSS BUNS

1 tablespoon sugar
¼ cup warm, not hot, water (lukewarm for compressed yeast)
1 package of active dry yeast, or
1 cake compressed yeast.
1 cup milk
1½ cups sifted all-purpose flour
¼ cup butter or margarine
¼ cup sugar
1 egg, well beaten
1/3 cup raisins
3 ¼ cups sifted all-purpose flour
½ teaspoon salt
1 teaspoon cinnamon
1 egg, slightly beaten
1 tablespoon water

Combine 1 tablespoon sugar and water (warm, not hot water for active dry yeast; lukewarm water for compressed yeast). Dissolve yeast in sweetened water. Scald milk and cool to lukewarm. Combine yeast mixture, milk and 1½ cups flour. Beat until smooth. Cover and let rise about 1 hour. Cream butter or margarine and ¼ cup sugar. Add egg and raisins. Mix well. Combine 3¼ cups flour, salt and cinnamon; add yeast mixture and raisin mixture. Turn out on lightly floured surface and knead lightly. Place in greased bowl. Cover and let rise until doubled in

bulk, about 2 hours. Shape into medium-sized buns. Place about 2 inches apart in well greased shallow pan. Cover and let rise until doubled in bulk, about 1 hour. Combine slightly beaten egg and water. Brush buns with egg-water mixture. Bake in hot oven (425° F.) 25-30 minutes. Decorate with confectioners' sugar glaze, as desired. Makes 24.

POPPY-SEED PASTE

1 cup ground poppy seed
½ cup water
1 tablespoon sugar
1 teaspoon flour

Combine ground poppy seed and water and sugar. Cook over low heat to boiling point, stirring constantly. Mix flour with small amount of water to form smooth paste and add to poppy-seed mixture. Cool. Spread on Kolacke as directed below.

KOLACKE

1½ cups milk
¾ cup butter
¼ cup shortening
½ cup sugar
4 egg yolks, beaten
2 packages active dry yeast, or 2 cakes compressed yeast
½ cup warm, not hot, water (lukewarm for compressed yeast)
1 teaspoon salt
¼ teaspoon mace
4-5 cups all-purpose flour (about)
Melted butter

Scald milk. Cool to lukewarm. Cream butter and shortening; add sugar and cream again. Add egg yolks. Dissolve yeast in water (warm, not hot, for active dry yeast; lukewarm for compressed yeast). Add lukewarm milk, salt and mace and stir in enough of the flour to make a soft dough. Cover, let rise until bulk is doubled. Drop by spoonfuls on floured board. Roll in balls and flatten to ½ inch thickness. Dent tops with fingers, making 3 dents in each cookie. Spread with poppy seed paste. Brush with melted butter. Let rise until doubled in size. Bake in hot oven (425° F.) about 20 minutes. Makes about 40.

Sandwiches

FILLINGS AND SPREADS

OYSTER-CHICKEN SPREAD

1 cup cooked chopped oysters
1 cup cooked chopped chicken
1 tablespoon chopped parsley
1 tablesoon grated onion
¼ teaspoon salt
⅛ teaspoon pepper
Salad dressing

Combine oysters, chicken, parsley, onion, salt and pepper; mix lightly. Add enough salad dressing to moisten. Makes about 2 cups.

AMISH APPLE BUTTER SANDWICH SPREAD

½ cup apple butter
1 8-ounce package cream cheese, softened
2 tablespoons chopped peanuts
2 tablespoons chopped celery

Combine all ingredients and beat until well blended. Makes about 1¼ cups.

BACON-PECAN FILLING

1 8-ounce package cream cheese
2 tablespoons mayonnaise
¼ cup cooked crumbled bacon
2 tablespoons chopped pecans

Combine all ingredients; mix well. Makes about 1 cup.

BAKED BEAN SANDWICH FILLING

1 cup canned baked beans
¼ cup chopped celery
1 tablespoon minced onion
3 tablespoons chili sauce
⅛ teaspoon salt

Combine all ingredients and mix well. Makes about 1¼ cups.

CHEESE, EGG AND OLIVE SANDWICH SPREAD

1 cup cottage cheese
2 hard-cooked eggs, chopped
¼ cup chopped stuffed olives
2 tablespoons mayonnaise
⅛ teaspoon salt
1 tablespoon chopped parsley

Combine all ingredients; mix lightly. Makes about 1¾ cups.

CHEESE-OLIVE SANDWICH FILLING

1½ cups grated Cheddar cheese
¼ cup chopped stuffed olives
1 tablespoon grated onion
⅛ teaspoon salt
Mayonnaise

Combine cheese, olives, onion and salt; mix lightly. Add enough mayonnaise to moisten. Makes about 1¼ cups.

CREAM CHEESE-PINEAPPLE SANDWICH SPREAD

1 8-ounce package cream cheese with chives
½ cup canned crushed pineapple
2 tablespoons orange juice
½ teaspoon grated orange rind
⅛ teaspoon salt

Combine all ingredients and mix well. Makes about 1 cup.

SOUR CREAM-CHEESE SANDWICH SPREAD

1 cup sour cream
1 cup finely diced American cheese
2 tablespoons chopped green pepper
1 tablespoon minced onion
1 tablespoon lemon juice
½ teaspoon salt
⅛ teaspoon paprika
½ teaspoon Worcestershire sauce

Combine all ingredients; mix well. Makes about 2 cups.

SWISS CHEESE SANDWICH SPREAD

½ pound Swiss cheese, grated
2 tablespoons salad dressing
1 tablespoon chopped onion
2 tablespoons chopped pimiento
1 teaspoon Worcestershire sauce
¼ cup chili sauce
¼ teaspoon salt
⅛ teaspoon pepper

Combine all ingredients; mix well. Makes about 2 cups.

CORNED BEEF-HORSERADISH SANDWICH FILLING

1½ cups chopped, cooked corned beef
½ cup chopped green pepper
1 tablespoon horseradish
Salad dressing

Combine corned beef, green pepper and horseradish; add enough salad dressing to moisten; mix lightly. Makes about 2 cups.

DUBLIN SANDWICH FILLING

1 cup chopped, cooked corned beef
1 cup shredded cabbage
1 tablespoon chopped dill pickle
Salad dressing

Combine corned beef, cabbage and pickle with enough salad dressing to moisten. Makes about 2 cups.

HAM AND CHEESE SANDWICH SPREAD

1½ cups cooked, chopped ham
1½ cups grated American cheese
1 tablespoon grated onion
2 tablespoons chili sauce
Mayonnaise

Combine ham, cheese, onion and chili sauce. Add enough mayonnaise to moisten. Makes about 3 cups.

CREAMY SHRIMP SANDWICH SPREAD

1 5-ounce can shrimp, chopped
1 cup sour cream
2 tablespoons catsup
1 teaspoon lemon juice
¼ teaspoon grated lemon rind
¼ teaspoon salt
⅛ teaspoon pepper
1 teaspoon horseradish

Combine all ingredients and mix well. Makes about 1½ cups.

ALMOND-TUNA SANDWICH SPREAD

1 7¾-ounce can tuna
½ cup mayonnaise
½ cup chopped almonds
1 tablespoon chopped pimiento
Dash Tabasco
¼ teaspoon salt

Combine all ingredients and mix well; chill. Makes about 2½ cups.

SOUR CREAM-PIMIENTO SANDWICH SPREAD

1 cup cottage cheese
¼ cup cream cheese
3 tablespoons sour cream
2 tablespoons chopped pimiento
¼ teaspoon salt

Combine all ingredients; mix lightly. Makes about 1½ cups.

WATER CRESS-BACON SPREAD

1 8-ounce package cream cheese
2 tablespoons light cream
½ cup cooked crumbled bacon
½ cup chopped water cress

Combine all ingredients and beat until well mixed. Makes about 1 cup.

HAM FILLING HAWAIIAN

1½ cups cooked ground ham
¼ cup drained canned crushed pineapple
1 tablespoon brown sugar
2 tablespoons mayonnaise
1 teaspoon horseradish

Combine all ingredients and mix well. Chill thoroughly. Makes about 1¾ cups.

LIVER SAUSAGE SPREAD

½ pound liver sausage
½ cup chopped celery
2 tablespoons sweet pickle relish
1 tablespoon chopped onion
2 hard-cooked eggs, chopped
Salad dressing

Combine liver sausage, celery, pickle relish, onion, eggs and enough salad dressing to moisten. Makes about 1½ cups.

HOT SANDWICHES

DEVILED HAMBURGERS

1 pound ground beef
2 tablespoons chili sauce
1 tablespoon catsup
1 teaspoon prepared mustard
1 teaspoon horseradish
1 tablespoon grated onion
½ teaspoon salt
6-8 slices bread

Combine beef, chili sauce, catsup, mustard, horseradish, onion and salt. Mix well. Toast bread on one side. Spread untoasted sides with beef mixture. Broil 3 or 4 inches from source of heat 5–7 minutes. Serves 6-8.

BROILED TUNA SANDWICHES

1 tablespoon butter
1 tablespoon all-purpose flour
½ cup milk
1 cup grated American cheese
1 egg, well beaten
1 cup flaked canned tuna
¼ teaspoon salt
6 slices bread

Melt butter and blend in flour. Gradually add milk and cook, stirring constantly, until thickened. Add cheese and stir until melted. Add a little of hot mixture to egg and mix well. Add egg mixture to hot mixture and cook, stirring constantly, 2 minutes. Add tuna and salt. Remove from heat. Toast bread on one side. Spread untoasted sides with tuna mixture. Broil 3 or 4 inches from source of heat, 3–5 minutes, or until lightly browned. Serves 6.

APPLESAUCE AND CHEESE SANDWICH

4 slices buttered toast
½ cup applesauce
1 teaspoon cinnamon
6 slices American cheese

Spread toast with applesauce. Sprinkle cinnamon over applesauce. Top with cheese slices. Broil 3 or 4 inches from source of heat 3–5 minutes or until cheese is melted. Serves 4.

GRILLED CHEESE AND TOMATO SANDWICH

¼ cup butter or margarine, softened
½ teaspoon celery seed
6 slices bread
3 medium-sized tomatoes, sliced
6 slices processed Swiss cheese

Combine butter or margarine and celery seed. Toast bread on one side. Spread untoasted sides with celery seed mixture. Arrange tomato slices over celery seed mixture. Top with cheese slices. Broil 3 or 4 inches from source of heat about 5 minutes or until lightly browned. Serves 6.

HOT CORNED BEEF HASH SANDWICHES

1 cup corned beef hash
1 tablespoon chili sauce
1 tablespoon grated onion
1 tablespoon prepared mustard
4 slices bread
4 slices American cheese

Combine hash, chili sauce, onion and mustard. Toast bread on one side; spread untoasted side with corned beef mixture. Top with cheese slices. Broil 3 or 4 inches from source of heat about 5 minutes or until cheese is melted. Serves 4.

CHEESE PUFF SANDWICHES

6 slices bread
6 slices American cheese
1/8 teaspoon salt
3 eggs, separated
1/4 cup mayonnaise

Toast bread on one side. Arrange cheese slices on untoasted side. Add salt to egg whites and beat until stiff. Combine mayonnaise and egg yolks. Beat until light. Fold yolk mixture into whites. Top cheese slices with egg mixture. Bake in moderate oven (350° F.) about 15 minutes or until lightly browned. Serve immediately. Serves 6.

HOT HAM SANDWICHES

1/4 cup chopped onion
2 tablespoons melted butter or margarine
8 slices boiled ham
1 8-ounce can tomato sauce
4 slices buttered toast

Cook onion in butter or margarine until tender. Add ham and brown on both sides. Add tomato sauce and heat to serving temperature. Serve over toast. Serves 4.

BROILED VEGETABLE-CHEESE SANDWICHES

2 cups chopped fresh tomatoes
2 tablespoons chopped celery
1 tablespoon chopped green pepper
2 tablespoons grated onion
4 slices buttered toast
4 slices American cheese

Combine tomatoes, celery, green pepper and onion. Place vegetable mixture on toast. Top with

cheese. Broil 3 or 4 inches from source of heat 4–5 minutes or until cheese is melted and lightly browned. Serves 4.

WESTERN SANDWICH

4 eggs, beaten
2 tablespoons minced onion
2 tablespoons chopped green pepper
1/4 cup minced, cooked ham
1/3 cup milk
1/8 teaspoon salt
2 tablespoons melted butter or margarine
8 slices buttered bread

Combine eggs, onion, green pepper, ham, milk and salt. Mix well. Cook over low heat in butter or margarine until set; arrange egg mixture on 4 slices bread. Top with remaining bread. Serves 4.

BROILED CRAB SANDWICHES

1 6 1/2-ounce can crab meat, flaked
1 tablespoon chopped green pepper
1 tablespoon grated onion
1/4 teaspoon salt
1/4 cup mayonnaise
1 teaspoon lemon juice
1 teaspoon horseradish
4 slices bread
4 slices American cheese

Combine crab meat, green pepper, onion, salt, mayonnaise, lemon juice and horseradish; mix well. Toast bread on one side. Spread untoasted sides with crab meat mixture. Top crab meat mixture with cheese slices. Broil 3 or 4 inches from source of heat, about 5 minutes, or until lightly browned. Serves 4.

BAKED FRANKFURTER SANDWICHES

8 slices buttered bread
2 tablespoons prepared mustard
1 cup grated American cheese
4 frankfurters, sliced
2 tablespoons chopped onion
1/4 teaspoon salt
1/8 teaspoon pepper
2 eggs, well beaten
3/4 cup milk

Arrange 4 slices of the bread in greased 8" x 8" baking pan. Combine mustard, cheese, frankfurter slices, onion, salt and pepper. Top bread slices in baking pan with frankfurter mixture. Top with remaining bread slices. Combine eggs and milk; pour milk mixture over sandwiches. Bake in moderate oven (350° F.) 45 minutes. Serves 4.

KRAUT AND FRANKFURTER ROLLS

¼ cup softened butter or margarine
1 tablespoon prepared mustard
4 frankfurters
1 No. 2 can sauerkraut
4 frankfurter rolls

Combine butter or margarine and mustard; mix well. Broil frankfurters 3 or 4 inches from source of heat about 5 minutes or until browned on both sides. Heat sauerkraut to serving temperature; drain. Split rolls lengthwise and spread with mustard mixture. Arrange frankfurters on rolls; top with sauerkraut. Serves 4.

COLD SANDWICHES

TONGUE AND CHEESE SANDWICH

8 slices buttered bread
1 8-ounce package cream cheese, softened
8 slices tongue
¼ cup horseradish

Spread 4 slices of the bread with cream cheese; arrange tongue over cheese. Top with horseradish and remaining bread slices. Serves 4.

ROAST BEEF AND ONION SANDWICH

8 slices buttered pumpernickel bread
¼ cup mayonnaise
8 slices roast beef
1 Bermuda onion, thinly sliced

Spread 4 slices bread with mayonnaise. Arrange roast beef over mayonnaise. Top with onion slices and remaining bread slices. Serves 4.

OPEN VEGETABLE AND HAM SANDWICH

2 cups shredded cabbage
¼ cup grated carrot
1 cup cooked beets
¼ teaspoon salt
1/8 teaspoon pepper
Mayonnaise
4 slices ham
4 slices buttered toast

Combine cabbage, carrot, beets, salt and pepper. Add enough mayonnaise to moisten and mix lightly. Arrange ham slices on toast. Top with cabbage mixture. Serves 4.

CHICKEN LIVER-BACON SANDWICHES

½ pound chicken livers, cooked
½ cup cooked crumbled bacon
1 tablespoon chopped onion
Mayonnaise
8 slices buttered rye bread

Chop chicken livers; combine chicken livers, bacon and onion. Add enough mayonnaise to moisten and mix lightly. Chill thoroughly. Spread on 4 slices of the bread. Top with remaining bread. Serves 4.

CRAB MEAT SANDWICH SPECIAL

1 6 ½-ounce can crab meat, flaked
2 tablespoons chopped green pepper
¼ cup chopped cucumber
3 tablesoons mayonnaise
2 tablesoons chili sauce
1 teaspoon lemon juice
2 drops Tabasco
6 buttered frankfurter rolls

Combine crab meat, green pepper, cucumber, mayonnaise, chili sauce, lemon juice and Tabasco; mix lightly. Fill rolls with crab-meat mixture. Serves 6.

AVOCADO-CHEESE SANDWICH

½ cup mashed avocado
1 cup cottage cheese
1 tablespoon minced onion
1/8 teaspoon celery salt
1/8 teaspoon salt
1 teaspoon lemon juice
½ teaspoon Worcestershire sauce
8 slices buttered rye bread

Combine avocado, cheese, onion, celery salt,
salt, lemon juice and Worcestershire sauce.
Spread cheese mixture on 4 slices of the bread.
Top with remaining bread. Serves 4.

CHEESE AND SALAMI SANDWICHES

8 slices buttered rye bread
1 tablespoon prepared mustard
4 slices Cheddar cheese
12 slices salami
1 medium-sized green pepper, cut in rings

Spread 4 slices of the bread with mustard.
Arrange cheese, salami and pepper rings over
mustard. Top with remaining bread slices. Serves
4.

TOMATO-PEANUT BUTTER SANDWICH

¾ cup peanut butter
¼ cup mayonnaise
1/8 teaspoon salt
8 slices buttered whole wheat bread
2 medium-sized tomatoes, thinly sliced

Combine peanut butter, mayonnaise and salt;
mix well. Spread peanut butter mixture on 4
slices of the bread. Top with tomato slices and
remaining bread. Serves 4.

BOLOGNA-BAKED BEAN SANDWICH

¼ pound bologna
1 1-pound can baked beans
1 tablespoon catsup
1 tablespoon prepared mustard
2 teaspoons grated onion
12 slices buttered bread

Chop bologna; add beans, catsup, mustard and
onion. Mix well. Spread bean mixture on 6 slices
of the bread. Top with remaining bread. Serves 6.

Eggs & Cheese

EGGS

SCOTCH WOODCOCK

2 tablespoons butter
1 tablespoon all-purpose flour
1 cup milk
4 hard-cooked eggs, chopped
1 tablespoon anchovy paste
¼ teaspoon salt
¼ teaspoon Worcestershire sauce
¼ teaspoon paprika

Melt butter; blend in flour. Gradually add milk and cook, stirring constantly, until thickened. Add remaining ingredients; heat to serving temperature. Serve over toast, as desired. Serves 4.

SCALLOPED EGGS WITH POTATO

2 tablespoons butter
2 tablespoons all-purpose flour
2 cups milk
2 tablespoons chopped parsley
1 teaspoon salt
6 medium-sized potatoes, cooked and sliced
6 hard-cooked eggs, sliced
1 cup cracker crumbs

Melt butter and blend in flour. Gradually add milk and cook, stirring constantly, until thickened. Add parsley, salt, potatoes and egg slices. Turn into greased 2-quart casserole. Top with crumbs. Bake in moderate oven (350° F.) 30–35 minutes. Serves 4–6.

BAKED EGGS ARKANSAS

4 slices Swiss cheese
8 slices bacon, cut in half
4 eggs
1 tablespoon minced scallions
½ teaspoon paprika
½ teaspoon salt
½ cup light cream

Arrange cheese slices in 4 greased individual baking dishes. Arrange bacon over cheese. Break eggs over bacon. Sprinkle scallions, paprika and salt over eggs. Pour 2 tablespoons cream over other ingredients. Bake in moderate oven (350° F.) about 15 minutes, or until eggs are set. Serves 4.

EGGS BAYOU

4 small tomatoes
½ teaspoon salt
⅛ teaspoon pepper
4 eggs
3 tablespoons butter
3 tablespoons all-purpose flour
1½ cups light cream
2 tablespoons chopped parsley
Dash Tabasco
4 slices toast

Remove stem ends from tomatoes and scoop out pulp. Sprinkle tomatoes with salt and pepper. Break 1 egg into each tomato. Place tomatoes in 4 greased baking cups. Bake in moderate oven (350° F.) 15–20 minutes, or until eggs are set. Melt butter and blend in flour. Gradually add cream and cook, stirring constantly, until thickened. Stir in parsley and Tabasco. Arrange tomatoes on toast slices and top with sauce. Serves 4.

GOLDEN EGG CROQUETTES

1 tablespoon minced onion
1/3 cup minced celery
3 tablespoons melted butter or margarine
1/3 cup all-purpose flour
1½ cups milk
2 cups cooked elbow macaroni
4 hard-cooked eggs, chopped
1 tablespoon chopped parsley
½ teaspoon salt
1/8 teaspoon pepper
¼ teaspoon poultry seasoning
Fine dry bread crumbs
3 tablespoons melted butter or margarine

Cook onion and celery in butter or margarine until tender. Blend in flour. Gradually add milk and cook, stirring constantly, until thickened. Add macaroni, eggs, parsley and seasonings. Chill thoroughly. Shape into croquettes and roll in bread crumbs. Cook in butter or margarine until browned on all sides. Serves 6.

NOVA SCOTIA POACHED EGGS

2 tablespoons butter
2 tablespoons all-purpose flour
1½ cups milk
1 teaspoon anchovy paste
1 teaspoon chopped pimiento
1/8 teaspoon Worcestershire sauce
4 slices smoked salmon
4 slices toast
4 poached eggs

Melt butter and blend in flour. Gradually add milk and cook, stirring constantly, until thickened. Add anchovy paste, pimiento and Worcestershire sauce. Arrange salmon on toast. Place poached eggs over salmon and top with anchovy sauce. Serves 4.

EGG POTATO PUFF

1/3 cup milk
1 cup mashed potatoes
1 teaspoon onion juice
½ teaspoon salt
1/8 teaspoon pepper
4 eggs, separated
¼ cup butter
12 slices cooked bacon

Combine milk, potatoes, onion juice, salt and pepper. Beat egg yolks and add potato mixture. Beat egg whites until stiff and fold into potato mixture. Melt butter and add potato mixture. Cook over low heat until browned on bottom. Broil 3 inches from source of heat until lightly browned. Serve with bacon. Serves 6.

EGGS SAN JOAQUIN

6 eggs, slightly beaten
½ teaspoon salt
1/8 teaspoon pepper
1/3 cup light cream
½ teaspoon Worcestershire sauce
¼ cup butter
1 medium-sized avocado, peeled and sliced
4 slices toast
8 slices cooked bacon

Combine eggs, salt, pepper, cream and Worcestershire sauce. Melt butter and cook until lightly browned. Add egg mixture and cook over low heat until eggs are set, stirring occasionally. Arrange avocado slices on toast. Top with eggs. Garnish with bacon. Serves 4.

BAKED CLAM OMELET

1 cup chopped clams
2 tablespoons melted butter
6 eggs, separated
½ teaspoon salt
2 tablespoons chopped parsley
½ cup light cream

Cook clams in butter 3 minutes over low heat. Beat egg yolks; add clam mixture, salt, parsley and cream. Beat egg whites until stiff and fold into clam mixture. Turn into well-greased skillet. Bake in moderate oven (350° F.) about 30 minutes. Serves 6.

IOWA MUFFIN PAN HASH

1 cup cooked, chopped beef
1 cup cooked, chopped potatoes
¼ cup chopped onion
1 teaspoon salt
1/8 teaspoon pepper
¼ cup beef broth
6 eggs

Combine beef, potatoes, onion, salt, pepper and broth. Mix thoroughly. Fill muffin pans 2/3 full with meat mixture. Bake in moderate oven (350° F.) 30 minutes. Break eggs over meat mixture and continue baking 10 minutes, or until eggs are set. Serves 6.

EGGS IN ISLANDS

4 slices bread
2 tablespoons butter
4 eggs

Remove centers from bread with small round cooky cutter. Melt butter. Add bread slices. Break eggs over bread so yolks fall in bread centers. Cook over low heat until eggs are set. Serves 4.

EGGS MARDI GRAS

⅓ cup chopped onion
⅓ cup chopped green pepper
2 tablesoons melted butter
1 No. 2 can tomatoes
2 cups water
1 cup rice
½ teaspoon salt
1/8 teaspoon pepper
6 eggs

Cook onion and green pepper in butter until tender. Add tomatoes and water. Heat to boiling point. Add rice, cover and cook over low heat until rice is tender. Add salt and pepper. Drop eggs over rice mixture. Cover and simmer until eggs are set. Serves 6.

DEVILED EGGS

4 hard-cooked eggs
2 tablespoons salad dressing
1 teaspoon grated onion
¼ teaspoon salt
1/8 teaspoon pepper

Cut eggs in half lengthwise. Remove yolks and mash. Combine yolks, salad dressing, onion, salt and pepper. Fill whites with yolk mixture. Top with chopped parsley, if desired. Serves 4.

EGGS ESPAGNOL

1 tablespoon butter
¼ pound dried beef, shredded
2 tablespoons grated American cheese
Dash of cayenne pepper
1 tablespoon chili sauce
1 cup cooked tomatoes
¼ teaspoon salt
4 eggs, well beaten

Melt butter, add beef and cheese. Toss lightly until beef is browned. Add remaining ingredients. Cook over low heat, stirring constantly, until thickened. Serves 4.

PIONEER EGG FRITTERS

1 cup cooked, minced tongue
1 cup cooked, minced ham
1 tablespoon chopped celery
1 tablespoon chopped stuffed olives
¼ teaspoon paprika
8 eggs, separated
¼ cup milk

Combine tongue, ham, celery, olives and paprika. Beat egg yolks well and add milk. Fold into tongue mixture. Beat egg whites until stiff and fold into tongue mixture. Drop by tablespoonfuls into hot fat, 1 inch deep. Cook about 2 minutes, or until browned on all sides. Drain on absorbent paper. Serves 8.

EGG-MUSHROOM SCRAMBLE

4 eggs
¼ cup light cream
Salt
½ teaspoon Worcestershire sauce
2 tablespoons melted butter
½ cup mushrooms, chopped
3 strips crisp cooked bacon, crumbled

Beat eggs with cream, salt to taste. Add Worcestershire sauce. Heat butter and add mushrooms. Cook 3 minutes over low heat. Add bacon and eggs. Stir eggs lightly until done. Serves 4.

SHIRRED EGGS POPEYE

2 cups cooked spinach
¼ cup cooked, crumbled bacon
4 eggs
½ teaspoon salt
1/8 teaspoon pepper
2 tablespoons fine dry bread crumbs

Combine spinach and bacon. Turn into greased 1-quart casserole. Drop eggs over spinach mixture. Season with salt and pepper. Sprinkle crumbs over eggs. Bake in moderate oven (350° F.) 20–25 minutes, or until eggs are set. Serves 4.

MUSHROOM-OYSTER OMELET

3 tablespoons butter
3 tablespoons all-purpose flour
1 cup light cream
1 cup small oysters
1 4-ounce can mushrooms, drained
½ teaspoon salt
1/8 teaspoon pepper
4 eggs, slightly beaten
¼ cup light cream
2 tablespoons butter

Melt the 3 tablespoons butter and blend in flour. Gradually add 1 cup cream and cook, stirring constantly, until thickened. Add oysters and mushrooms, and cook over low heat until edges of oysters curl. Combine salt, pepper, eggs and ¼ cup cream. Melt the 2 tablespoons butter. Add egg mixture and cook over low heat until omelet is firm. Pour half of oyster mixture over omelet. Fold over and turn out on platter. Pour remaining oysters around omelet. Serves 4.

HOOSIER EGG CASSEROLE

¼ cup butter
¼ cup all-purpose flour
2 cups milk
1 tablespoon prepared mustard
2½ cups cooked green beans
4 hard-cooked eggs, chopped
Salt and pepper to taste
2 tablespoons buttered bread crumbs

Melt butter and blend in flour. Gradually add milk and cook, stirring constantly, until thickened. Add mustard, beans and eggs. Season with salt and pepper. Turn into greased 1½-quart casserole. Top with crumbs. Bake in moderate oven (350° F.) 30-40 minutes. Serves 6.

SUNDAY BREAKFAST OMELET

¼ cup butter
2 cups dry bread cubes
4 eggs, well beaten
1 tablespoon cream
1 teaspoon salt
Dash Tabasco
1 tablespoon chopped celery

Melt butter. Add bread cubes and cook over low heat until browned. Combine eggs, cream, salt, Tabasco and parsley. Pour over bread cubes and continue cooking until eggs are set Serves 4.

DEEP SEA SCRAMBLED EGGS

6 eggs, slightly beaten
½ cup light cream
Salt and pepper to taste
1 tablespoon lemon juice
1 tablespoon chopped chives
1 cup diced cooked salmon
2 tablespoons melted butter

Combine eggs, cream, salt, pepper, lemon juice, chives and salmon. Cook in butter over low h«at, stirring constantly, until eggs are set. Serves 4.

CHEESE

WELSH RABBIT

1 tablespoon butter
2 8-ounce packages natural Cheddar cheese, grated
½ to 1 cup ale or beer
1 teaspoon Worcestershire sauce
½ teaspoon dry mustard
1/8 teaspoon cayenne pepper
½ teaspoon salt

In chafing dish or double boiler over hot (not boiling) water, melt butter and cheese. As cheese begins to melt, gradually stir in ale or beer to make desired consistency. Cook only until smooth and hot. Stir in seasonings and serve on hot crisp toast or heated crackers. Serves 4-6.

CHEESE FONDUE

4 eggs, well beaten
2 cups milk
2 cups soft bread crumbs
2 cups grated American or Swiss cheese
1 tablespoon melted butter
½ teaspoon salt
1/8 teaspoon paprika

Combine all ingredients and mix lightly. Turn into greased 2-quart baking dish. Bake in moderate oven (350° F.) 30 minutes or until lightly browned. Serves 4.

CHEESE SOUFFLÉ

3 tablespoons butter or margarine
3 tablespoons flour
1 cup milk
¼ teaspoon salt
Dash of cayenne pepper
1/8 teaspoon dry mustard
1 cup grated cheese
4 eggs, separated

Melt butter or margarine. Stir in flour. Gradually add milk, stirring until well blended. Cook until sauce is thick. Add salt, cayenne, mustard and cheese; stir until cheese melts. Beat egg yolks, gradually add to cheese sauce stirring constantly. Cool. Beat egg whites until stiff but not dry. Fold egg yolk mixture into beaten egg whites. Pour into ungreased 1½-quart baking dish. Bake in a moderate oven (350° F.) 45 minutes. Serve immediately. Serves 4.

Fish

BAKED FLOUNDER

1 3-pound flounder, cleaned
1 teaspoon salt
1/8 teaspoon pepper
1/3 cup chopped onions
1 bay leaf, crushed
2 tablespoons chopped parsley
1/4 teaspoon thyme
1 cup dry white wine
2 tablespoons butter
2 tablespoons all-purpose flour
6 medium-sized tomatoes, chopped
1/4 teaspoon celery salt
1/4 cup buttered cracker crumbs
Paprika

Sprinkle flounder with salt and pepper. Combine onions, bay leaf, parsley and thyme. Spread onion mixture evenly over bottom of greased shallow baking pan. Place flounder over onion mixture. Pour wine over flounder. Bake in moderate oven (350° F.) 25 minutes. Melt butter. Add flour and brown. Add tomatoes and celery salt. Cook over low heat, stirring constantly, 10 minutes. Pour tomato mixture over flounder. Top with crumbs. Continue baking 10 minutes. Sprinkle with paprika. Serves 6.

BROILED SHAD

1 3-pound shad, cleaned and split
1/4 cup melted butter
1 teaspoon salt
1/4 teaspoon pepper
1/4 cup chopped water cress
1/2 cup melted butter
2 tablespoons lemon juice

Brush shad with the 1/4 cup butter. Broil, skin side down, 3 inches from source of heat 8–12 minutes, or until fish flakes easily when tested with a fork. Meanwhile, combine remaining ingredients. Heat to serving temperature. Pour over fish. Serves 6–8.

MINNESOTA BAKED PIKE

1 3-pound pike
Salt
2 cups soft bread crumbs
1 tablespoon melted bacon drippings
1 cup well-drained cooked tomatoes
1 teaspoon poultry seasoning
1 teaspoon salt
1/4 teaspoon paprika
6 bay leaves
4 slices bacon
Lemon wedges
Parsley

Clean fish and rub with salt. Combine bread crumbs, bacon drippings, tomatoes, poultry seasoning, the 1 teaspoon salt and paprika. Stuff fish with tomato mixture and fasten with toothpicks. Place fish in greased baking pan. Top with bay leaves and bacon. Bake in moderate oven (350° F.) 45 minutes, or until fish flakes easily when tested with a fork. Garnish with lemon and parsley. Serves 6.

ISLANDERS' BAKED BASS

1 4-pound bass
1 cup olive oil
1 cup canned tomatoes
1/4 cup chopped parsley
1 clove garlic, chopped fine
1/2 cup cracker meal

Clean, wash and salt fish. Place in a shallow baking pan. Mix olive oil, tomatoes, parsley and garlic and spread part of this mixture over fish. Sprinkle fish with half of cracker meal, pour on rest of the sauce and cover with remaining cracker meal. Bake fish in hot oven (400° F.) about 1 hour, basting occasionally. Serves 4–6.

COD ANTIGUA

½ cup chives, chopped
2 cloves garlic, chopped
2 tablespoons olive oil
2 pounds cod, shredded
3 raw potatoes, sliced thin
2 tomatoes, peeled and sliced
1 green pepper, chopped
1 cup grated American cheese
Salt and pepper
1 cup water

Saute chives and garlic in olive oil 5 minutes. Add cod and mix thoroughly. Place ½ of cod mixture in bottom of 2-quart casserole. Arrange potatoes, tomato slices, green pepper and cheese over fish. Season to taste with salt and pepper and cover with remaining fish. Add water; cover and bake in moderate oven (350° F.) 1 hour. Serves 6.

FISH FILLET CASSEROLE

1 medium-sized onion, thinly sliced
¼ cup melted butter or margarine
1½ pounds fish fillets
1 teaspoon salt
1/8 teaspoon pepper
½ cup buttered bread crumbs
2 tablespoons chopped parsley
½ cup cooked, crumbled bacon

Cook onion in butter or margarine until tender. Arrange fillets in a greased shallow baking dish. Arrange onion over fish. Add remaining ingredients. Bake in moderate oven (350° F.) 25–30 minutes. Serves 6.

BAKED SALMON PORTLAND

1 5-pound piece fresh salmon
Salt
Lemon juice
3 cups cracker crumbs, crushed
¼ cup melted butter or margarine
½ teaspoon salt
2 tablespoons vinegar
1 bay leaf, crushed
1 teaspoon Worcestershire sauce
2 tablespoons chopped chives
¼ teaspoon poultry seasoning

Rub fish inside and out with salt. Sprinkle with lemon juice. Combine remaining ingredients and pile into fish. Sew together. Place fish on rack in shallow pan. Bake, uncovered, in moderate oven (350° F.) about 1 hour. Serves 6–8.

FRESH SALMON CASSEROLE

2 pounds salmon steaks, cut 1-inch thick
2 teaspoons salt
Dash pepper
1½ cups chopped celery
½ cup onion rings
3 tablespoons chopped green pepper
¼ cup butter, melted
2 cups whole-kernel corn
2 tablespoons soy sauce

Sprinkle salmon on both sides with 1 teaspoon of the salt, and pepper. Place steaks in shallow well-greased casserole. Cook celery, onion and green pepper in butter until tender. Add corn and soy sauce; pour over salmon. Sprinkle with remaining salt, and bake, covered, in moderate oven (350° F.) for 25–30 minutes. Serves 6.

SALMON MOUSSE

2 egg yolks, slightly beaten
1 teaspoon salt
½ teaspoon dry mustard
¼ teaspoon paprika
¼ cup lemon juice
1 tablespoon butter
1 cup milk
1 envelope unflavored gelatin
¼ cup cold water
2½ cups cooked flaked salmon

Combine egg yolks, salt, mustard, paprika, lemon juice, butter and milk. Cook over low heat, stirring constantly, until thickened. Soften gelatin in water. Add gelatin to milk mixture and stir until dissolved. Chill until slightly thickened. Fold in salmon. Pour into 1-quart mold and chill until firm. Serves 4–6.

SHEPHERD SALMON PIE

1 1-pound can salmon
1/3 cup butter
1/3 cup all-purpose flour
½ teaspoon salt
¼ teaspoon paprika
Milk
1 tablespoon chopped onion
1 cup cooked mushrooms
3 cups seasoned mashed potatoes

Drain and flake salmon; reserve liquid. Melt butter and blend in flour, salt and paprika. Add enough milk to salmon liquid to make 2 cups. Gradually add milk mixture to butter mixture.

Cook, stirring constantly, until thickened. Add onion and mushrooms. Line well-greased 9" pie pan with 2 cups of the potatoes. Pour salmon mixture over potatoes. Top with remaining potatoes. Bake in hot oven (400° F.) 15–20 minutes, or until lightly browned. Serves 6.

BAKED STUFFED SMELTS

36 smelts
12 anchovies, skinned, boned and chopped
¾ cup fine dry bread crumbs
½ cup melted butter
½ teaspoon Worcestershire sauce

Remove head and backbone (if desired) from smelts. Place ½ of smelts in greased shallow baking pan. Top with anchovies. Top with remaining smelts. Sprinkle bread crumbs over smelts. Combine butter and Worcestershire sauce; pour over smelts. Bake in moderate oven (350° F.) 35–40 minutes, or until fish flakes easily when tested with a fork. Serves 6.

SOUTHERN RED SNAPPER

¼ cup minced onion
1 cup chopped green pepper
1 clove garlic, minced
2 tablespoons cooking oil
6 medium-sized tomatoes, chopped
½ cup chopped shrimp
4 pounds red snapper, cleaned
1 cup dry white wine
1 teaspoon salt
¼ teaspoon pepper
2 tablespoons chopped parsley

Cook onion, green pepper and garlic in oil until onion is tender. Add tomatoes and cook over low heat 20 minutes; stir in shrimp. Place red snapper in greased shallow baking pan. Pour wine over fish. Add tomato mixture. Sprinkle with salt, pepper and parsley. Bake in moderate oven (350° F.) 30 minutes, or until fish is tender. Serves 6.

CURRIED SOLE

2 pounds tomatoes, peeled
½ cup chopped onions
¼ teaspoon Worcestershire sauce
1 tablespoon curry powder
1/8 teaspoon pepper
¼ teaspoon salt
1 tablespoon chopped green pepper

1 tablespoon chopped pimiento
6 tablespoons butter
12 sole fillets
½ cup all-purpose flour
½ cup chopped parsley
½ cup light cream

Combine tomatoes, onions and Worcestershire sauce. Cook over low heat 1 hour. Add curry powder, pepper, salt, green pepper and pimiento. Melt butter. Dip fish in flour and cook in butter until browned on both sides. Sprinkle with parsley. Arrange on platter. Combine cream with tomato mixture. Heat to serving temperature. Pour over fish. Serves 6.

SAUTÉED STURGEON STEAK

1½ pounds sturgeon steak
2 tablespoons melted butter
½ cup lemon juice
½ teaspoon salt
1/8 teaspoon pepper
2 tablespoons horseradish
1 egg
2 tablespoons water
½ cup fine dry bread crumbs
¼ cup melted fat

Soak fish in hot water 5 minutes; drain. Combine butter, lemon juice, salt, pepper and horseradish; add fish and chill several hours. Beat egg with water. Drain fish and dip in egg mixture. Coat with crumbs. Cook in fat until browned on both sides and fish is tender. Serves 4.

WENDISH FISH HASH

1 salt herring
2 cups cooked cubed potatoes
2 tablespoons chopped onion
2 tablespoons melted butter
½ cup heavy cream
½ cup milk
1/8 teaspoon black pepper
1/8 teaspoon paprika
1/8 teaspoon celery salt

Clean herring and soak in cold water for several hours. Remove skin and bones. Cut in cubes. Brown potatoes and onion in butter. Add herring and brown lightly. Add remaining ingredients and cook over low heat, stirring occasionally, until fish is tender. Serves 4.

TROUT DELICIOUS

1 cup blanched slivered almonds
¼ cup melted butter
3 tablespoons brown sugar
½ cup sherry
1 tablespoon chopped parsley
4 mountain trout
3 tablespoons melted butter

Add almonds to the ¼ cup butter and cook over low heat until lightly browned. Add brown sugar, sherry and parsley. Mix well and heat thoroughly. Cook trout in the 3 tablespoons butter until browned on both sides. Continue cooking until fish flakes easily when tested with a fork. Serve with almond sauce. Serves 4.

BAKED TROUT WITH TOMATO SAUCE

3 pounds lake trout
1 No. 2 can tomatoes
¼ cup chopped onion
¼ cup chopped celery
1 tablespoon butter
1 teaspoon salt ft teaspoon pepper
1 tablespoon all-purpose flour
1 egg yolk
½ cup milk
1/8 teaspoon Tabasco

Arrange trout in greased shallow baking pan. Combine tomatoes, onion and celery. Pour tomato mixture over trout. Dot with butter. Sprinkle salt and pepper over tomato mixture. Bake in moderate oven (350° F.) 40 minutes, or until fish flakes easily when tested with a fork. Remove fish; strain tomato mixture. Combine flour, egg yolk, milk and Tabasco; mix well. Add flour mixture to tomato mixture and cook over low heat, stirring constantly, 5 minutes. Serve tomato sauce over trout. Serves 6.

PLANKED WHITEFISH

1 3-pound whitefish
1/3 cup butter or margarine
2 tablespoons lemon juice
1 teaspoon grated lemon rind
2 teaspoons salt
¼ teaspoon pepper
4 cups seasoned mashed potatoes

Clean fish and split down back. Remove bones. Place skin side down on preheated oiled plank.

Combine butter or margarine, lemon juice and rind. Spread lemon mixture evenly over fish. Sprinkle with salt and pepper. Broil 3 inches from source of heat 5 minutes. Arrange potatoes around fish. Continue broiling about 5 minutes, or until potatoes are browned and fish flakes easily when tested with a fork. Serves 6.

SUNDAY CODFISH CAKES

2 cups cooked salt codfish
2 cups seasoned mashed potatoes
2 tablespoons melted butter
1 egg, well beaten
1 cup milk
1/8 teaspoon pepper
¼ cup melted bacon drippings

Combine fish, potatoes, butter, egg, milk and pepper. Chill several hours. Shape into cakes and cook in drippings until well browned on both sides. Serve with bacon, as desired. Serves 4.

FROGS' LEGS BIARRITZ

12 pairs frog's legs
1½ cups white wine
4 sprigs parsley
2 bay leaves
1 clove garlic, crushed
¼ cup all-purpose flour
1 teaspoon salt
1/8 teaspoon pepper
½ cup butter
¼ cup chopped shallots
3 tablespoons all-purpose flour
1 cup light cream
2 tablespoons minced parsley
Lemon quarters

Combine frog's legs, wine, the 4 sprigs parsley, bay leaves and garlic. Let stand several hours. Remove frogs' legs. Combine the ¼ cup flour, salt and pepper. Coat frogs' legs with flour mixture. Melt butter; add frogs' legs and cook until lightly browned. Remove frogs' legs. Add shallots to butter and cook until lightly browned. Blend in the 3 tablespoons flour. Gradually add cream and cook until thickened, stirring constantly. Strain wine mixture; add to cream mixture and heat to serving temperature, stirring constantly. Garnish frogs' legs with minced parsley and lemon quarters. Serve with wine sauce. Serves 4.

HALIBUT-BEET HASH

¾ cup flaked cooked halibut
¾ cup chopped cooked potatoes
2 cooked medium beets, chopped
1 tablespoon minced onion
1 tablespoon minced parsley
½ teaspoon salt
1/8 teaspoon black pepper
1 teaspoon soy sauce
3 tablespoons milk
1½ tablespoons butter

Mix all ingredients except butter. Cook in butter, stirring until hot; then press lightly with pancake turner and cook until underside is well browned. Fold. Serves 4–6.

STUFFED HALIBUT STEAKS

2½ cups soft bread cubes
1 teaspoon salt
¼ cup grated onion
1/3 cup melted butter
2 tablespoons chopped parsley
1 can tomato soup
1 cup grated Cheddar cheese
2 1-pound halibut steaks

Combine bread cubes, salt, onion, butter, parsley, soup and cheese; mix well. Place 1 halibut steak in a greased shallow baking pan. Cover with tomato mixture. Place remaining halibut steak over tomato mixture. Bake in moderate oven (350° F.) 1 hour, or until fish flakes easily when tested with a fork. Serves 6.

FISHERMAN'S HALIBUT HASH

2 cups cooked flaked halibut
2 cups diced cooked potatoes
2 tablespoons minced onion
1 egg, beaten
1 teaspoon salt
1/8 teaspoon pepper
¼ cup chopped celery
¼ cup melted bacon drippings

Combine halibut, potatoes, onion, egg, salt, pepper and celery. Mix well. Cook in bacon drippings until well browned on both sides. Serves 4.

Shellfish

ABALONE CASSEROLE

2 eggs
2 tablespoons water
2 pounds abalone, sliced
1½ cups cracker crumbs
1/3 cup melted fat
1 cup water
¼ cup chopped onion
2/3 cup tomato juice
2 tablespoons lemon juice
1 teaspoon salt
1/8 teaspoon pepper

Beat eggs with the 2 tablespoons water. Dip fish in egg mixture and coat with crumbs. Cook in fat until browned on both sides; arrange in greased baking dish. Combine remaining ingredients with fish drippings and cook 10 minutes. Pour over fish. Bake in moderate oven (350° F.) 1 hour, or until fish is tender. Serves 6.

OREGON CLAM CAKES

2 cups ground clams
2 eggs, well beaten
½ cup fine dry bread crumbs
½ teaspoon salt
¼ teaspoon thyme
¼ cup grated onion
Fine dry bread crumbs
2 tablespoons melted fat

Combine clams, eggs, the ½ cup crumbs, salt, thyme and onion. Chill and shape into cakes. Coat with crumbs. Cook in fat over low heat until browned on both sides. Serves 4.

CLAM AND CORN CASSEROLE

1 7-ounce can minced clams
Milk
3 eggs, well beaten
1¼ cups canned cream-style corn
2 tablespoons grated onion
2 tablespoons finely chopped parsley

1 tablespoon melted butter
¼ teaspoon salt
1/8 teaspoon pepper

Drain clams; reserve liquid. Add enough milk to clam liquid to make 1 cup. Add clams and remaining ingredients. Mix well and turn into greased 1½-quart casserole. Bake in moderate oven (350° F.) about 50 minutes. Serves 4–6.

CLAMS GUILFORD

1 cup soft bread crumbs
2 cups chopped clams
1 teaspoon salt
¼ teaspoon paprika
2 tablespoons chopped parsley
2 tablespoons chopped onion
¼ cup light cream
½ cup clam juice
1 tablespoon butter

Alternate layers of bread crumbs and clams in a greased 1-quart casserole. Season with salt and paprika. Sprinkle parsley and onion over clam mixture. Pour cream and clam juice over clam mixture. Dot with butter. Bake in moderate oven (350° F.) 30 minutes. Serves 4.

ALASKAN CLAM PIE

1 7-ounce can minced clams
1/3 cup butter
1/3 cup all-purpose flour
Water
½ teaspoon Worcestershire sauce
1 tablespoon chopped parsley
1 cup milk
¼ teaspoon salt
1/8 teaspoon black pepper
1 9" baked pastry shell
2 tablespoons melted butter
½ cup fine dry bread crumbs

Drain clams and reserve liquor. Melt the 1/3 cup butter and blend in flour. Add enough water to clam liquor to make 1 cup. Add clam liquor, Worcestershire sauce, parsley and milk to flour mixture. Cook over low heat, stirring constantly, until thickened. Add salt, pepper and clams and mix well; pour into pastry shell. Combine the 2 tablespoons butter and crumbs; sprinkle over clam mixture. Bake in hot oven (400° F.) 12–15 minutes. Serves 6.

CLAM EGGPLANT CASSEROLE

1 medium-sized eggplant
2 tablespoons chopped onion
2 tablespoons butter or margarine, melted
2 7-ounce cans minced clams
2 cups fine cracker crumbs
1 teaspoon salt
1/8 teaspoon pepper
1 tablespoon butter or margarine
1/4 cup light cream
1/2 teaspoon Worcestershire sauce

Peel and cube eggplant. Cook, covered, in small amount of boiling water 10 minutes; drain. Cook onion in melted butter or margarine until tender. Drain clams; reserve liquor. Alternate layers of eggplant, clams and cracker crumbs in greased 1½-quart casserole. Sprinkle layers with salt and pepper. Dot with butter or margarine. Combine clam liquor, cream and Worcestershire sauce. Pour over other ingredients. Bake in moderate oven (350° F.) 40 minutes. Serves 4–6.

MARBLEHEAD CLAM FRITTERS

2 cups sifted all-purpose flour
2 teaspoons baking powder
1/4 teaspoon salt
2 eggs, well beaten
1/2 cup milk
1/2 cup clam liquor
2 tablespoons chopped parsley
2 cups cooked chopped clams

Sift flour, baking powder and salt together. Combine eggs, milk and clam liquor; add to sifted ingredients and mix until blended. Add parsley and clams; mix lightly. Drop by tablespoonfuls into deep, hot fat (365° F.) and fry until browned on all sides. Drain on absorbent paper. Serves 6.

EASTERN SHORE SOFT-SHELLS

1/4 cup melted butter
3 tablespoons lemon juice
Salt and pepper
1/4 teaspoon cayenne pepper
6 soft-shell crabs
Flour
Parsley

Combine butter, lemon juice, salt, pepper and cayenne pepper. Roll crabs in butter mixture. Roll in flour. Broil over hot coals 8 minutes, turning once. Garnish with parsley. Serves 6.

CRAB-STUFFED AVOCADO

3 large avocados
3 tablespoons lime juice
1 teaspoon salt
3 tablespoons butter
6 tablespoons flour
1/8 teaspoon paprika
1/8 teaspoon black pepper
1½ cups milk
3/4 cup cooked sliced celery
1/4 cup minced pimiento
1 cup cooked crab meat

Cut avocados lengthwise into halves and peel. Sprinkle with lime juice and IA teaspoon of the salt. Melt butter, blend in flour, add remaining seasonings and milk; cook until thickened, stirring constantly. Add celery, pimiento and crab meat. Fill avocados with crab meat mixture. Place in baking pan, pour in water to depth of ½ inch and bake in moderate oven (350° F.) 15 minutes. Serves 6.

CRAB WITH NOODLES

2 tablespoons butter
1/4 cup chopped green pepper
1/4 cup chopped pimiento
3 tablespoons all-purpose flour
1 teaspoon prepared mustard
1 cup cooked tomatoes
1/2 pound Swiss cheese, grated
1 egg, well beaten
3/4 cup milk
1½ cups cooked, flaked crab meat
Salt and pepper to taste
4 cups cooked noodles

Melt butter, add green pepper and pimiento, and cook 5 minutes. Blend in flour and mustard. Add tomatoes and cook until thickened, stirring constantly. Add cheese and egg. Stir until smooth. Add milk and crab meat. Season with salt and pepper. Serve with noodles. Serves 4.

CRAB SUPREME

3 cups cooked flaked crab meat
Salad greens
1 cup salad dressing
1/3 cup heavy cream, whipped
1/3 cup catsup
1/4 cup chopped green pepper
1/4 cup grated onion
1/4 cup chopped sweet pickles
1/4 teaspoon salt
1 tablespoon lemon juice

Arrange crab meat on salad greens. Combine remaining ingredients and pour over crab meat. Serves 4.

PAELLA

1 frying chicken, cut up
4 hot sausages
1/3 cup olive oil
1 clove garlic
1 cup rice
1 cup boiling water
2 cups peas
1/2 bay leaf
Pinch of saffron
Salt and pepper
4-ounce can pimiento
1/2 pound shrimp, cleaned
6-8 clams in shell, scrubbed

In a large skillet, brown chicken and sausages in olive oil. Add garlic and rice, cook about 5 minutes. Add boiling water and remaining ingredients. Cover and cook until rice has absorbed all the water and is fluffy and tender. Stir frequently during cooking. Turn into casserole or serve from skillet. Serves 4.

CRAB CAKES MARYLAND

1 pound crab meat, flaked
1 egg yolk
1 teaspoon salt
1/4 teaspoon pepper
1 teaspoon dry mustard
2 teaspoons Worcestershire sauce
1 tablespoon mayonnaise
1 tablespoon chopped parsley
1 teaspoon lemon juice
1 tablespoon melted butter
Fine dry bread crumbs
2 tablespoons melted butter

Combine crab meat, egg yolk, salt, pepper, mustard, Worcestershire sauce, mayonnaise, parsley, lemon juice and the 1 tablespoon butter. Shape into cakes and coat with crumbs. Cook in the 2 tablespoons melted butter over low heat until browned on both sides. Serves 6.

SHRIMP CROQUETTES

1 pound shrimp
1 tablespoon lemon juice
1 tablespoon Worcestershire sauce
1 tablespoon butter
1/8 teaspoon nutmeg
1 teaspoon salt
1/8 teaspoon pepper
2 tablespoons melted fat

Peel shrimp and remove black vein. Grind shrimp and combine with lemon juice, Worcestershire sauce, butter, nutmeg, salt and pepper. Chill thoroughly. Shape into patties. Cook patties in fat over low heat until browned on both sides. Serves 4.

SHRIMP CURRY, HAWAIIAN STYLE

6 tablespoons butter
2 teaspoons onion, finely chopped
6 tablespoons flour
2 cups milk
2 cups shredded coconut
1 1/4 teaspoons salt
3 teaspoons curry powder
2 teaspoons chopped preserved ginger
1 1/2 pounds fresh shrimp, shelled and cleaned
1 tablespoon lime juice

Melt butter, add onion and cook about 2 minutes; stir in flour. Gradually add milk, stirring constantly, and cook until thickened. Add coconut, salt, curry powder and ginger. Cook over low heat about 30 minutes. Add shrimp and cook, stirring constantly, about 5 minutes or until shrimp are cooked. Stir in lime juice. Serve with rice, as desired. Serves 4–6.

PAPILLON FRIED SHRIMP

2 pounds shrimp
2 eggs, eaten
½ teaspoon celery salt
⅛ teaspoon pepper
1½ cups cracker crumbs

Peel shrimp and remove black vein. Combine eggs, celery salt and pepper. Dip shrimp in egg mixture and coat with crumbs. Fry in deep hot fat (375° F.) until lightly browned on all sides. Drain on absorbent paper. Serves 6.

DEVILED CRABS

¼ cup minced onion
3 tablespoons melted butter
2 tablespoons all-purpose flour
1 cup milk
¼ teaspoon salt
1 teaspoon prepared mustard
1 tablespoon lemon juice
1 tablespoon Worcestershire sauce
1 egg, beaten
1 pound crab meat
½ cup buttered cracker crumbs

Cook onion in butter until tender. Blend in flour. Gradually add milk and cook, stirring constantly, until thickened. Add salt, mustard, lemon juice, Worcestershire sauce, egg and crab meat. Mix well. Turn into 6 greased individual baking dishes. Top with crumbs. Bake in moderate oven (350° F.) 20 minutes, or until lightly browned. Serves 6.

SHRIMP FRICASSEE OVER RICE

2 pounds shrimp, cooked
2 cups chopped fresh tomatoes
2 tablespoons chopped onions
1 bay leaf
¼ cup chopped green pepper
¼ cup butter or margarine
¼ cup all-purpose flour
2 cups tomato juice
Salt and pepper to taste
Cooked rice

Combine shrimp, tomatoes, onions, bay leaf and green pepper. Melt butter or margarine and blend in flour. Remove from heat, gradually add tomato juice and cook until thickened, stirring constantly. Add shrimp mixture and heat to serving temperature, stirring occasionally. Season with salt and pepper. Remove bay leaf. Serve over rice. Serves 6.

MARDI GRAS SHRIMP

¼ cup chopped onion
¼ cup chopped green pepper
¼ cup chopped celery
1 clove garlic, minced
¼ cup melted butter
3 tablespoons all-purpose flour
½ teaspoon chili powder
1 bay leaf
⅛ teaspoon pepper
1 No. 2 can tomatoes
1½ pounds shrimp, cooked and cleaned
4 cups cooked hot rice

Cook onion, green pepper, celery and garlic in butter until onion is tender. Blend in flour and seasonings. Gradually add tomatoes, and cook, stirring constantly, over low heat until thickened. Add shrimp and heat just to serving temperature. Remove bay leaf. Arrange rice on serving platter. Top with shrimp mixture. Serves 6.

GOURMET SHRIMP

1/3 cup sherry
2 tablespoons chopped chives
1/3 cup chopped parsley
1 clove garlic, minced
1 cup chopped mushrooms
4 medium-sized tomatoes, peeled and diced
1 cup beef bouillon
1 teaspoon chili powder
1 teaspoon salt
⅛ teaspoon pepper
½ teaspoon Worcestershire sauce
¼ cup chopped green pepper
1 cup tomato sauce
3 pounds shrimp
½ cup melted butter

Combine all ingredients except shrimp and butter. Cover and cook over low heat, 30 minutes. Peel shrimp and remove black vein. Cook shrimp in butter until Jinn and pink, about 5 minutes. Serve with sauce. Serves 6–8.

SHRIMP JAMBALAYA

2 tablespoons butter
2 tablespoons all-purpose flour
2 cups cooked tomatoes
1 small onion, sliced
¼ teaspoon thyme
½ cup chopped green pepper
1 tablespoon chopped parsley
1 teaspoon salt
1/8 teaspoon pepper
1/8 teaspoon paprika
1 teaspoon Worcestershire sauce
1 red pepper, chopped
4 cups water
1 cup rice
3 cups cleaned shrimp

Melt butter in large saucepan; blend in flour. Add tomatoes. Cook over low heat, stirring constantly, 3 minutes. Add remaining ingredients except shrimp and cook, covered, over low heat 25-30 minutes or until water is absorbed. 10 minutes before cooking time is up, arrange shrimp on surface, cover and continue cooking. To serve, stir shrimp into rice mixture. Serves 6.

SHRIMP LOUISIANA

½ cup French dressing
¼ cup horseradish
¼ teaspoon chili powder
1 tablespoon dry mustard
¼ teaspoon thyme
1½ pounds cooked cleaned shrimp

Combine French dressing, horseradish, chili powder, mustard and thyme. Beat until thoroughly blended. Add shrimp. Chill several hours. Drain and serve. Serves 4.

OYSTERS ROCKEFELLER

¼ cup melted butter
¼ cup cooked chopped spinach
3 tablespoons minced onion
2 tablespoons minced lettuce
1 tablespoon minced celery
¼ cup fine dry bread crumbs
¼ teaspoon anchovy paste
¼ teaspoon salt
1/8 teaspoon pepper
2 dozen oysters on half shells

Combine butter, spinach, onion, lettuce, celery, bread crumbs, anchovy paste, salt and pepper. Cook over low heat, stirring occasionally, 5 minutes. Remove oysters from shells. Clean shells thoroughly. Place an oyster in each shell. Broil 4 inches from source of heat 5 minutes. Top oysters with spinach mixture. Continue broiling 2-5 minutes. Serves 4-6.

BILOXI SCALLOPED OYSTERS

1/3 cup melted butter
1½ cups cracker crumbs
1 pint oysters
1 teaspoon salt
1/8 teaspoon pepper
2 tablespoons oyster liquor
¼ cup light cream

Combine butter with crumbs. Alternate layers of crumb mixture and oysters in greased 1-quart casserole. Sprinkle with salt and pepper. Pour oyster liquor and cream over other ingredients. Bake in moderate oven (350° F.) 30 minutes. Serves 4.

SKEWERED OYSTERS

1½ cups fine bread crumbs
½ cup finely minced celery
¼ cup minced parsley
¼ teaspoon salt
1/8 teaspoon black pepper
1/8 teaspoon paprika
36 large oysters, shucked
2 eggs, slightly beaten
4-6 slices bacon, cut in 1" pieces
3 tablespoons melted butter
½ teaspoon Worcestershire sauce
Toast

Mix crumbs, celery, parsley and seasonings. Drain oysters; dip into eggs, then in crumb mixture until well covered. Place oysters and bacon on skewers, allowing 6 oysters to each. Mix butter with Worcestershire sauce. Broil oysters 4 inches from source of heat until browned on both sides. Baste with butter mixture. Serve hot on toast. Serve with remaining butter mixture. Serves 6.

OYSTER-STUFFED POLLOCK

1 4-pound pollock
Salt
2 cups finely chopped oysters
1/2 cup cracker crumbs
1/2 cup milk
1/4 teaspoon salt
1/8 teaspoon pepper
1/8 teaspoon cayenne pepper
1 tablespoon melted butter
1/4 cup chopped parsley

Clean pollock and rub with salt. Combine remaining ingredients and mix lightly. Stuff pollock with oyster mixture and fasten with skewers or cord. Place in greased shallow baking pan. Add enough water to cover bottom of pan. Bake in moderate oven (350° F.) 40 minutes, or until fish flakes easily when tested with a fork. Serves 6.

SEA FOOD COCKTAIL SAUCE

1 cup catsup
2 tablespoons chili sauce
2 tablespoons vinegar
1 tablespoon horseradish
1 tablespoon minced celery
1 tablespoon grated onion
1/2 teaspoon salt
1 teaspoon Worcestershire sauce
Dash Tabasco

Combine all ingredients; chill thoroughly. Serve with sea foods, as desired. Makes about 1¼ cups.

MARINATED SCALLOPS

1/4 cup lemon juice
1 tablespoon olive oil
1 teaspoon salt
1/4 teaspoon pepper
1 quart scallops
1/3 cup finely shredded soft bread crumbs
1/4 cup cooked minced ham
1 teaspoon minced chives
1 egg, slightly beaten

Combine lemon juice, olive oil, salt and pepper. Pour oil mixture over scallops and let stand 1 hour. Drain scallops. Combine bread crumbs, ham and chives. Dip scallops in egg and coat with crumb mixture. Fry in deep hot fat (375° F.) until browned on all sides. Serves 4-6.

SCALLOP MUSHROOM KABOBS

1 pound scallops
1 pound small mushrooms
1/2 cup melted butter
1 cup cracker meal
1 teaspoon salt
1/2 teaspoon celery seed
1/4 teaspoon thyme
Lemon wedges

Dip scallops and caps of mushrooms in butter. Combine cracker meal, salt, celery seed and thyme. Roll scallops in meal mixture. Alternate scallops and mushroom caps on skewers. Broil 3 inches from source of heat 3 minutes. Turn and continue broiling 3-4 minutes or until golden brown. Serve with lemon wedges. Serves 4-6.

SCALLOP SAUTÉ MONTAUK

1/4 cup all-purpose flour
1/2 teaspoon salt
1/8 teaspoon pepper
1 pound scallops
1/4 cup melted fat
2 tablespoons melted butter
2 tablespoons lemon juice
1 teaspoon lemon rind
1 tablespoon chopped parsley

Combine flour, salt and pepper. Coat scallops with flour mixture. Cook scallops in fat over low heat until lightly browned on all sides and tender. Combine butter, lemon juice, rind and parsley. Heat to serving temperature. Pour over scallops. Serves 4.

OLYMPIA OYSTER PAN ROAST

2 cups small oysters
1/3 cup butter or margarine, melted
1½ teaspoons lemon juice
Salt and pepper

Cook oysters in butter or margarine until edges curl. Remove from heat. Sprinkle with lemon juice, salt and pepper. Serves 4-6.

BROILED OYSTERS

12 large oysters
½ cup melted butter
¼ teaspoon salt
Dash cayenne pepper
¾ cup fine dry bread crumbs
4 slices buttered toast
Lemon slices

Dip oysters in butter and sprinkle with salt and cayenne pepper. Roll in bread crumbs. Broil 3–4 inches from source of heat until browned on both sides, brushing occasionally with remaining butter. Arrange oysters on toast. Serve with lemon slices. Serves 4.

CASCO BAY LOBSTER

¼ cup butter or margarine, melted
1 teaspoon Worcestershire sauce
¼ teaspoon salt
1/8 teaspoon pepper
1 tablespoon lemon juice
1 tablespoon prepared mustard
2 cups cooked diced lobster
4 slices buttered toast

Combine butter or margarine, Worcestershire sauce, salt, pepper, lemon juice, mustard and lobster. Cook over low heat, stirring, until thoroughly heated. Serve over toast. Serves 4.

LOBSTER CROQUETTES

¼ cup butter
¼ cup all-purpose flour
1 cup milk
1 egg yolk, beaten
2 cups cooked diced lobster
1 tablespoon chopped parsley
1 tablespoon catsup
½ teaspoon salt
2 eggs, beaten
Fine dry bread crumbs

Melt butter and blend in flour. Gradually add milk and cook, stirring constantly, until thickened. Add a little of hot mixture to egg yolk and mix well; stir into hot mixture and cook, stirring constantly 2 minutes. Remove from heat; add lobster, parsley, catsup and salt. Chill thoroughly. Shape into croquettes. Dip in eggs and coat with crumbs. Fry in deep, hot fat (375° F.) until browned on all sides. Drain on absorbent paper. Serves 6.

LOBSTER NEWBURG

2½ cups cooked, diced lobster
5 tablespoons butter
2 tablespoons sherry
2 tablespoons all-purpose flour
¼ teaspoon salt
1/8 teaspoon paprika
1/8 teaspoon cayenne pepper
¼ teaspoon nutmeg
2 cups light cream
2 egg yolks, slightly beaten
4 slices toast

Heat lobster with 3 tablespoons of the butter. Add sherry. Melt remaining 2 tablespoons butter and blend in flour and seasonings. Gradually add cream and cook over low heat, stirring constantly, until thickened. Stir a little of sauce into egg yolks and mix well. Stir into sauce and continue cooking, stirring constantly, 2 minutes. Add lobster mixture and mix well. Serve over toast. Serves 4.

LOBSTER STEW

3 cups diced cooked lobster
1 quart milk
2 cups clam broth
2 tablespoons butter or margarine
1/8 teaspoon cayenne pepper
1½ teaspoons salt

Combine all ingredients and heat to serving temperature, stirring occasionally. Serves 6.

CURRIED MUSSELS

1 pint mussels
3 tablespoons minced onion
2 tablespoons butter, melted
½ cup dry white wine
1 tablespoon chopped parsley
¼ teaspoon celery seed
1 teaspoon curry powder
¼ cup sour cream
1/8 teaspoon pepper

Drain mussels and reserve liquid. Cook onion in butter until tender. Add mussel liquid, wine, parsley, celery seed and curry powder. Simmer 5 minutes. Add mussels, sour cream and pepper. Heat to serving temperature, stirring constantly. Serves 4.

OYSTERS AND BACON ON SHELL

24 oysters in shells
4 slices bacon, diced
Salt
Pepper
2 tablespoons chopped parsley

Remove oysters from shells and drain. Place oysters on half shells and top with bacon. Sprinkle salt, pepper and parsley over bacon. Bake in very hot oven (450° F.) about 10 minutes. Serves 4–6.

BAKED OYSTERS

2 dozen large oysters in shells
1 egg, beaten
¼ teaspoon salt
1/8 teaspoon pepper
1 tablespoon water
1 cup dry bread crumbs
2 tablespoons butter

Remove oysters from shells. Combine egg, salt, pepper and water. Dip oysters in egg mixture and roll in crumbs. Place oysters in shells. Dot with butter. Bake in hot oven (400° F.) 15–20 minutes. Serves 6.

MAINE BAKED LOBSTER

2 cups cracker crumbs
¼ teaspoon salt
1/8 teaspoon pepper
¼ cup butter or margarine, melted
¼ cup milk
2 cups cooked flaked crab meat
4 2-pound lobsters, cleaned and split
½ cup melted butter or margarine
¼ cup grated Parmesan cheese

Combine crumbs, salt, pepper, the ¼ cup butter or margarine, milk and crab meat. Mix lightly. Stuff lobsters with crab meat mixture. Pour the ½ cup butter over stuffing and sprinkle with cheese. Bake in hot oven (400° F.) 20–25 minutes. Serves 4.

BOILED LOBSTER

Salt
Boiling water
4 lobsters
1 cup melted butter
¼ cup lemon juice

Add 1 tablespoon salt to each quart boiling water. (There should be enough water to cover lobsters.) Drop lobsters, head first, one at a time into water. Let water come to boiling point after each lobster is added. Cover and cook 20 minutes. Combine butter and lemon juice. Heat to serving temperature and serve with lobster. Serves 4.

Poultry

CHICKEN TETRAZZINI

½ pound spaghetti, cooked
½ pound mushrooms, sliced
4 tablespoons butter or margarine
1 teaspoon lemon juice
2 tablespoons all-purpose flour
2 cups milk
2 tablespoons sherry
1 teaspoon salt
2 cups diced cooked chicken
2 tablespoons grated Parmesan cheese

Arrange half of spaghetti in shallow baking dish. Cook mushrooms in 2 tablespoons of the butter or margarine until tender; add lemon juice. Arrange mushroom mixture over spaghetti in baking dish. Melt remaining 2 tablespoons butter or margarine; blend in flour. Gradually add milk and cook, stirring constantly, until thickened. Add sherry, salt and chicken. Pour chicken mixture over mushroom mixture. Top with remaining spaghetti. Sprinkle with cheese. Bake in hot oven (400° F.) about 20 minutes, or until lightly browned. Serves 4.

SUNDAY SUPPER CHICKEN LOAF

¼ cup butter or margarine
¼ cup all-purpose flour
1 cup chicken stock
½ cup milk
2 tablespoons chopped onion
2 tablespoons chopped green pepper
¼ cup chopped celery
2 tablespoons melted butter or margarine
3 cups soft bread crumbs
4 cups chopped cooked chicken
1 teaspoon salt

Melt the ¼ cup butter or margarine; blend in flour. Gradually add stock and milk. Cook, stirring constantly, until thickened. Remove from heat. Cook onion, green pepper and celery in the 2 tablespoons butter or margarine until onion is tender. Combine sauce, vegetable mixture, crumbs, chicken and salt; mix lightly. Turn into greased 9" x 5" x 3" baking pan. Bake in moderate oven (350° F.) 1½ hours, or until firm. Serves 6.

SAVOY CHICKEN

1 5-pound fowl
2 carrots
2 stalks celery
1 medium-sized onion, chopped
1 bay leaf
½ teaspoon black pepper
1 teaspoon salt
4 sprigs parsley
¼ cup butter
¼ cup all-purpose flour
2 cups chicken stock
½ cup dry white wine

Cover fowl with hot water, add remaining ingredients. Simmer, covered, about 2 hours or until chicken is tender. Remove skin from chicken and cut into serving pieces. Strain stock and reserve. Melt butter and blend in flour. Gradually add chicken stock, and cook, stirring constantly, until thickened. Add wine and cook 3 minutes, stirring constantly. Add chicken and heat to serving temperature, stirring occasionally. Serve with rice or noodles, as desired. Serves 6.

SMOTHERED CHICKEN CHARLESTON

1 3-pound chicken
½ cup all-purpose flour
1 teaspoon salt
1/8 teaspoon pepper
¼ cup melted butter or margarine
½ cup sliced onions
1 cup chicken stock
½ cup light cream
2 tablespoons melted butter or margarine
2 tablespoons all-purpose flour

Cut chicken into serving pieces. Combine the ½ cup flour, salt and pepper; coat chicken with flour mixture. Brown chicken on all sides in the ¼ cup butter or margarine. Add onions, stock and cream. Cover and simmer about 45 minutes, or until chicken is tender. Remove chicken. Combine the 2 tablespoons butter or margarine and the 2 tablespoons flour. Add to chicken liquid and cook, stirring constantly, until thickened; strain. Serve gravy over chicken. Serves 4.

CHICKEN SOUFFLÉ

¼ cup butter or margarine
½ cup all-purpose flour
2 cups milk
1 cup chicken stock
½ cup soft bread crumbs
3 cups chopped cooked chicken
1 tablespoon chopped parsley
2 tablespoons chopped celery
1 teaspoon salt
4 eggs, separated

Melt butter or margarine; blend in flour. Gradually add milk and stock; cook, stirring constantly, until thickened. Remove from heat. Add crumbs, chicken, parsley, celery and salt. Beat egg yolks until thick and fold into chicken mixture. Beat egg whites until stiff; fold into chicken mixture. Turn into greased 2½-quart baking dish. Bake in moderate oven (350° F.) about 1¼ hours, or until firm. Serves 6.

SOUTHERN CHICKEN AND DUMPLINGS

1 5-pound stewing chicken
1 medium onion
2 stalks celery
3 tablespoons salt
½ teaspoon pepper
2 cups sifted all-purpose flour
1 teaspoon salt
1½ teaspoons baking powder
2 tablespoons shortening
2 eggs, beaten slightly
1 cup milk (about)

Cover chicken with boiling water. Add onion, celery, the 3 tablespoons salt and pepper. Cover and cook until tender, about 3 hours. Remove chicken, reserve stock. While chicken is cooking, prepare dumplings. Sift together flour, salt and baking powder. Cut in shortening. Stir in eggs and enough milk to make a soft dough. Turn out on floured board and roll dough very thin. Cut into strips 1½" wide and about 3" long. Drop dough strips one at a time into boiling stock. Cook about 15 minutes. Serve with chicken. Makes 6-8 servings.

CHICKEN TIMBALES

3 tablespoons butter or margarine
3 tablespoons all-purpose flour
1½ cups light cream
3 eggs, well beaten
3 cups ground cooked chicken
1 tablespoon minced onion
1 tablespoon chopped parsley
½ teaspoon salt
1/8 teaspoon pepper

Melt butter or margarine; blend in flour. Gradually add cream and cook, stirring constantly, until thickened. Add a little of hot mixture to eggs and mix well. Stir into remaining hot mixture and cook, stirring constantly, 2 minutes. Add remaining ingredients and mix well. Turn into greased individual baking cups. Place cups in pan of hot water. Bake in moderate oven (350° F.) 25-30 minutes, or until firm. Serve with tomato or mushroom sauce (pages 88, 85), as desired. Serves 6.

CHICKEN TURNOVERS

¼ cup butter or margarine
¼ cup all-purpose flour
1 cup milk
2 cups minced cooked chicken
1 teaspoon grated onion
1/2 teaspoon salt
1/8 teaspoon pepper
1 recipe plain pastry

Melt butter or margarine; blend in flour. Gradually add milk and cook, stirring constantly, until thickened. Add chicken, onion, salt and pepper; mix lightly. Roll pastry out to 1/8" thickness on lightly floured surface. Cut into 6" squares; top with chicken mixture. Fold over to form triangles and seal edges. Prick tops. Place on baking sheet. Bake in hot oven (400° F.) 25-30 minutes or until lightly browned. Serve with mushroom sauce (page 85), if desired. Serves 4-6.

GOOSE FARM STYLE

8-pound domestic goose
2 onions, sliced
2 heads cabbage, chopped fine
1 medium-sized apple, cored and chopped
Salt and pepper to taste

Cut goose into serving pieces. Place on rack in roasting pan and bake in slow oven (325° F.) until almost tender, about 2½ hours. Pour off fat. Cook onions in fat. Add cabbage and apple. Cook 10 minutes; season. Arrange goose over cabbage. Cover and cook 1 hour or until goose is tender. Serves 6.

ROAST GOOSE

1 8-pound domestic goose
2 teaspoons salt

Stuff goose as desired. Sprinkle with salt. Place on rack in roasting pan. Bake in slow oven (325° F.) about 3 ½ hours, or until tender. Drain off fat occasionally during baking period. Baste with drippings frequently. Serves 6–8.

NEW MEXICO BAKED CHICKEN

3 cups diced cooked chicken
1 cup cooked rice
2 tablespoons chopped green olives
2 tablespoons chopped pimiento
1 teaspoon salt
3 eggs, slightly beaten
1½ cups chicken stock
½ cup corn cereal flakes

Combine chicken, rice, olives, pimiento, salt, eggs and stock; mix well. Turn into greased 8" x 8" baking pan. Top with cereal flakes. Place in pan of hot water. Bake in moderate oven (350° F.) about 40 minutes, or until firm. Serves 6.

BARBECUED CHICKEN MEXICALI

2 medium-sized broiling chickens
¼ cup melted butter
1 tablespoon sugar
1 tablespoon all-purpose flour
¼ teaspoon dry mustard .
1/8 teaspoon cayenne pepper
1 teaspoon salt
1 cup vinegar
1 cup water
1 cup chili sauce

Cut chickens in quarters; brown on all sides in butter. Place in shallow baking pan and sprinkle with sugar, flour, mustard, cayenne pepper and salt. Mix vinegar, water and chili sauce and pour over chicken. Bake in moderate oven (350° F.) 1 hour or until chicken is tender. Baste occasionally during baking period. Serves 6.

BROWNED CHICKEN WITH COCONUT AND SPINACH

1 cup shredded coconut
1 cup milk
2 tablespoons peanut oil
2½-pound chicken, boned and cut into 1½"
  cubes
2 teaspoons salt
½ cup water
1½ pounds spinach, cooked
3 tablespoons butter
1/8 teaspoon nutmeg

Combine coconut and milk. Bring to boil, remove from heat. Let stand 30 minutes. Press very thoroughly through wire strainer (you don't use the pulp). Heat oil. Add chicken cubes and brown on all sides. Add salt and water. Cook, covered, over low heat 20 minutes or until chicken is tender. Drain. Combine chicken with spinach, butter, nutmeg, and coconut milk. Cook over low heat 5 minutes. Serves 4.

CHICKEN CACCIATORE

1 3 ½-pound frying chicken
½ cup cooking oil
½ cup thinly sliced onions
1 No. 2½ can tomatoes
1 can tomato paste
1 bay leaf
1 clove garlic, minced
1 teaspoon salt
¼ teaspoon pepper
2 tablespoons chopped parsley
½ cup white wine

Cut chicken into serving pieces. Brown chicken on all sides in oil. Add remaining ingredients. Cover and cook over low heat 45-50 minutes, or until chicken is tender. Serves 4.

CREAMED CHICKEN AND AVOCADO

3 tablespoons butter or margarine
3 tablespoons all-purpose flour
2 cups milk
½ teaspoon salt
2 tablespoons chopped parsley
2 cups diced cooked chicken
2 tablespoons lemon juice
3 avocados, cut in halves
1 tablespoon chopped pimiento

Melt butter or margarine; blend in flour; gradually add milk and cook, stirring constantly, until thickened. Add salt, parsley and chicken; heat to serving temperature. Brush lemon juice over avocados. Sprinkle with pimiento. Serve chicken mixture over avocados. Serves 6.

ARROZ CON POLLO

1 medium-sized frying chicken
½ cup cooking oil
1 cup rice
¼ cup chopped onion
½ cup chopped green pepper
1 clove garlic, minced
1 cup tomato sauce
1 No. 2½ can tomatoes
1 teaspoon salt
1½ teaspoons chili powder
¼ teaspoon oregano
¼ cup chopped stuffed olives

Cut chicken into serving pieces; brown on all sides in oil; remove chicken; add rice, onion, green pepper and garlic. Cook, stirring occasionally, until rice is lightly browned. Add remaining ingredients and chicken; cover and cook over low heat about 30 minutes or until chicken is tender. Serves 4.

CHICKEN À LA KING

1/3 cup butter or margarine
1/3 cup all-purpose flour
1 cup chicken stock
2 cups light cream
2 egg yolks, slightly beaten
¼ cup chopped green pepper
½ cup sliced mushrooms
1 teaspoon minced onion
2 tablespoons melted butter or margarine
3 cups diced cooked chicken
¼ cup chopped pimiento

½ teaspoon salt
4 slices buttered toast

Melt the 1/3 cup butter or margarine; blend in flour. Gradually add stock and cream and cook, stirring constantly, until thickened. Add a little of hot mixture to egg yolks and mix well. Add to sauce and cook 2 minutes, stirring constantly. Remove from heat. Cook green pepper, mushrooms and onion in the 2 tablespoons butter or margarine until pepper is tender. Combine sauce, green pepper mixture, chicken, pimiento and salt. Heat to serving temperature, stirring constantly. Serve over toast. Serves 4.

CHICKEN CROQUETTES

¼ cup butter or margarine
1/3 cup all-purpose flour
1 cup milk
½ cup chicken stock
½ cup chopped mushrooms
3 cups ground cooked chicken
1 tablespoon minced onion
2 tablespoons chopped parsley
½ teaspoon salt
1/8 teaspoon pepper
¼ teaspoon nutmeg
1 egg, slightly beaten
1 tablespoon water
Fine dry bread crumbs
Deep hot fat

Melt butter or margarine; blend in flour. Gradually add milk and stock. Cook, stirring constantly, until thickened. Add mushrooms, chicken, onion, parsley, salt, pepper and nutmeg; chill thoroughly. Shape into croquettes. Combine egg and water. Dip croquettes in egg mixture and roll in crumbs. Fry in deep hot fat (350° F.) about 4–5 minutes, or until browned on all sides. Drain on absorbent paper. Serves 4–6.

DEVILED CHICKEN
WITH MUSHROOMS

1 4-pound frying chicken
1 teaspoon salt
½ teaspoon pepper
½ cup melted butter or margarine
2 tablespoons all-purpose flour
1 cup chicken bouillon
1 cup chopped mushrooms
1 tablespoon prepared mustard
1 tablespoon chili sauce

½ teaspoon paprika
½ cup dry white wine
2 cups seasoned mashed potatoes
Paprika

Cut chicken into serving pieces; sprinkle with salt and pepper. Brown chicken on all sides in butter or margarine; remove chicken. Blend flour into chicken drippings; add chicken bouillon and cook, stirring constantly, until thickened. Add mushrooms, mustard, chili sauce, paprika and wine. Add chicken and cook, covered, over low heat about 45 minutes or until chicken is tender. Arrange potatoes over chicken mixture. Broil 3 or 4 inches from source of heat 3–5 minutes or until potatoes are lightly browned. Sprinkle with paprika. Serves 4.

VIENNESE CHICKEN DIVAN

1 package frozen broccoli, cooked
4 chicken breasts, cooked
2 tablespoons butter or margarine
2 tablespoons all-purpose flour
1 cup chicken stock
2 egg yolks, well beaten
2 tablespoons sherry
½ teaspoon salt
2 tablespoons grated
Parmesan cheese

Arrange broccoli and chicken in greased shallow baking pan. Melt butter or margarine; blend in flour. Gradually add stock and cook, stirring constantly, until thickened. Add a little of hot mixture to egg yolks and mix well. Stir into hot mixture and cook 2 minutes, stirring constantly. Add sherry and salt; pour over broccoli-chicken mixture. Top with cheese. Bake in moderate oven (350° F.) 25–30 minutes, or until lightly browned. Serves 4.

CHICKEN AND LIGHT DUMPLINGS

1 5-pound fowl
1 medium-sized onion, chopped
1 carrot, finely chopped
1 teaspoon salt
½ teaspoon paprika
Water
1 cup sifted all-purpose flour
1½ teaspoons baking powder
¼ teaspoon salt
½ cup milk

Cut fowl into serving pieces. Place in kettle with onion, carrot, the 1 teaspoon salt, paprika and enough water to cover. Cover and simmer about 2 hours, or until fowl is tender. Sift flour, baking powder and the ¼ teaspoon salt together. Add milk and mix only until ingredients are moistened. Drop by tablespoonfuls into boiling chicken liquid. Cover and cook over low heat 20 minutes. Serves 4.

CHICKEN LIVERS EN BROCHETTE

1 pound chicken livers
6 slices bacon
½ pound mushrooms
1 teaspoon salt
¼ teaspoon pepper

Cut chicken livers in quarters. Cut bacon into 1" pieces. Alternate livers, bacon and mushrooms on skewers. Sprinkle with salt and pepper. Broil 3 or 4 inches from source of heat 5 minutes. Turn and broil 3–5 minutes, or until bacon is crisp. Serves 4–6.

CHICKEN MARYLAND

3 broiling chickens, cut into quarters
2 tablespoons salad oil
¾ cup all-purpose flour
1 teaspoon salt
1/8 teaspoon black pepper
3 slices salt pork, finely chopped
2 cups light cream

Brush chicken quarters with oil and dredge with flour, salt and pepper. Fry salt pork until brown. Add chicken, cook until browned on all sides. Add 1 cup cream. Cook uncovered until cream is thickened, about 5 minutes. Add remaining cream. Cover and cook over low heat about 15 minutes, or until tender. Serve with cream gravy. Serves 6–8.

CHICKEN PAPRIKA BUDAPEST

2 medium-sized broiling chickens
2 tablespoons all-purpose flour
1 teaspoon salt
¼ cup melted butter
1 large onion, chopped
1 cup chicken stock
2 teaspoons paprika
1 cup sour cream

Cut chickens into serving pieces. Combine flour and salt and coat chicken with flour mixture. Brown chicken on all sides in butter. Add onion and cook until tender. Add stock and simmer, covered, 30 minutes or until chicken is tender. Stir paprika into chicken liquid. Add sour cream. Heat to serving temperature. Serve with wide noodles or dumplings, as desired. Serves 4.

SAUTERNE SIMMERED CHICKEN

1 medium-sized frying chicken
½ cup all-purpose flour
1 teaspoon salt
¼ teaspoon paprika
¼ teaspoon pepper
¼ cup olive oil
¾ cup white wine
2 tablespoons chopped parsley

Cut chicken into serving pieces. Combine flour, salt, paprika and pepper. Sprinkle flour mixture over chicken. Brown chicken in oil. Add wine and parsley. Cover and cook over low heat about 30 minutes, or until chicken is tender. Serves 4.

CURRIED CHICKEN LIVERS

1 pound chicken livers, ground
1 cup light cream
½ teaspoon curry powder
6 eggs, slightly beaten
2 tablespoons chopped parsley
¼ teaspoon salt
1/8 teaspoon pepper
3 cups cooked noodles

Combine all ingredients, except noodles, and mix well. Turn into greased 9" ring mold. Place mold in pan of hot water. Bake in moderate oven (350° F.) about 1 hour, or until firm. Unmold and fill center with noodles. Serves 6.

SAUTÉED CHICKEN LIVERS

1½ pounds chicken livers
1 teaspoon salt
1/8 teaspoon pepper
¼ cup all-purpose flour
¼ cup melted butter or margarine
6 slices buttered toast
¼ cup chopped parsley

Sprinkle livers with salt, pepper and flour. Cook in butter or margarine about 10 minutes, or until browned on all sides. Arrange livers on toast.

Pour liver drippings over livers. Sprinkle with parsley. Serves 6.

KENTUCKY FRIED CHICKEN

1 5-pound roasting chicken
2 teaspoons salt
1 cup fine dry bread crumbs (approx.)
3 eggs, slightly beaten
3 tablespoons water
Deep hot fat

Cut chicken into serving pieces, sprinkle with salt. Arrange chicken in skillet; add enough water to cover bottom of pan. Cover and cook over low heat about thirty minutes or until chicken is tender. Chill chicken. Roll chicken pieces in crumbs; combine eggs and water; dip chicken in egg mixture and coat with crumbs. Fry in hot deep fat (350° F) about 8 minutes or until browned on all sides. Drain on absorbent paper. Serves 4.

CHICKEN LIVER BALLS

2 slices dry white bread
¼ cup milk, approx.
4 eggs, slightly beaten
2 tablespoons chopped parsley
½ teaspoon salt
2 tablespoons melted butter or margarine
1 cup chopped cooked chicken livers
1 quart chicken stock

Crumble bread; add enough milk to cover and let stand 5 minutes. Combine bread mixture, eggs, parsley and salt. Cook in butter or margarine until thickened, stirring constantly. Add livers and cool. Shape into balls; heat stock to boiling point; add liver balls and cook, covered, over low heat 25 minutes. Serves 4.

BAKED CHICKEN WITH OYSTERS

1 broiling chicken, split
½ cup all-purpose flour
1 teaspoon salt
1/8 teaspoon pepper
½ teaspoon nutmeg
1 cup chicken stock or bouillon
1 cup light cream
¼ cup melted butter or margarine
2 cups oysters

Sprinkle chicken with flour, salt, pepper and nutmeg. Arrange chicken in greased shallow baking pan. Pour stock or bouillon over chicken. Cover and bake in moderate oven (350° F.) about 1 hour, or until chicken is tender. Add cream, butter or margarine, and oysters. Cover and bake about 10 minutes, or until oyster edges curl. Serves 4–6.

BAKED CHICKEN IN SCALLOP SHELLS

1 tablespoon melted butter or margarine
1 teaspoon temon juice
¼ pound mushrooms, sliced
2 cups diced cooked chicken
1 can condensed cream of mushroom soup
6 greased scallop shells or ramekins
Salt and pepper to taste
2 tablespoons fine dry bread crumbs
6 tablespoons diced bacon

Combine butter or margarine, and lemon juice. Add mushrooms and cook until tender. Add chicken and soup; mix well. Turn into scallop shells or ramekins. Sprinkle with salt and pepper. Top with crumbs and bacon. Bake in moderate oven (350° F.) 25–30 minutes. Serves 6.

BARBECUED TURKEY WINGS

4 medium-sized turkey wings
2 tablespoons brown sugar
½ teaspoon chili powder
1 teaspoon salt
2 tablespoons lemon juice
1 tablespoon Worcestershire sauce
⅓ cup chili sauce
1 cup water

Combine all ingredients and mix lightly. Cover and cook over low heat about 1½ hours or until turkey wings are tender. Serves 4.

CAROLINA TURKEY WITH BISCUITS

2 tablespoons butter or margarine
2 tablespoons all-purpose flour
1 cup milk
1 cup turkey gravy
½ teaspoon salt
2 cups diced cooked turkey
1 cup cooked peas
4 hot baking powder biscuits

Melt butter or margarine; blend in flour. Gradually add milk and cook, stirring constandy, until thickened. Add gravy, salt, turkey and peas. Heat to serving temperature. Split biscuits and top with turkey mixture. Serves 4.

TURKEY MUSHROOM HASH

2 cups cooked diced turkey
1 cup potatoes, diced
1 egg
2 tablespoons chopped onion
½ cup chopped mushrooms
Salt and pepper
¼ cup melted butter

Combine turkey, potatoes, egg, onion and mushrooms. Salt and pepper to taste. Brown in butter on both sides over low heat. Serves 4.

BAKED TURKEY CROQUETTES

¼ cup butter or margarine
¼ cup all-purpose flour
1 cup milk
1 egg, beaten
1½ cups ground, cooked turkey
¼ cup chopped pecans
1 cup seasoned mashed potatoes
2 tablespoons grated onion
2 tablespoons minced pimiento
½ teaspoon salt
⅛ teaspoon pepper

Melt butter or margarine; blend in flour; gradually add milk and cook, stirring constantly, until thickened. Add a little of hot mixture to egg and mix well; stir into hot mixture and cook, stirring constantly 1 minute. Add remaining ingredients and mix lightly. Chill thoroughly. Shape into croquettes and arrange in greased shallow baking pan. Bake in moderate oven (350° F.) 25–30 minutes or until lightly browned. Serves 4.

DE LUXE CREAMED TURKEY

½ pound mushrooms, sliced
¼ cup melted butter or margarine
¼ cup all-purpose flour
½ teaspoon salt
1/8 teaspoon pepper
1 tablespoon grated onion
1 cup light cream
1 cup chicken bouillon
2½ cups diced cooked turkey
2 tablespoons chopped green pepper
¼ cup chopped pimiento
2 tablespoons sherry
½ cup cooked small white onions

Cook mushrooms in butter or margarine until tender; blend in flour, salt, pepper and onion. Gradually add cream and bouillon; cook, stirring constantly, until thickened. Add remaining ingredients and mix well. Turn into greased 1-quart baking dish. Bake in moderate oven (350° F.) 35–40 minutes, or until lightly browned. Serves 4.

SQUAB IN CASSEROLE

4 squabs
½ cup melted butter or margarine
1 teaspoon salt
2 cups cooked potato balls
2 cups cooked peas
2 cups sliced cooked carrots
1 cup small white onions, cooked

Arrange squabs in shallow baking pan. Brush with butter or margarine and sprinkle with salt. Cover and bake in moderate oven (350° F.) 40 minutes. Arrange remaining ingredients around squabs. Bake, uncovered, 15–20 minutes, or until vegetables are thoroughly heated. Serves 4.

ROAST SQUAB

4 squabs
1 teaspoon salt
½ cup melted butter or margarine
¼ cup melted currant jelly

Arrange squabs on rack in shallow baking pan. Sprinkle with salt and brush with butter or margarine. Brush with jelly. Bake in moderate oven (350° F.) about 45 minutes, or until tender. Brush frequently with drippings during baking period. Serves 4.

Stuffings

BAYOU SHRIMP STUFFING

(for Turkey or Fish)

2 slices bacon
1 cup chopped celery
½ cup chopped onions
2 cups chopped cooked shrimp
2 eggs, slightly beaten
3 cups cracker crumbs
¼ cup sherry
1 teaspoon salt
¼ teaspoon pepper

Cook bacon until crisp; drain on absorbent paper and crumble. Add celery and onion to bacon drippings and cook until tender. Combine all ingredients and mix lightly. Makes about 6 cups.

APPLE-ORANGE STUFFING

(for Game)

½ cup chopped salt pork
1½ cups chopped celery
½ cup chopped onions
4 cups diced apples
1 cup sugar
2 cups fine dry bread crumbs
1 teaspoon salt
¼ teaspoon pepper
1 tablespoon grated orange rind

Cook salt pork until crisp; remove pork. Add celery, onions and apples. Cover and cook until tender. Add remaining ingredients and salt pork; mix lightly. Makes about 5 cups.

MUSHROOM STUFFING

(for Meat or Fish)

1 cup chopped mushrooms
¼ cup melted butter or margarine
1 cup fine dry bread crumbs
1 tablespoon minced parsley
½ teaspoon salt
1/8 teaspoon pepper
½ teaspoon sage
14 teaspoon marjoram

Cook mushrooms in butter or margarine until tender. Add remaining ingredients and mix lightly. Makes about 2 cups.

ORANGE-CRANBERRY STUFFING

(for Poultry or Crown Roast of Pork)

2 cups ground cranberries
½ cup melted butter or margarine
1/3 cup sugar
8 cups soft bread cubes
1 teaspoon salt
1/8 teaspoon pepper
1 tablespoon sage
½ cup chopped celery
1 cup water
2 tablespoons grated orange rind

Cook cranberries in butter or margarine 5 minutes; add sugar and mix well. Add remaining ingredients and cook over low heat, stirring constantly, 10 minutes. Makes 6 cups.

OYSTER STUFFING

(for Turkey)

1½ pints oysters
¾ cup melted butter or margarine
¼ cup chopped parsley
2 tablespoons chopped onion
2½ quarts soft bread crumbs
½ teaspoon poultry seasoning
½ teaspoon celery seed
1/8 teaspoon garlic salt
2 teaspoons salt

Cook oysters in butter or margarine until edges curl; remove oysters. Add parsley and onion to butter or margarine and cook until onion is tender. Add remaining ingredients and oysters. Mix lightly but thoroughly. Makes enough for 10-12 pound turkey.

PEACH PECAN STUFFING

(for Duck)

2 cups fine dry bread crumbs
½ cup melted butter or margarine
½ cup chopped stewed dried peaches
½ cup chopped pecans
1 teaspoon salt
1/8 teaspoon pepper
¼ teaspoon poultry seasoning

Combine all ingredients and mix lightly. Makes about 2½ cups.

PYRENEES BROWN RICE PUDDING

(for Poultry)

2 cups brown rice, cooked
2 tablespoons grated onion
1 cup finely chopped mushrooms, cooked
3 slices crisp bacon, crumbled
2 tablespoons melted butter or margarine
1 poultry giblet, cooked and chopped
½ teaspoon poultry seasoning
1/8 teaspoon pepper
1/8 teaspoon paprika

Combine all ingredients and mix lightly. Makes about 6 cups.

EGG STUFFING

(for Fish)

1 cup soft whole wheat bread crumbs
2 tablespoons melted butter or margarine
2 hard-cooked eggs, chopped
1 tablespoon minced chives
Salt and pepper

Combine all ingredients and mix lightly. Makes about 1½ cups.

CELERY STUFFING

(for Goose)

¾ cup chopped parsley
1 cup chopped onions
½ Vi cup melted butter or margarine
2 quarts soft bread crumbs
3 cups chopped celery
1 teaspoon celery seed
½ teaspoon poultry seasoning
2 teaspoons salt
¼ teaspoon pepper

Cook parsley and onions in butter or margarine until onions are tender. Add remaining ingredients and mix lightly. Makes enough for 10–12-pound goose.

BROWNED STUFFING BALLS

(for Poultry or Fish)

1 loaf whole wheat bread
2 eggs, beaten
¼ cup melted butter or margarine
1 teaspoon salt
2½ cups chicken stock
1 tablespoon minced chives
¼ teaspoon freshly ground pepper
½ teaspoon poultry seasoning
1/8 teaspoon paprika

Crumb bread. Add eggs and butter or margarine; mix well. Add salt, stock, chives, pepper, poultry seasoning and paprika. Shape into balls. Arrange in greased shallow pan. Bake in hot oven (400° F.) 25–30 minutes. Serve with poultry or fish. Serves 6–8.

OLD-FASHIONED BREAD STUFFING

(for Chicken)

3 cups soft bread crumbs
½ teaspoon salt
¼ teaspoon pepper
¼ teaspoon sage
2 tablespoons chopped onion
1 tablespoon chopped raisins
1/3 cup melted butter or margarine

Combine all ingredients and mix lightly. Makes enough for 5-pound chicken.

OZARK CORN BREAD STUFFING

(for Chicken)

1 cup chopped celery
2 tablespoons chopped parsley
2 tablespoons chopped onion
1/3 cup melted butter or margarine
4 cups corn bread crumbs
¼ teaspoon thyme
1 teaspoon salt
1/8 teaspoon pepper

Cook celery, parsley and onion in butter or margarine until onion is tender. Add remaining ingredients and mix lightly. Makes enough for 5-pound chicken.

CORN AND BACON STUFFING

(for Poultry)

6 slices bacon, diced
1 cup chopped onions
1 cup chopped celery
1 cup fine dry bread crumbs
4 cups cooked corn
½ teaspoon poultry seasoning
1 teaspoon salt
¼ teaspoon pepper
½ cup milk

Cook bacon until crisp; remove bacon and drain on absorbent paper. Cook onions and celery in bacon drippings until tender. Add remaining ingredients and bacon; mix lightly. Makes about 5 cups.

AVOCADO STUFFING

(for Fish)

¼ cup butter
½ cup chopped mushrooms
1 tablespoon chopped chives
1 ripe avocado, peeled and mashed
2 tablespoons chopped pimiento
2 tablespoons all-purpose flour
½ cup lemon juice
½ cup beef stock or bouillon
1 teaspoon poppy seeds
2 egg yolks

Heat butter. Add mushrooms and chives; sauté until tender. Add avocado, pimiento and flour; mix well. Cook over low heat 3 minutes. Add lemon juice, beef stock or bouillon and poppy seeds; mix well. Cook 10 minutes over low heat or until thickened, stirring occasionally. Add egg yolks gradually. Cook, stirring constantly, until thickened. Makes about 4 cups.

Meat

BEEF

CHILI CON CARNE

1 pound ground beef
¼ cup chopped onion
¼ cup chopped green pepper
2 tablespoons melted butter or margarine
1 No. 2 can kidney beans, drained
2 cans tomato soup
1 cup water
2 tablespoons chili powder
1 teaspoon salt
Dash cayenne pepper

Cook beef, onion and green pepper in butter or margarine until onion is tender. Add remaining ingredients and mix well. Cook, covered, over low heat 1 hour, stirring occasionally. Serves 4–6.

LONE STAR FAVORITE CASSEROLE

½ cup chopped green pepper
½ cup sliced onions
3 tablespoons melted salt pork drippings
¾ pound ground round steak
2 tablespoons chopped parsley
¼ teaspoon sugar
3 cups cooked tomatoes
1 teaspoon Worcestershire sauce
2 cups cooked rice
½ teaspoon chili powder
1 teaspoon salt
⅛ teaspoon freshly ground pepper

Cook green pepper and onions in drippings until tender. Add ground round steak and brown. Add remaining ingredients and mix lightly. Turn into greased 2-quart baking dish. Bake in moderate oven (350° F.) 30 minutes. Serves 4–6.

CORNED BEEF WITH MUSTARD SAUCE

4 pounds corned beef
¼ cup butter or margarine
2 tablespoons chopped onion
3 tablespoons all-purpose flour
½ teaspoon salt
⅛ teaspoon pepper
¼ cup prepared mustard
1½ cups milk
2 egg yolks, well beaten
3 tablespoons lemon juice

Cover corned beef with cold water. Cover and simmer 3½–4 hours or until tender. Drain. Melt butter or margarine; add onion and cook until tender. Blend in flour, salt, pepper and mustard. Gradually add milk and cook over low heat, stirring constantly, until thickened. Add a little of hot mixture to egg yolks and stir well. Stir into hot mixture and cook 1 minute, stirring constantly. Remove from heat; stir in lemon juice. Serve sauce with corned beef. Serves 8.

GOULASH BOHEMIAN

2 pounds round beef
¼ cup chopped onion
2 tablespoons butter or margarine
⅛ teaspoon cloves
1 small onion, thinly sliced
1 teaspoon sugar
1 cup water
¼ cup chili sauce
1 teaspoon salt
⅛ teaspoon pepper

Cut beef into 3-inch cubes. Cook onion in butter or margarine until tender; add beef and brown. Add remaining ingredients and cook, covered, over low heat about 1 hour, or until beef is tender. Add more water during cooking period, if necessary. Serves 6.

MEAT BALLS À LA DENMARK

3 slices bread
1 cup cold water
½ pound ground beef
½ pound ground veal
1 tablespoon chopped chives
1 teaspoon salt
1/8 teaspoon pepper
¼ teaspoon nutmeg
1 egg
1/3 cup all-purpose flour
¼ cup butter, melted
1 cup hot beef stock or bouillon

Soak bread in cold water, squeeze dry. Add beef, veal, chives, salt, pepper, nutmeg and egg; mix well. Shape into 1" balls. Coat with flour. Brown on all sides in butter. Add beef stock or bouillon. Cover, and cook over low heat 30 minutes. Serves 6.

BARNYARD BARBECUE

1 pound round steak, cubed
1 pound pork, cubed
¼ cup melted shortening
½ cup sliced onions
½ cup chopped celery
1½ cups chili sauce
1 No. 2 can tomatoes
1 teaspoon salt
¼ teaspoon pepper
1 teaspoon chili powder

Cook beef and pork in shortening until well browned on all sides. Add remaining ingredients and mix well. Cover and cook over low heat about 1# hours, or until meat is tender. Uncover and cook 1 hour. Serves 6.

NEW ENGLAND BOILED DINNER

Boiling water
4 pounds corned beef
1 medium-sized head cabbage, cut in quarters
6 medium-sized carrots, scraped
6 medium-sized onions, peeled
6 medium-sized potatoes, peeled
1 medium-sized turnip, peeled and cubed

Add enough boiling water to cover corned beef. Cover and cook over low heat 3–4 hours or until meat is tender. Add cabbage, carrots, onions, potatoes and turnip. Cover and cook about 30 minutes or until vegetables are tender. Serves 6–8.

SHORT RIBS OF BEEF

2 pounds short ribs
3 tablespoons melted shortening
1 medium-sized onion, thinly sliced
2 tablespoons melted butter or margarine
2 tablespoons lemon juice
1 tablespoon brown sugar
½ cup chili sauce
1 tablespoon Worcestershire sauce
1 tablespoon prepared mustard
½ cup water
1 cup chopped celery
1 teaspoon salt
¼ teaspoon pepper

Brown short ribs on all sides in shortening. Combine remaining ingredients and heat to boiling point. Pour sauce over short ribs; cover and cook over low heat 1½–2 hours or until meat is tender. Serves 4–6.

STEAK MANDARIN

1 pound top round steak, cut 1 inch thick
½ cup sliced onions
1 cup cooked bamboo sprouts
2 tablespoons melted shortening
1 small clove garlic, crushed
1½ teaspoons sugar
1 teaspoon salt
1/8 teaspoon pepper
1 tablespoon soy sauce
1 cup beef bouillon
I tablespoon cornstarch
¼ cup cold water

Cut meat into thin strips. Cook meat, onions and bamboo sprouts in shortening until meat is cooked; add garlic, sugar, salt, pepper, soy sauce and bouillon. Cover and cook over low heat 10 minutes. Combine cornstarch and cold water. Add to meat mixture and cook, stirring constantly, until thickened. Serves 4–6.

IOWA BEEF STEW

1 pound beef chuck, cut in 1 inch pieces
3 tablespoons melted shortening
¼ cup chopped onion
1 clove garlic, minced
1 No. 2 can tomatoes
1 teaspoon salt
1/8 teaspoon pepper
1 cup canned lima beans
1 cup canned whole kernel corn

Brown beef on all sides in shortening. Add onion, garlic, tomatoes, salt and pepper. Cover and cook over low heat 1½–2 hours or until meat is tender. Add lima beans and corn. Heat to serving temperature. Thicken liquid, as desired. Serves 4.

BEEF STROGANOFF

1 pound beef round, cut in 1 inch cubes
2 tablespoons melted shortening
2 cups chopped onions
½ teaspoon salt
1 teaspoon celery seed
3 cups noodles
1 4-ounce can mushrooms
½ cup sour cream
3 cups tomato juice
1 tablespoon Worcestershire sauce

Cook beef in shortening until it is well browned on all sides. Add onions and cook until tender. Add salt and celery seed. Add noodles and mushrooms. Combine remaining ingredients and pour over beef mixture. Cover and simmer 30 minutes. Serves 4.

FLEMISH CARBONADE

2½ pounds boneless beef chuck, cut in cubes
½ cup all-purpose flour
2 teaspoons salt
½ teaspoon pepper
2 tablespoons shortening
¼ cup butter or margarine
4 medium onions, sliced
1 12-ounce can or bottle beer
1 clove garlic, peeled
3 sprigs parsley
1 bay leaf
¼ teaspoon dried thyme
2 2-inch pieces celery

Dredge meat with flour, then sprinkle with salt and pepper. Heat shortening in a Dutch oven or heavy skillet until very hot. Add meat and brown on all sides. Meanwhile, melt butter or margarine in a skillet and sauté onion slices until tender. Add sauteed onions, beer and garlic clove speared with a wooden pick. Place parsley, bay leaf and thyme in the curve of one piece of celery. Cover with second piece of celery. Tie securely with a white string. Add to carbonade. Cover and cook over low heat 1¼ hours, or until tender. Discard garlic and celery mixture. Skim off the surface fat. Serves 4–6.

CLASSIC MEAT LOAF

1 pound ground beef
½ pound ground pork
2 cups fine dry bread crumbs
1 egg, well beaten
1 cup milk
½ cup chopped onions
1 teaspoon salt
1 tablespoon Worcestershire sauce

Combine all ingredients and mix well. Pack into greased 9" x 5" x 3" baking pan. Bake in moderate oven (350° F.) 1½ hours. Serves 6–8.

BEEF CHOW MEIN

½ cup sliced onions
½ cup chopped mushrooms
1½ cups diced celery
3 tablespoons melted butter or margarine
1½ tablespoons all-purpose flour
1 cup beef stock
2 cups diced, cooked beef
1 cup sliced water chestnuts
¼ teaspoon salt
¼ teaspoon soy sauce
Chinese noodles

Separate onion slices into rings; cook onion rings, mushrooms and celery in butter or margarine until tender. Blend in flour. Gradually add stock and cook, stirring constantly, until thickened. Add beef, water chestnuts, salt and soy sauce. Heat to serving temperature. Serve over noodles. Serves 4.

SAUERBRATEN

1 clove garlic, cut in half
3 pounds beef round
1 tablespoon salt
¼ teaspoon pepper
2 cups vinegar
2 cups water
½ cup sliced onions
1 bay leaf
1 teaspoon peppercorns
¼ cup sugar
3 tablespoons melted shortening

Rub cut side of garlic over meat. Sprinkle meat with salt and pepper. Combine vinegar, water, onions, bay leaf, peppercorns and sugar; heat to boiling point. Pour over meat and chill at least 4 days. Drain meat and reserve liquid. Brown meat well in shortening. Add half of liquid. Cover and simmer 2½–3 hours or until meat is tender. Add more liquid during cooking period if necessary. Serves 6–8.

ROAST BEEF HASH

¼ cup chopped onion
1 cup diced celery
2 tablespoons melted shortening
1½ cups ground, cooked roast beef
1 cup diced, cooked potatoes
½ cup fine dry bread crumbs
2 tablespoons chopped parsley
1 teaspoon salt
1 cup milk

Cook onion and celery in shortening until tender. Add remaining ingredients and mix well. Turn into greased shallow baking pan. Bake in hot oven (400° F.) 25 minutes. Serves 6.

GOURMET PORTERHOUSE STEAK

1 3-pound porterhouse steak, cut 1½ inches thick
½ cup crumbled blue cheese
¼ cup light cream
1 tablespoon grated onion
1 teaspoon lemon juice
1 teaspoon Worcestershire sauce
⅛ teaspoon salt

Broil steak 3 or 4 inches from source of heat 15–20 minutes (depending upon desired degree of doneness), turning once. Combine blue cheese with remaining ingredients and spread over steak. Broil until cheese melts. Serves 4.

SAVORY SWISS STEAKS

2 pounds round steak, cut 1½ inches thick
1½ cups all-purpose flour
2 tablespoons melted shortening
¼ cup sliced onion
1 cup tomato juice
1 cup tomato sauce
¼ cup lemon juice
1 teaspoon sugar
½ teaspoon dry mustard
½ teaspoon chili powder
1 teaspoon salt
¼ cup sliced stuffed olives

Cut steak into serving pieces; coat with flour. Brown meat on both sides in shortening.

Combine remaining ingredients and pour over meat. Cover and simmer 2–2½ hours or until meat is tender. Serves 6.

RED FLANNEL HASH

1½ cups cooked chopped corned beef, or 12-ounce can
¼ teaspoon salt
2½ cups cooked chopped potatoes
1 cup cooked chopped beets
½ cup finely chopped onions
1 tablespoon chili sauce
2 tablespoons butter or margarine

Combine all ingredients and mix lightly. In skillet melt butter or margarine; add corned-beef mixture, spread evenly. Cook over low heat until lightly browned on under side. Serves 4.

LAMB

POTATO LAMB HASH

2 cups ground, cooked lamb
2 tablespoons grated onion
2 tablespoons chopped pimiento
2 cups mashed potatoes
2 tablespoons chili sauce
1 teaspoon salt
3 tablespoons melted shortening

Combine lamb, onion, pimiento, potatoes, chili sauce and salt. Mix well. Cook in shortening over low heat until well browned on both sides. Serves 4.

CURRIED LEG OF LAMB

1 tablespoon fat
2 onions, sliced
1 bay leaf
1½ teaspoons salt
1 4-pound leg of lamb
1 tablespoon curry powder
1½ cups light cream
¼ cup lemon juice

Melt fat in iron kettle. Add onions, bay leaf and salt. Brown meat on all sides; cover and cook 10 minutes. Add curry powder, cream and lemon juice. Cover and cook over low heat about 1½ hours, or until lamb is tender. Serves 6–8.

PICNIC LAMB LOAF

1½ pounds ground lamb shoulder
2 cups cooked rice
½ cup canned tomatoes
2 eggs, slightly beaten
¼ cup chopped onion
1 teaspoon celery seed
1 tablespoon prepared mustard
1 tablespoon chili sauce

Combine all ingredients and mix lightly. Pack into greased 9" x 5" x 3" pan. Bake in slow oven (325° F.) about 1½ hours. Serves 6.

APRICOT-MINT LAMB ROAST

1 4-pound leg of lamb
½ teaspoon salt
1/8 teaspoon pepper
1 teaspoon ginger
¼ teaspoon nutmeg
1 cup apricot nectar
1 tablespoon mint jelly

Place lamb on rack in shallow baking pan. Combine remaining ingredients; pour over lamb. Bake in slow oven (325° F.) 2 hours, or until done. Baste frequently during baking with apricot mixture. Serves 6–8.

BRAISED LAMB SHANKS

2 pounds lamb shanks
¼ cup melted shortening
1 tablespoon Worcestershire sauce
1 teaspoon salt
¼ teaspoon pepper
2 cups water
1 cup diced carrots
1 cup diced potatoes
½ cup chopped celery
¼ cup grated onion

Brown lamb shanks in shortening. Add Worcestershire sauce, salt, pepper and water. Cover and simmer 1½ hours. Add vegetables. Cover and cook about 25 minutes, or until vegetables are tender. Thicken stock as desired. Serves 4.

DUBLIN LAMB STEW

2 pounds lamb shoulder
Boiling water
1 cup diced turnip
2 cups cubed potatoes
½ cup sliced onions
1 cup diced carrots
1 teaspoon salt
1/8 teaspoon pepper
1 bay leaf

Cut meat in small pieces. Add enough boiling water to cover. Cover and cook over low heat about 2 hours. Add remaining ingredients and cook, covered, about 25 minutes, or until vegetables are tender. Thicken as desired. Serve with dumplings, as desired. Serves 6.

SHISH KABOB

1½ pounds lean lamb, cut in 1 inch cubes
2 medium-sized tomatoes, cut in wedges
¼ pound mushrooms, cut in halves
2 small onions, cut in ¼-inch slices
2 tablespoons oil
1 teaspoon salt
1/8 teaspoon pepper

Alternate lamb, tomato wedges, mushrooms, and onions on skewers. Brush with oil and sprinkle with salt and pepper. Broil 3 or 4 inches from source of heat 10 minutes on each side. Serves 6.

PORK AND HAM

SWEET AND SOUR SPARERIBS

3 pounds spareribs
¼ cup melted shortening
¼ teaspoon ginger
2 teaspoons salt
¼ teaspoon pepper
1 tablespoon sugar
1 cup white vinegar
3 tablespoons soy sauce
¼ cup chopped onion
1 orange, thinly sliced

Brown spareribs in shortening. Combine ginger, salt, pepper, sugar, vinegar and soy sauce. Heat to boiling point. Pour over spareribs. Top with onion and orange slices. Cover and simmer 1–1½ hours, or until meat is tender. Serves 4.

GLORIA'S HAM AND YAM CASSEROLE

2 cups diced, cooked ham
2 cups cooked green beans
1 can condensed cream of mushroom soup
4 medium-sized yams, cooked and peeled
¼ teaspoon nutmeg
¼ teaspoon cinnamon
¼ teaspoon salt
1 tablespoon butter or margarine

Combine ham, beans and soup. Turn into greased 1½-quart baking dish. Mash yams and beat until light and fluffy. Fold in spices, salt, and butter or margarine. Pile yam mixture over ham mixture. Bake in moderate oven (350° F.) 30–35 minutes. Serves 6.

PORK CANTONESE

½ cup all-purpose flour
½ teaspoon salt
1/8 teaspoon pepper
1 pound pork, cut in 1-inch cubes
1 egg, slightly beaten
2 tablespoons melted shortening
3 tablespoons water
1 tablespoon cornstarch
¼ cup sugar
¾ cup chopped green pepper
¾ cup canned pineapple chunks
¾ cup pineapple juice
3 cups cooked, hot rice

Combine flour, salt and pepper. Dip pork into flour mixture, then in egg. Coat with flour mixture. Brown on all sides in shortening. Add water and cook over low heat, covered, 20 minutes. Cook, uncovered, 10 minutes. Combine cornstarch and sugar; add green pepper, pineapple and pineapple juice. Cook over low heat, stirring constantly, until thickened. Add pork. Serve over rice. Serves 4.

CELERY-STUFFED PICNIC SHOULDER

1 5-pound smoked ham shoulder, with bone
2 tablespoons chopped onion
1 cup diced celery
2 tablespoons melted butter or margarine
1 cup fine dry bread crumbs
½ teaspoon salt
1/8 teaspoon pepper

Cover ham shoulder (also called picnic shoulder) with water. Cover and simmer 2–2½ hours or until tender. Cool thoroughly. Remove bone and skin. (Or return meat to butcher and ask him to remove bone so that cavity can be stuffed.) Cook onion and celery in butter or margarine until tender. Add bread crumbs, salt and pepper; mix lightly. Stuff shoulder with bread-crumb mixture. Fasten with skewers. Place on rack in shallow baking pan. Bake in moderate oven (350° F.) 30 minutes. Serves 8.

MUSHROOM AND PORK TETRAZZINI

¾ cup sliced mushrooms
2 tablespoons chopped onion
1 tablespoon chopped pimiento
¼ cup melted butter or margarine
3 tablespoons all-purpose flour
¼ teaspoon salt
1/8 teaspoon pepper
2½ cups milk
2 cups cooked, diced pork
1 8-ounce package egg noodles, cooked

Cook mushrooms, onion and pimiento in butter or margarine until onion is tender. Blend in flour; add salt and pepper. Gradually add milk and cook over low heat, stirring constantly, until thickened. Add pork and mix well. Turn noodles into greased shallow baking dish. Top with pork mixture. Bake in hot oven (400° F.) about 15 minutes. Serves 6.

SCHNITZ UN KNEPP

2 cups dried apples
1 3½–4 pound ham butt
¼ cup firmly packed brown sugar
1 cup sifted all-purpose flour
1 teaspoon baking powder
1/8 teaspoon salt
1/3 cup milk
2 tablespoons melted butter or margarine
1 egg, well beaten

Soak apples in enough water to cover several hours. Cook ham butt, covered, in enough water to cover over low heat until almost tender. Add apples and brown sugar and cook, covered, 30 minutes. Sift flour, baking powder and salt together; add remaining ingredients and mix well. Drop by tablespoonfuls into ham mixture. Cover and simmer 15–20 minutes. Serves 6.

FRESH HAM WITH APPLE STUFFING

1 6 ½-pound fresh ham
1 No. 2½ can sauerkraut
¼ cup finely chopped onion
2 small apples, cored, pared and chopped
Salt and pepper

Ask butcher to remove bone from ham so that bone area can be stuffed. Drain sauerkraut. Combine sauerkraut, onion and apples; mix well. Stuff ham with sauerkraut mixture. Fasten with skewers. Score rind and sprinkle with salt and pepper. Place fat side up on rack in shallow baking pan. Bake in moderate oven (350° F.) 3–3½ hours or until tender. Serves 8–10.

DELUXE HAM FRITTERS

1 cup sifted all-purpose flour
1 teaspoon baking powder
½ teaspoon salt
1/8 teaspoon pepper
2 cups ground cooked ham
2 cups cooked peas
2 eggs, separated
¼ cup melted shortening

Sift flour, baking powder and salt together. Add pepper, ham and peas. Beat egg yolks well and add to ham mixture. Mix lightly. Beat egg whites until stiff and fold into ham mixture. Drop by tablespoons into shortening and cook until well browned on both sides. Serves 6.

SAUSAGE PATTIES

4 medium-sized potatoes, peeled, cooked and chopped
½ pound sausage, ground
1 tablespoon grated onion
2 eggs, slightly beaten
2 tablespoons chopped parsley
½ teaspoon salt
1/8 teaspoon pepper
½ cup fine dry bread crumbs
3 tablespoons melted shortening

Combine potatoes and sausage. Add onion, eggs, parsley, salt and pepper. Mix well. Shape into 8 patties. Coat with bread crumbs. Cook in shortening over low heat 10 minutes; turn patties and cook 10–15 minutes. Serves 4.

BRAISED PORK AND KRAUT

1 cup sliced onions
¼ cup melted butter or margarine
1½ pounds pork tenderloin, cut in 1-inch cubes
2 cups sauerkraut
1 teaspoon salt
¼ teaspoon nutmeg
1 cup sour cream

Cook onions in butter or margarine until tender. Remove onions from pan. Add pork to pan and brown well on all sides. Add onions, sauerkraut and salt. Cover and cook over low heat 40 minutes. Add nutmeg and sour cream and mix lightly. Heat to serving temperature, stirring occasionally. Serves 4–6.

SPARERIBS ORCHARD STYLE

2 onions, chopped
6 tart apples, chopped
¼ cup firmly packed brown sugar
1 cup toasted bread crumbs
3 pounds spareribs, in 2 parts
¼ teaspoon salt
1/8 teaspoon black pepper

Combine onions, apples, sugar and crumbs. Cover 1 part of ribs with stuffing. Place other section on top and season with salt and pepper. Bake, uncovered, in moderate oven (350° F.) until tender, about 1½ hours. Serves 6.

PORK CHOP SKILLET

4 loin pork chops
2 tablespoons melted shortening
¾ cup rice
2 medium-sized tomatoes, cut in halves
1 green pepper, cut in thin strips
1 teaspoon salt
¼ teaspoon pepper
1 can beef bouillon

Brown chops on both sides in shortening. Turn into greased 2-quart casserole. Arrange rice, tomatoes and pepper strips over chops. Sprinkle with salt and pepper. Pour bouillon over other ingredients. Cover and bake in moderate oven (350° F.) 45–50 minutes. Serves 4.

APPLE-HAM CASSEROLE

3 cups diced cooked ham
2 tablespoons prepared mustard
2 apples, cored and sliced
2 tablespoons lemon juice
½ cup brown sugar, firmly packed
1 teaspoon grated orange rind

Arrange ham in greased shallow baking dish. Spread mustard over ham. Arrange apple slices over ham mixture and brush with lemon juice. Combine sugar and orange rind; sprinkle over ham mixture. Bake in moderate oven (350° F.) 30–35 minutes. Serves 4.

BEAN AND SAUSAGE CASSEROLE

4 cups cooked navy beans
½ cup chili sauce
1 tablespoon prepared mustard
1 tablespoon prepared horseradish
1 cup firmly packed brown sugar
3 tablespoons chopped onion
1 pound pork sausage links

Combine beans, chili sauce, mustard, horseradish, sugar and onion. Turn into greased 1½-quart baking dish. Arrange sausage links over bean mixture. Bake in moderate oven (350° F.) 50 minutes. Serves 6.

HAM STEAK WAIKIKI

4½-pound ham steaks
4 slices canned pineapple
2 tablespoons toasted almonds
2 tablespoons honey
I cup orange juice
½ cup white wine
½ cup crushed pineapple

Grease large heated skillet with a piece of fat trimmed from ham steak. Brown ham steaks in skillet. Add pineapple slices, almonds, honey, orange juice, wine and crushed pineapple. Cover and simmer until ham is tender, about 30 minutes. Serves 4.

CITY SCRAPPLE

1 cup white corn meal
1 quart boiling water
1 teaspoon salt
1 pound pork sausage
¼ teaspoon thyme
¼ teaspoon sage

Gradually add cornmeal to boiling water. Add remaining ingredients and mix wrell. Cook over hot water, covered, 1½ hours, stirring frequently. Pour into loaf pan and chill until firm. Serves 6.

HAM LOAF

1 pound ground ham
1 pound ground pork
1 cup crushed wheat cereal flakes
2 eggs, slightly beaten
1 cup milk
½ teaspoon salt
1/8 teaspoon pepper

Combine all ingredients and mix well. Pack into 9" x 5" x 3" pan. Bake in moderate oven (350° F.) about 1½ hours. Serves 6-8.

BROILED HAM AND BEANS AU GRATIN

1 slice ham, cut 1-inch thick
1 No. 2 can green beans, drained
1 cup grated Swiss cheese

Broil ham 3 inches from source of heat 10 minutes. Turn ham and broil 8 minutes. Arrange beans over ham; top with cheese. Broil 4 or 5 inches from source of heat about 3 minutes, or until cheese is melted. Serves 4.

LIVER, HEART, KIDNEY, SWEETBREADS, TRIPE AND TONGUE

TORY BEEF AND KIDNEY STEW

2 pounds round steak
¼ cup all-purpose flour
2 tablespoons melted shortening
1 beef kidney
3 cups water
1 teaspoon salt
1 teaspoon Worcestershire sauce
2 cups sliced carrots
½ cup sliced onions
2 tablespoons chopped parsley

Cut round steak into 1" cubes. Coat with flour. Brown well in shortening. Remove membrane and fat from kidney. Cut into cubes. Combine beef, kidney, water, salt and Worcestershire sauce. Cover and cook over low heat 1½ hours. Add remaining ingredients; cook covered about 20 minutes, or until vegetables are tender. Serves 6.

CALF'S LIVER CHIANTI

1 pound calf's liver, thinly sliced
3 tablespoons melted butter
¼ teaspoon salt
1/8 teaspoon pepper
¼ cup chopped celery
¼ cup chopped chives
½ cup red wine

Brown liver on both sides in butter. Add remaining ingredients. Cover and bake in slow oven (325° F.) 25–30 minutes. Serves 4.

SAUTÉED LIVER PATTIES

1 pound beef liver
1 small onion
1 tablespoon all-purpose flour
1 egg, slightly beaten
½ teaspoon salt
1 teaspoon Worcestershire sauce
½ cup fine dry bread crumbs
3 tablespoons melted butter or margarine

Cut liver into thin slices. Cover liver with boiling water and cook over low heat 10 minutes. Drain. Put liver and onion through meat grinder; add flour, egg, salt and Worcestershire sauce. Mix well. Shape into 4 patties. Coat with crumbs. Cook patties in butter or margarine over low heat until well browned on both sides. Serves 4.

SAVORY TONGUE DIVAN

½ cup vinegar
2 teaspoons salt
2 tablespoons sugar
2 bay leaves
1 teaspoon whole cloves
½ cup sliced onions
4 quarts boiling water
1 5-pound tongue

Combine all ingredients. Cover and simmer 3½–4 hours, or until tongue is tender. Drain and remove outer skin. Slice diagonally to serve. Serves 6–8.

SWEETBREADS À LA POULETTE

1 pair sweetbreads
1 tablespoon vinegar
1 teaspoon salt
1 quart boiling water
2 cups diced, cooked veal
¼ cup butter or margarine
3 tablespoons all-purpose flour
2 cups milk
1/8 teaspoon pepper
¼ teaspoon salt

Soak sweetbreads in ice water 20 minutes; drain. Add vinegar and the 1 teaspoon salt to boiling water and add sweetbreads. Cook, covered, over low heat, 30 minutes. Drain and place again in ice water. Drain. Separate sweetbreads. Remove fat and connecting tissue and fine membrane. Dry. Break sweetbreads into pieces and combine with veal. Melt butter or margarine and blend in flour; gradually add milk and cook, stirring constantly, until thickened. Add veal, sweetbreads, pepper and the ¼ teaspoon salt. Heat to serving temperature. Serves 4.

PHILADELPHIA TRIPE CAKES

1 pound boiled tripe
1 egg
½ cup dry bread crumbs
1 teaspoon onion juice
1 teaspoon lemon juice
1 teaspoon salt
1/8 teaspoon black pepper

Grind tripe and combine with remaining ingredients. Shape into patties and fry in greased skillet until browned on both sides. Serves 4.

VEAL

BUDAPEST CABBAGE ROLLS

½ pound ground veal
½ pound ground pork
2 tablespoons chopped onion
2 tablespoons melted butter or margarine
1 cup soft bread crumbs
¼ cup beef bouillon
2 egg yolks, slightly beaten

8 large cabbage leaves, blanched
2 cups cooked tomatoes
½ teaspoon salt

Combine veal, pork, onion, butter or margarine, bread crumbs, bouillon and egg yolks. Mix well. Spread meat mixture over cabbage leaves. Roll up and fasten with toothpicks. Arrange cabbage rolls in greased shallow baking pan; pour tomatoes over cabbage rolls. Sprinkle with salt. Bake in moderate oven (350° F.) 1 hour. Serves 4.

VEAL PAPRIKA

1 cup grated carrots
¼ cup melted butter
½ teaspoon salt
1 teaspoon paprika
½ teaspoon pepper
2 pounds veal shoulder, diced
2 cups beef stock or bouillon
1 tablespoon all-purpose flour
½ cup sour cream

Cook carrots in butter until tender. Add salt, paprika, pepper, veal and stock or bouillon. Cover and cook over low heat about 1 hour, or until veal is tender. Combine flour and sour cream. Add to veal mixture and cook, stirring constantly, until mixture boils. Serve with dumplings if desired. Serves 6–8.

FRENCH HAM AND VEAL LOAF

2½ pounds ground veal
½ pound ground ham
1 cup soft bread crumbs
¾ cup chopped mushrooms
½ cup finely chopped green pepper
2 tablespoons prepared horseradish
1 tablespoon prepared mustard
1 tablespoon Worcestershire sauce
Dash of Tabasco
1 egg, well beaten

Combine all ingredients and mix well. Pack into greased 9" x 5" x 3" pan. Bake in slow oven (325° F.) 1) 1½–2 hours. Serves 6.

VEAL STEW CHAMPIGNON

2 pounds boneless veal shoulder, cut in 1-inch cubes
3 tablespoons melted shortening
1½ teaspoons salt
1/8 teaspoon pepper

¼ teaspoon paprika
2 cups water
1 4-ounce can mushrooms, drained
1 package frozen mixed vegetables
3 tablespoons all-purpose flour
½ cup water

Brown meat in shortening. Add salt, pepper, paprika and 2 cups water. Cover and cook over low heat 1½ hours. Add mushrooms and vegetables. Cover and cook about 15 minutes or until vegetables are tender. Combine flour and ½ cup water; add to meat mixture and cook, stirring constantly, until thickened. Serves 6–8.

VEAL SCALLOPINI

¼ cup all-purpose flour
1 teaspoon salt
¼ teaspoon pepper
1½ pounds veal cutlet, thinly sliced
1/3 cup olive oil
¼ cup minced onion
¼ cup chopped green pepper
1½ cups tomato sauce
¼ cup water

Combine flour, salt and pepper. Coat veal with flour mixture. Heat olive oil; add onion and green pepper and cook until tender. Remove onion and pepper; reserve drippings. Brown meat on both sides in drippings. Combine tomato sauce and water. Pour over veal. Add onion and green pepper. Cook, covered, over low heat 15–20 minutes. Serves 6.

VEAL FRICASSEE

2 pounds veal rump, cut in 1-inch cubes
¼ cup all-purpose flour, approx.
3 tablespoons melted shortening
½ cup hot water
½ cup sliced onions
1 cup diced celery
2 cups cubed potatoes
1 cup sliced carrots
1 teaspoon salt
¼ teaspoon pepper

Coat veal with flour; brown on all sides in shortening. Add water; cover and cook over low heat about 40 minutes. Add remaining ingredients; cover and cook 20–25 minutes, or until vegetables are tender. Serves 6.

VEAL CHOPS WITH PINEAPPLE

6 shoulder veal chops
¼ cup melted shortening
1 teaspoon salt
6 slices canned pineapple
1 cup pineapple juice

Brown chops on both sides in shortening; sprinkle with salt. Arrange pineapple slices over chops. Add pineapple juice. Cover and simmer 45-50 minutes or until chops are tender. Serves 4.

BRAISED VEAL LYON

1 3-pound veal shoulder, boned and rolled
2 tablespoons melted shortening
1 teaspoon salt
⅛ teaspoon pepper
1 medium-sized orange, thinly sliced
¾ cup orange juice

Brown veal shoulder on all sides in shortening. Season with salt and pepper; arrange orange slices over veal. Add orange juice. Cover and cook over low heat about 2½ hours, or until veal is tender. Serves 6.

DRIED BEEF, FRANKS

SPANISH FRANKFURTERS

½ cup finely chopped onions
¼ cup chopped celery
¼ cup chopped green pepper
3 tablespoons melted butter or margarine
1 can condensed tomato soup
1 tablespoon brown sugar
2 tablespoons Worcestershire sauce
2 tablespoons vinegar
1 tablespoon prepared mustard
8 frankfurters

Cook onions, celery and green pepper in butter or margarine until onions are tender. Add soup, sugar, Worcestershire sauce, vinegar and mustard. Mix well. Cook over low heat, stirring occasionally, 10 minutes. Add frankfurters and heat to serving temperature. Serves 4.

FRANKFURTER-POTATO CASSEROLE

1 pound frankfurters, cut in 1-inch pieces
2 tablespoons chopped onion
¼ cup chopped green pepper
½ cup chopped celery
¼ cup melted butter or margarine
3 tablespoons all-purpose flour
1 ¼ cups milk
1 teaspoon salt
⅛ teaspoon pepper
2 cups mashed, seasoned potatoes

Cook frankfurters, onion, green pepper and celery in butter or margarine until onion is tender; blend in flour. Gradually add milk and cook, stirring constantly, until thickened. Add salt and pepper. Turn into greased 1½-quart casserole. Arrange potatoes over frankfurter mixture. Bake in moderate oven (350° F.) 35 minutes. Serves 4.

OLIVE-CHIPPED BEEF CASSEROLE

¼ pound chipped beef
3 tablespoons melted butter or margarine
2 tablespoons all-purpose flour
2 cups milk
1 cup chopped celery
½ cup sliced ripe olives
½ cup grated American cheese
2 cups cooked egg noodles

Cook beef in butter or margarine 5 minutes. Blend in flour. Gradually add milk and cook, stirring constantly, until thickened. Add remaining ingredients and mix lightly. Turn into greased 1½-quart baking dish. Bake in moderate oven (350° F.) 30 minutes. Serves 6.

Macaroni & Spaghetti

Macaroni

NEAPOLITAN MACARONI SALAD

1 8-ounce package elbow macaroni, cooked
1 cup diced celery
2 tablespoons grated onion
¼ cup chopped green pepper
¼ cup sweet pickle relish
1 cup grated carrot
¼ teaspoon garlic salt
1 teaspoon Worcestershire sauce
2 tablespoons vinegar
½ cup salad dressing
2 hard-cooked eggs, chopped

Combine all ingredients, mix lightly. Chill thoroughly. Serves 6.

QUICK SAUCEPAN MACARONI AND CHEESE

1 tablespoon salt
3 quarts boiling water
2 cups elbow macaroni (8 ounces)
¼ cup butter or margarine
2 cups grated processed American cheese
(about ½ pound)
¼ cup finely chopped onion
Salt and pepper to taste
Pimiento-stuffed green olives

Add 1 tablespoon salt to rapidly boiling water. Gradually add macaroni so that water continues to boil. Cook uncovered, stirring occasionally, until tender. Drain in colander. Combine macaroni, butter or margarine, cheese, onion and salt and pepper to taste. Cook over low heat until cheese is melted. Serve immediately, garnished with olives, as desired. Serves 4-6.

MACARONI AND GREEN PEPPER AU GRATIN

3 medium-sized green peppers
1 tablespoon salt
3 quarts boiling water
2 cups elbow macaroni (8 ounces)
1 cup light cream
2 cups grated, processed American cheese
(about ½ pound)
1 teaspoon Worcestershire sauce
1 teaspoon prepared mustard
Salt and pepper to taste

Quarter peppers and remove seeds and membranes. Cover and cook in small amount of boiling salted water until tender, about 10 minutes. Drain. Add the 1 tablespoon salt to rapidly boiling water. Gradually add macaroni so that water continues to boil. Cook uncovered, stirring occasionally, until tender. Drain in colander. Combine cream and cheese. Cook over low heat until cheese is melted, stirring constantly. Add peppers, macaroni and remaining ingredients. Mix well and turn into greased 2-quart casserole. Bake in moderate oven (350° F.) 30 minutes. Serves 4-6.

BOHEMIAN MACARONI

1 1-pound jar pickled red cabbage
2 medium-sized onions, thinly sliced
1 tablespoon butter or margarine
1 cup grated processed Swiss cheese, (about ¼ pound)
1 tablespoon salt
3 quarts boiling water
2 cups elbow macaroni (8 ounces)
Salt and pepper to taste

Combine cabbage, onions, butter or margarine and cheese. Cook over medium heat until cheese is melted, stirring occasionally. Add the 1 tablespoon salt to rapidly boiling water. Gradually add macaroni so that water continues to boil. Cook uncovered, stirring occasionally, until tender. Drain in colander. Combine macaroni and cabbage mixture; toss lightly. Season to taste with salt and pepper. Serves 4–6.

MACARONI CHEESE LOAF

1 tablespoon salt
3 quarts boiling water
2 cups elbow macaroni (8 ounces)
1 14 ½-ounce can evaporated milk
2 cups grated Cheddar cheese (about ½ pound)
1 4-ounce can pimientos, drained and chopped
½ cup chopped parsley
1 tablespoon grated onion
1½ teaspoons salt
Freshly ground pepper

Add 1 tablespoon salt to rapidly boiling water. Gradually add macaroni so that water continues to boil. Cook uncovered, stirring occasionally, until tender. Drain in colander. Combine macaroni and remaining ingredients. Mix lightly but thoroughly. Turn into greased 9" x 5" x 3" loaf pan. Place in pan of hot wrater. Bake in slow oven (325° F.) 45–50 minutes, or until firm. To serve, unmold and slice. Serves 4–6.

VEGETABLE-MACARONI MEDLEY

¼ pound elbow macaroni, cooked
1 cup cooked green beans
2 onions, chopped
2 green peppers, chopped
½ cup diced cooked carrots
2 cups canned tomatoes
1 cup diced American cheese
½ cup cracker crumbs
1 teaspoon salt
¼ teaspoon pepper

Alternate layers of macaroni, vegetables and cheese in greased 1½-quart casserole. Top with crumbs. Add salt and pepper. Bake in moderate oven (375° F.) 35–40 minutes. Serves 6.

DEEP-SEA MACARONI

1 clove garlic, minced
1 cup sliced mushrooms
½ cup melted butter
½ cup chopped parsley
¾ cup diced shrimp

¾ cup diced oysters
¼ teaspoon salt
1 8-ounce package shell macaroni, cooked

Combine garlic, mushrooms, butter and parsley. Cover and cook over low heat 15 minutes. Add shrimp, oysters and salt; cook 5 minutes. Arrange macaroni on serving platter and top with shrimp-oyster mixture. Serves 4.

NOODLES

LYONNAISE NOODLES

1 tablespoon salt
3 quarts boiling water
8 ounces medium egg noodles (about 4 cups)
¼ cup butter or margarine
¼ cup finely chopped onion
1½ teaspoons paprika
2 tablespoons chopped chives

Add the 1 tablespoon salt to rapidly boiling water. Gradually add noodles so that water continues to boil. Cook uncovered, stirring occasionally, until tender. Drain in colander. Meanwhile, melt butter or margarine over low heat; add onion and cook until tender. Add paprika and mix thoroughly. Combine noodles, and butter or margarine mixture; mix thoroughly. Sprinkle with chopped chives. Serve with pot roast, as desired. Serves 6.

NUTTY NOODLES

2 tablespoons blanched slivered almonds
1 tablespoon melted butter
1½ cups cooked, diced beef
1 beef bouillon cube
½ cup hot water
1 teaspoon salt
8 ounces medium egg noodles, cooked
1 cup sour cream

Cook almonds in butter until lightly browned. Add beef and brown. Combine bouillon cube and water; stir until dissolved. Add bouillon, salt and noodles to beef mixture. Cook over low heat, stirring occasionally, 10 minutes. Add sour cream and mix lightly. Heat to serving temperature. Serves 4.

NOODLES WITH CLAMS

1 10 ½-ounce can minced clams
½ cup diced celery
3 tablespoons butter or margarine
½ cup chopped onions
1 small clove garlic, finely chopped
3 tablespoons all-purpose flour
1½ cups milk
2 cups grated sharp Cheddar cheese
  (about ½ pound)
1 No. 303 can peas, drained
Salt and pepper to taste
1 tablespoon salt
3 quarts boiling water
8 ounces medium egg noodles (about 4 cups)

Combine clams and celery; heat to boiling point and cook 10–15 minutes, or until celery is tender. Melt butter or margarine over low heat. Add onions and garlic and sauté 5 minutes. Add flour and blend. Gradually add milk and clam mixture and cook until thickened, stirring constantly. Add cheese and stir until cheese is melted. Add peas and salt and pepper to taste. Meanwhile, add the 1 tablespoon salt to rapidly boiling water. Gradually add noodles so that water continues to boil. Cook uncovered, stirring occasionally, until tender. Drain in colander. Serve sauce over noodles. Serves 4–6.

NOODLE AND LETTUCE TOSS

1 tablespoon salt
3 quarts boiling water
8 ounces medium egg noodles (about 4 cups)
¼ cup butter or margarine
6 cups shredded lettuce (1 medium-sized
  head)
¼ cup grated Parmesan cheese
Salt and pepper

Add the 1 tablespoon salt to rapidly boiling water. Gradually add noodles so that water continues to boil. Cook uncovered, stirring occasionally, until tender. Drain in colander. Meanwhile, melt butter or margarine and add lettuce. Cook over low heat 5 minutes, tossing lightly. Combine lettuce, noodles and cheese; season with salt and pepper. Toss lightly but thoroughly. Serves 4–6.

LAMB AND NOODLE LOAF

4 ounces egg noodles
2 cups cooked, ground lamb
¼ cup chopped green pepper
2 tablespoons grated onion
1 teaspoon salt
1/8 teaspoon pepper
1 tablespoon chopped pimiento
1 cup light cream

Cook noodles according to package directions. Drain. Add remaining ingredients and mix lightly. Turn into greased 9" x 5" x 3" pan. Bake in moderate oven (350° F.) 1¼ hours. Serves 4–6.

SAUTÉED NOODLES AND ALMONDS

6 tablespoons butter or margarine
8 ounces medium egg noodles (about 4 cups)
1 large onion, thinly sliced
2/3 cup chopped, toasted almonds
3 cups milk
Salt and pepper to taste

Melt butter or margarine and add noodles, onion and almonds. Cook over medium heat, stirring occasionally, until noodles are browned. Add milk and cook, stirring occasionally, 15–20 minutes, or until noodles are tender. Season with salt and pepper. Serves 4.

NOODLE CHEESE DESSERT

8 ounces egg noodles, cooked
4 eggs, beaten
2 cups cottage cheese
¾ cup sugar
2 teaspoons cinnamon
½ teaspoon nutmeg
¼ teaspoon ground ginger
1 cup crushed salted almonds
½ cup melted butter

Combine all ingredients and mix lightly. Turn into greased 1½-quart baking dish. Bake in moderate oven (350° F.) 20–30 minutes, or until lightly browned. Serves 6.

TURKEY NOODLE BAKE

6 **tablespoons butter or margarine**
6 **tablespoons all-purpose flour**
3 **cups milk**
3 **cups cooked noodles**
¼ **cup grated onion**
1 **cup cooked peas and carrots**
2 **cups diced cooked turkey**
½ **cup grated cheddar cheese**
¼ **cup buttered cracker crumbs**

Melt butter or margarine; blend in flour; gradually add milk and cook, stirring constantly, until thickened. Add noodles, onion, peas and carrots, turkey and cheese; mix lightly. Turn into greased 2-quart casserole. Top with crumbs. Bake in moderate oven (350° F.) about 1 hour. Serves 6.

NOODLES WITH TOASTED NUTS

3 **tablespoons butter**
½ **cup chopped Brazil nuts**
3 **cups cooked noodles**
1 **tablespoon chopped chives**

Melt butter. Add nuts. Cook until lightly browned. Pour butter mixture over noodles. Sprinkle with chives Serves 4.

SPAGHETTI

SPAGHETTI WITH TOMATO AND MUSHROOM SAUCE

2 **tablespoons olive or salad oil**
2 **large onions, chopped**
2 **cloves garlic, finely chopped**
1 **pound button mushrooms**
1 **No. 2½ can tomatoes**
1 **No. 2 can tomato juice**
1/3 **cup tomato paste**
1/3 **cup water**
1½ **teaspoons salt**
¼ **teaspoon pepper**
2 **tablespoons salt**
4-6 **quarts boiling water**
1 **pound spaghetti**
Grated Parmesan cheese

Heat oil over medium heat. Add onions and garlic and cook until tender. Add mushrooms; cover and cook over low heat 20 minutes, stirring occasionally. Add tomatoes, tomato juice, tomato paste and water. Heat to boiling point over high heat. Reduce heat and cook 1 hour, stirring occasionally. Add the 1½ teaspoon salt and pepper. Add the 2 tablespoons salt to rapidly boiling water about 10 minutes before sauce is done. Gradually add spaghetti so that water continues to boil. Cook uncovered, stirring occasionally, until tender. Drain in colander. Serve sauce over spaghetti. Sprinkle with grated cheese, if desired. Serves 8.

NEAPOLITAN SPAGHETTI SAUCE

1 **pound ground beef**
1 **cup sliced mushrooms**
1 **small clove garlic, minced**
½ **cup chopped onions**
¼ **cup melted butter or margarine**
1/8 **teaspoon oregano**
1/8 **teaspoon basil**
1 **No. 2½ can tomatoes**
1 **can tomato paste**
½ **teaspoon salt**
1/8 **teaspoon pepper**

Cook beef, mushrooms, garlic and onions in butter or margarine until onions are tender. Add remaining ingredients and simmer 1–2 hours. Serve with spaghetti, as desired. Makes about 6 cups.

SPAGHETTI WITH CHICKEN LIVERS

1 **clove garlic, minced**
¼ **cup cooking oil**
¼ **cup minced chives**
1 **cup chopped chicken livers**
1 **cup cooked tomatoes**
¼ **cup sliced mushrooms**
½ **cup white wine**
½ **teaspoon salt**
1/8 **teaspoon pepper**
½ **teaspoon Worcestershire sauce**
1 **pound spaghetti, cooked**
¼ **cup butter or margarine**

Cook garlic in oil 5 minutes. Add chives and chicken livers; cook 5 minutes. Add tomatoes, mushrooms, wine, salt, pepper and Worcestershire sauce. Simmer 20 minutes.

Combine hot spaghetti and butter or margarine; serve chicken liver sauce over spaghetti. Serves 4.

PARSLEY SPAGHETTI

1 tablespoon salt
3 quarts boiling water
8 ounces spaghetti
¼ cup butter or margarine
3 tablespoons finely chopped onion
½ cup finely chopped parsley
¼ teaspoon sweet basil
1 teaspoon salt

Add the 1 tablespoon salt to rapidly boiling water. Gradually add spaghetti so that water continues to boil. Cook uncovered, stirring occasionally, until tender. Drain in colander. While spaghetti is cooking, melt butter or margarine over low heat; add onion, parsley, basil and the 1 teaspoon salt. Cook over low heat 10 minutes. Remove from heat and pour over spaghetti; mix lightly. Serves 4–6.

Gravies & Sauces

CAPER SAUCE PESCADERO

2 tablespoons butter or margarine
2 tablespoons all-purpose flour
2 cups chicken stock or bouillon
1 teaspoon lemon juice
¼ teaspoon salt
½ cup capers

Melt butter or margarine; blend in flour. Gradually add stock or bouillon and cook, stirring constantly, until thickened. Add remaining ingredients and heat to serving temperature, stirring constantly. Serve with fish, as desired. Makes about 2½ cups.

BARBECUE SAUCE

¼ cup chopped onions
1 tablespoon butter, melted
1½ cups chili sauce
1½ cups water
3 tablespoons lemon juice
1 tablespoon brown sugar
1½ tablespoons Worcestershire sauce
1 tablespoon prepared mustard
1 teaspoon salt
1 cup minced celery

Combine all ingredients and simmer over low heat until celery and onion are tender. Serve with hamburgers, as desired. Makes about 4 cups.

HOLLANDAISE SAUCE

¼ cup butter or margarine
2 tablespoons lemon juice
3 egg yolks, well beaten
1/8 teaspoon salt
¼ cup butter or margarine
¼ cup butter or margarine
Dash cayenne pepper

Combine ¼ cup butter or margarine, lemon juice, egg yolks and salt in top of double boiler. Cook over hot water, beating constantly, until butter melts. Add the second ¼ cup butter or margarine and continue cooking, beating

constantly, until mixture begins to thicken. Add remaining ¼ cup butter or margarine and cayenne pepper; cook, stirring constantly, until thickened. Serve immediately, with fish and vegetables, as desired. Makes about ¾ cup.

HORSERADISH BUTTER SAUCE

½ cup butter or margarine
3 tablespoons horseradish
1/8 teaspoon salt
Dash of cayenne

Combine all ingredients. Cook over low heat, stirring constantly, until butter melts. Serve with steaks and chops, as desired. Makes about 2/3 cup.

SAUCE DIABLE

¼ cup melted butter or margarine
2 tablespoons water
¼ cup chili sauce
2 teaspoons sugar
½ clove garlic, minced
1 tablespoon Worcestershire sauce
½ teaspoon salt
1/8 teaspoon Tabasco

Combine all ingredients and heat to serving temperature. Serve with lobster or crab. Makes about ½ cup.

EGG AND ANCHOVY SAUCE

3 hard-cooked eggs, chopped
3 anchovies, chopped
1 tablespoon chopped stuffed olives
1 teaspoon grated onion
2 egg yolks
1½ teaspoons prepared mustard
¼ teaspoon salt
3 tablespoons white vinegar

Combine all ingredients and beat until well blended. Chill thoroughly. Serve with fish, as desired. Makes about ¾ cup.

GAME SAUCE

3 tablespoons butter
¼ cup chopped mushrooms
3 tablespoons all-purpose flour
1 cup beef stock
1 cup water
½ teaspoon salt
1/8 teaspoon paprika
2 tablespoons chopped chives
2 tablespoons red wine

Melt butter, add mushrooms and cook until tender. Blend in flour. Gradually add stock and water. Cook over low heat, stirring constantly, until thickened. Add remaining ingredients and heat to serving temperature, stirring constantly. Makes about 3 cups.

ANCHOVY BUTTER SAUCE

1/3 cup butter or margarine
1 tablespoon chopped parsley
¼ teaspoon salt
1/8 teaspoon pepper
1 teaspoon anchovy paste
½ teaspoon prepared mustard
1 tablespoon lemon juice
1 teaspoon Worcestershire sauce

Melt butter or margarine; add remaining ingredients and heat to serving temperature. Serve with fish, as desired. Makes about 1/3 cup.

BROWN GRAVY

¼ cup all-purpose flour
¼ cup melted meat or poultry drippings
2 cups meat or vegetable stock
¼ teaspoon salt
1/8 teaspoon pepper

Blend flour into drippings and cook over low heat until browned. Gradually add stock and cook, stirring constantly, until thickened. Season with salt and pepper. Serve with meat and poultry, as desired. Makes about 2 cups.

RAISIN SAUCE

½ cup raisins
1 cup water
¼ teaspoon cloves
¾ cup firmly packed brown sugar
2 teaspoons cornstarch
1/8 teaspoon salt
1 tablespoon butter or margarine
1 tablespoon lemon juice
1 tablespoon orange juice

Combine raisins, water and cloves. Cook over low heat ten minutes. Combine sugar, cornstarch and salt. Add cornstarch mixture to raisin mixture, and cook, stirring constantly, until thickened. Add remaining ingredients and heat to serving temperature, stirring constantly. Serve with ham or tongue, as desired. Makes about 2 cups.

FLEMISH CARROT SAUCE

¼ cup butter or margarine
¼ cup all-purpose flour
1 cup chicken stock
1 cup light cream
¾ cup grated carrots
¼ teaspoon salt
¼ teaspoon paprika

Melt butter or margarine; blend in flour. Gradually add stock and cream and cook, stirring constantly, until thickened. Add remaining ingredients. Heat to serving temperature, stirring constantly. Serve with fish and vegetables, as desired. Makes about 2¾ cups.

BRUSSELS MUSHROOM SAUCE

½ cup sliced mushrooms
¼ cup melted butter or margarine
¼ cup all-purpose flour
1 cup milk
1 cup light cream
2 tablespoons chopped parsley
¼ teaspoon salt

Cook mushrooms in butter or margarine until tender. Remove mushrooms. Blend in flour. Gradually add milk and cream and cook, stirring constantly, until thickened. Add mushrooms, parsley and salt. Serve with meats, fish, poultry and vegetables, as desired. Makes about 2 cups.

ALMOND SAUCE

1/3 **cup slivered blanched almonds**
1/2 **cup melted butter**
2 **tablespoons lemon juice**
1/8 **teaspoon garlic salt**

Cook almonds in butter until lightly browned. Add remaining ingredients and heat to serving temperature. Serve with game, fish, or vegetables, as desired. Makes about 1 cup.

VELOUTE SAUCE

2 **tablespoons butter or margarine**
2 **tablespoons all-purpose flour**
1 **cup chicken stock**
1/4 **cup light cream**
1/4 **teaspoon salt**
1/8 **teaspoon pepper**

Melt butter or margarine; blend in flour. Gradually add stock and cream and cook, stirring constantly, until thickened. Season with salt and pepper. Serve with poultry, vegetables and fish, as desired. Makes about 1 cup.

FRENCH VINAIGRETTE SAUCE

1/2 **cup French dressing**
1 **tablespoon chopped green pepper**
1 **teaspoon grated onion**
1 **tablespoon chopped parsley**
1 **tablespoon chopped dill pickle**

Combine all ingredients and beat well. Serve with meats and vegetables, as desired. Makes about 3/4 cup.

WINE SAUCE

1 **tablespoon butter**
1/2 **cup currant jelly**
2 **tablespoons lime juice**
Dash cayenne pepper
1/2 **cup water**
1 **teaspoon salt**
1/2 **cup sherry wine**

Combine butter, jelly, lime juice, cayenne pepper, water and salt. Simmer 5 minutes. Add sherry wine. Heat to serving temperature. Serve with game, or tongue. Makes about 1½ cups.

ALL-PURPOSE CHEESE SAUCE

3 **tablespoons butter or margarine**
3 **tablespoons all-purpose flour**
1½ **cups milk**
1 **cup grated Cheddar or American cheese**
1 **tablespoon Sherry**
1/8 **teaspoon salt**

Melt butter or margarine; blend in flour. Gradually add milk and cook, stirring constantly, until thickened. Add remaining ingredients and stir until cheese is melted. Serve with meat, fish and vegetables, as desired. Makes about 3 cups.

DANISH CREAM CHEESE SAUCE

1 **8-ounce package cream cheese**
2 **egg yolks**
1/4 **cup lemon juice**
1/8 **teaspoon salt**
1/8 **teaspoon pepper**

Soften cream cheese and blend in remaining ingredients. Cook over low heat, stirring constantly, until thoroughly heated. Serve with green vegetables and fish, as desired. Makes about 1½ cups.

BOG CRANBERRY SAUCE

4 **cups cranberries**
1½ **cups water**
2 **cups sugar**
1/8 **teaspoon salt**
1 **tablespoon lemon juice**

Wash cranberries. Add ¾ cup of the water and cook until cranberries are very tender. Press through sieve. Combine sugar, salt, lemon juice and remaining ¾ cup water; cook 10 minutes. Add strained cranberries and cook 10 minutes. Strain and pour into molds. Chill until firm. Serve with fowl and meat. Makes about 4 cups.

PINEAPPLE CHUTNEY SAUCE

1/2 **cup pineapple jam**
2 **tablespoons chopped cucumber pickles**
1/4 **cup sherry**
1 **tablespoon butter or margarine**
1 **teaspoon chopped pimiento**

Combine all ingredients and heat to serving temperature, stirring constantly. Serve with lamb and ham, as desired. Makes about ¾ cup.

DINARD CUCUMBER ONION SAUCE

½ cup chopped cucumber, drained
2 tablespoons grated onion
1 tablespoon vinegar
½ cup heavy cream, whipped
¼ teaspoon salt

Combine cucumber, onion and vinegar. Fold in cream and salt. Chill thoroughly. Serve with fish, as desired. Makes about 1¼ cups.

CHATEAUBRIAND SAUCE

2 tablespoons butter
1 tablespoon lime juice
½ teaspoon salt
1 teaspoon minced parsley
2 cups tomato sauce
Dash Tabasco

Combine butter, lime juice, salt and parsley. Add tomato sauce and Tabasco. Heat to serving temperature. Serve with steak or roast beef. Makes about 2 cups.

HORSERADISH SAUCE FOR SHRIMP

1 cup catsup
1 tablespoon horseradish
2 tablespoons chili sauce
2 tablespoons white vinegar
Dash Tabasco

Combine all ingredients and chill. Makes about 1¼ cups.

INDONESIAN CURRY SAUCE

1 tablespoon chopped onion
2 tablespoons melted butter or margarine
2 tablespoons all-purpose flour
1 tablespoon curry powder
2 cups chicken stock
¼ teaspoon salt

Cook onion in butter or margarine until tender. Blend in flour and curry powder. Gradually add stock and cook, stirring constantly, until thickened. Season with salt. Serve with meats, fish and poultry, as desired. Makes about 2 cups.

WHITE WINE SAUCE

3 tablespoons butter or margarine
3 tablespoons all-purpose flour
¾ cup water
¼ cup dry white wine
1 cup light cream
1 tablespoon Sherry
¼ teaspoon salt

Melt butter or margarine; blend in flour. Gradually add water, white wine, cream, Sherry and salt. Cook, stirring constantly, until thickened. Serve with fish, as desired. Makes about 1¼ cups.

PARISIENNE PARSLEY BUTTER SAUCE

¼ cup butter or margarine
¼ teaspoon garlic salt
¼ teaspoon celery salt
¼ teaspoon paprika
2 tablespoons chopped parsley

Combine all ingredients and cook, stirring occasionally, until butter or margarine melts. Serve with green vegetables, as desired. Makes about 1 cup.

FROZEN HORSERADISH SAUCE

½ cup horseradish
1 tablespoon sugar
¼ teaspoon salt
½ cup salad dressing
1 cup heavy cream, whipped

Combine horseradish, sugar, salt and salad dressing. Fold in cream. Turn into refrigerator tray and freeze until firm. Serve with cold meats, as desired. Makes about 2 cups.

CANTONESE LOBSTER SAUCE

½ cup sliced mushrooms
3 tablespoons melted butter or margarine
2 tablespoons all-purpose flour
1 1/3 cups beef stock
½ cup chopped, cooked lobster
¼ teaspoon salt

Cook mushrooms in butter or margarine until tender. Remove mushrooms. Blend in flour. Gradually add stock and cook, stirring constantly, until thickened. Add mushrooms, lobster and salt. Heat to serving temperature, stirring constantly. Serve with fish croquettes and loaves, as desired. Makes about 2 cups.

SAUCE MOULIN

4 onions, sliced
2 tablespoons melted butter
2 tablespoons all-purpose flour
1 cup beef stock
1 tablespoon dry white wine
1 tablespoon chili sauce
¼ teaspoon paprika
Salt and pepper to taste

Cook onions in butter until browned. Remove onions. Stir in flour. Gradually add stock, wine and remaining ingredients and cook until thickened, stirring constantly. Serve with meats or sea food. Makes about 1½ cups.

SOUR CREAM GRAVY

2 tablespoons butter or margarine
2 tablespoons all-purpose flour
½ cup meat or vegetable stock
¾ cup sour cream
¼ teaspoon black pepper
¼ teaspoon salt
¼ teaspoon nutmeg
1 tablespoon chopped parsley

Melt butter or margarine; blend in flour. Gradually add stock and cook over low heat, stirring constantly, until thickened. Add remaining ingredients and heat to serving temperature, stirring constantly. Serve with beef and veal. Makes about 1½ cups.

STEAK SAUCE

½ cup butter or margarine
1 tablespoon Worcestershire sauce
1 tablespoon prepared mustard
2 tablespoons chili sauce
½ teaspoon paprika
2 tablespoons vinegar

Combine all ingredients and heat to serving temperature, stirring occasionally. Serve with steak, as desired. Makes about ¾ cup.

MARSHALL'S SWEET AND SOUR GRAPE SAUCE

1 teaspoon cornstarch
2/3 cup water
½ cup grape jelly
1 tablespoon onion juice
2 tablespoons horseradish

2 tablespoons butter or margarine
1/8 teaspoon salt

Combine cornstarch and water; add remaining ingredients and cook, stirring constantly, until thickened. Serve with meats, as desired. Makes about 1¼ cups.

TOMATO SAUCE

1 No. 2 can tomatoes
¼ teaspoon salt
1/8 teaspoon pepper
1 bay leaf
1 tablespoon chopped onion
2 tablespoons butter or margarine
2 tablespoons all-purpose flour

Combine tomatoes, salt, pepper, bay leaf and onion. Cook over low heat ten minutes; remove bay leaf. Force tomato mixture through sieve. Melt butter and blend in flour. Gradually add tomato mixture and cook, stirring constantly, until thickened. Serve with meat, fish and vegetables, as desired. Makes 1 cup.

OYSTER CHIVE SAUCE

¼ cup butter
¾ cup oysters
¼ cup all-purpose flour
2 cups milk
2 tablespoons sherry
1 tablespoon chopped chives
¼ teaspoon salt

Melt butter, add oysters and cook until edges curl, about 2 minutes. Remove oysters. Stir in flour. Gradually add milk and cook, stirring constantly, until thickened. Add oysters and remaining ingredients and heat to serving temperature, stirring constantly. Serve with fish. Makes about 2½ cups.

MINT SAUCE

1/3 cup finely chopped mint leaves
2 teaspoons powdered sugar
½ cup white vinegar

Combine all ingredients and stir until sugar is dissolved. Let stand thirty minutes. Serve with lamb, as desired. Makes about ¾ cup.

HUNTERS ORANGE SAUCE

2 tablespoons butter or margarine
2 tablespoons all-purpose flour
1¼ cups orange juice
¼ teaspoon grated orange rind
1/8 teaspoon salt
1 teaspoon sugar

Melt butter or margarine and blend in flour. Gradually add orange juice and cook, stirring constantly, until thickened. Add remaining ingredients and heat to serving temperature, stirring constantly. Serve with game and poultry, as desired. Makes about 1¼ cups.

MUSTARD SAUCE

1 tablespoon butter or margarine
1 tablespoon all-purpose flour
2 tablespoons dry mustard
1 tablespoon sugar
¼ teaspoon salt
1/3 cup boiling water
1/3 cup vinegar
½ teaspoon Worcestershire sauce

Melt butter or margarine; blend in flour, mustard, sugar and salt. Remove from heat and gradually add remaining ingredients. Cook over low heat, stirring constantly, until thickened. Serve with meats and fish, as desired. Makes about 1 cup.

MUSHROOM GRAVY

¾ cup chopped mushrooms
¼ cup melted meat or poultry drippings
3 tablespoons all-purpose flour
2 cups meat, poultry or vegetable stock
2 tablespoons chopped parsley
¼ teaspoon salt

Cook mushrooms in drippings until tender. Blend in flour. Gradually add stock and cook, stirring constantly, until thickened. Add parsley and salt. Heat to serving temperature, stirring constantly. Serve with meat or poultry, as desired. Makes 2 cups.

SWEET AND SOUR CURRANT SAUCE

½ cup currant jelly
½ cup prepared mustard
½ teaspoon horseradish

Melt jelly over low heat. Add remaining ingredients and cook, stirring constantly, until thoroughly heated. Serve with meats or game, as desired. Makes about 1½ cups.

NEWBURGH SAUCE

1 tablespoon butter or margarine
1 tablespoon all-purpose flour
1 cup milk
1 egg yolk
1 tablespoon Sherry
1/8 teaspoon salt
1/8 teaspoon paprika

Melt butter or margarine; blend in flour. Gradually add milk and cook, stirring constantly, until thickened. Add a little of hot mixture to egg yolk and mix well. Stir into hot mixture and cook, stirring constantly, 1 minute. Add Sherry, salt and paprika. Serve with fish, as desired. Makes about 1 cup.

AUSTRIAN POPPY SEED SAUCE

½ cup butter or margarine
2 tablespoons lemon juice
½ teaspoon grated lemon rind
1 teaspoon poppy seed
1/8 teaspoon salt

Combine all ingredients and cook, stirring occasionally, until butter or margarine melts. Serve with green vegetables, as desired. Makes about ½ cup.

MARINARA SAUCE

1 No. 2½ can tomatoes
¾ cup water
2 tablespoons butter or margarine
½ teaspoon garlic salt
½ teaspoon oregano

Combine all ingredients and simmer 1 hour. Serve with spaghetti and macaroni. Makes about 3 cups.

CREOLE TOMATO SAUCE

2 **tablespoons chopped onion**
2 **tablespoons chopped green pepper**
1 **tablespoon salad oil**
1 **can condensed tomato soup**
¼ **cup water**
1 **teaspoon chili powder**
¼ **teaspoon salt**

Cook onion and green pepper in oil until onion is tender. Add remaining ingredients and heat to serving temperature, stirring frequently. Serve with meat, fish and vegetables, as desired. Makes about 1½ cups.

MISSOURI CREAM GRAVY

¼ **cup all-purpose flour**
¼ **cup melted chicken drippings**
1 **cup chicken or vegetable stock**
1 **cup light cream**
¼ **teaspoon salt**
1/8 **teaspoon pepper**

Blend flour into drippings and cook over low heat until browned. Gradually add stock and cream; cook, stirring constantly, until thickened. Season with salt and pepper. Serve with chicken. Makes about 2 cups.

TARTARE SAUCE

2 **tablespoons chopped parsley**
1 **teaspoon capers**
¼ **cup sweet pickle relish**
1 **cup salad dressing**

Combine all ingredients; chill. Serve with fish, as desired. Makes about 1¼ cups.

TURKEY GIBLET GRAVY

½ **cup all-purpose flour**
1½ **cups melted turkey drippings**
3 ½ **cups turkey or vegetable stock**
Turkey giblets, cooked
1½ **teaspoons salt**
1/8 **teaspoon pepper**

Blend flour into drippings. Gradually add stock and cook, stirring constantly, until thickened. Add remaining ingredients and heat to serving temperature, stirring constantly. Serve with turkey, as desired. Makes about 4 cups.

ONION GRAVY

½ **cup chopped onions**
¼ **cup melted meat or poultry drippings**
¼ **cup all-purpose flour**
2 **cups meat, poultry or vegetable stock**
¼ **teaspoon salt**
1/8 **teaspoon pepper**

Cook onions in drippings until tender. Blend in flour. Gradually add stock and cook, stirring constantly, until thickened. Season with salt and pepper. Serve with meats or poultry, as desired. Makes 2 cups.

Vegetables

ASPARAGUS VINAIGRETTE

1 package frozen asparagus
1 tablespoon vinegar
½ teaspoon prepared mustard
3 tablespoons melted butter or margarine
¼ teaspoon paprika
¼ teaspoon salt
1 teaspoon grated onion
1 hard-cooked egg, chopped

Cook asparagus according to package directions. Drain and chill. Combine remaining ingredients and mix well. Pour vinegar mixture over asparagus. Serves 4.

ARTICHOKES, ITALIAN STYLE

3 small artichokes
2 tablespoons olive oil
½ teaspoon salt
1/8 teaspoon pepper
3 tablespoons water
6 eggs, slightly beaten
1 tablespoon grated Parmesan cheese

Wash artichokes and trim. Remove tough upper portions of petals. Cut in half and remove chokes. Cut petals into thin lengthwise strips. Cook in oil until wilted. Add salt, pepper and water. Cover and cook over low heat 15–20 minutes, or until tender. Add eggs and cook until firm, stirring occasionally. Sprinkle with cheese. Serves 6.

BOSTON BAKED BEANS

1 quart pea beans
Water
½ pound salt pork
1 teaspoon salt
2 tablespoons brown sugar
1/8 teaspoon ginger
¼ cup molasses
½ teaspoon dry mustard
Boiling water

Wash beans; soak overnight in water to cover. Without draining, simmer 2 to 3 hours until skins wrinkle. Cut pork into thin slices. Alternate layers of undrained beans and pork in bean pot. Add salt, sugar, ginger, molasses and mustard. Add enough boiling water to cover. Cover and bake in slow oven (250° F.) about 6 hours, or until beans are tender. Add boiling water during baking period as needed to cover beans. Uncover for last half hour of baking. Serves 8-10.

BAKED BEAN CROQUETTES

2 cups baked beans
2 tablespoons minced onion
½ teaspoon salt
1/8 teaspoon pepper
1 teaspoon molasses
1 egg, slightly beaten
1 tablespoon water
Fine dry bread crumbs

Mash beans with onion, salt, pepper and molasses. Shape into croquettes. Combine egg and water. Dip croquettes in egg mixture and roll in bread crumbs. Fry in deep hot fat (375° F.) 1½–2 minutes, or until browned on all sides. Drain on absorbent paper. Serves 4.

JERUSALEM ARTICHOKES

1 pound Jerusalem artichokes
1/3 cup melted butter or margarine
3 tablespoons lemon juice
2 tablespoons chopped parsley
¼ teaspoon salt

Wash and pare artichokes. Cook, covered, in small amount of boiling salted water 15–25 minutes or until tender. Drain. Add remaining ingredients and heat to serving temperature, stirring frequently. Serves 4-6.

BAKED BEETS WITH ORANGE

6 medium-sized beets, sliced
½ cup water
½ teaspoon salt
1 tablespoon orange juice
1 teaspoon grated orange rind
1 tablespoon butter
Dash of pepper

Combine all ingredients and turn into greased 1-quart casserole. Bake, covered, in moderate oven (350° F.) 45 minutes, or until beets are tender. Serves 4.

BEET GREENS WITH CREAM

3 cups cooked chopped beet greens
1 tablespoon grated onion
½ cup light cream
1 tablespoon prepared mustard
2 tablespoons prepared horseradish
½ teaspoon salt
⅛ teaspoon pepper

Combine all ingredients and heat to serving temperature, stirring frequently. Serves 6.

GREEN BEANS WITH CELERY

1 cup chopped celery
½ cup chopped green pepper
3 tablespoons melted butter or margarine
3 cups green beans
1 teaspoon salt
½ cup water

Cook celery and green pepper in butter or margarine until tender. Add beans and salt. Turn into greased 1½-quart casserole. Pour water over other ingredients. Cover and bake in moderate oven (375° F.) about 20 minutes or until beans are tender. Serves 6.

SOUR CREAM LIMA BEANS

¼ cup chopped onion
2 tablespoons melted butter
½ cup sour cream
2 tablespoons chopped pimiento
¼ teaspoon salt
⅛ teaspoon pepper
2 cups cooked hot lima beans
½ teaspoon paprika

Cook onion in butter until tender. Add sour cream, pimiento, salt and pepper. Cook, stirring constantly, until thoroughly heated. Arrange beans in serving dish. Pour sour-cream mixture over beans. Sprinkle with paprika. Serves 4.

CARROT FLUFF

4 cups mashed cooked carrots
⅛ teaspoon pepper
¼ teaspoon salt
¼ teaspoon paprika
2 tablespoons butter, melted
¼ cup hot milk

Combine all ingredients. Beat until light. Serves 6.

SWEET AND SOUR CARROTS

4 cups sliced carrots
2 tablespoons melted fat
1 cup boiling water
3 tablespoons vinegar
3 tablespoons sugar
1 teaspoon salt
2 tablespoons cornstarch
¼ cup water
¼ teaspoon soy sauce

Cook carrots in fat three minutes, stirring constantly. Add boiling water, vinegar, sugar and salt; simmer for 10 minutes. Mix cornstarch with water and soy sauce; add to carrots and cook, stirring constantly, until thickened. Serves 6.

BAKED CAULIFLOWER

1 large head cauliflower, cooked
3 eggs, well beaten
¼ cup chopped onion
¼ cup chopped parsley
1 small clove garlic, minced
1 cup canned tomatoes
¼ cup cooking oil
1 teaspoon salt
¼ teaspoon pepper
1 cup grated sharp cheese

Separate cauliflower into flowerets. Arrange in greased 2½-quart casserole. Combine remaining ingredients and pour over cauliflower. Bake in moderate oven (350° F.) 35–40 minutes. Serves 6.

CARROT POTATO BALLS

4 medium-sized carrots, grated
4 medium-sized potatoes, grated
3 tablespoons all-purpose flour
¼ cup milk
1 tablespoon onion, grated
¼ teaspoon salt
1/8 teaspoon pepper
¼ cup melted shortening

Combine carrots, potatoes, flour, milk, onion, salt and pepper. Shape into small balls. Cook in shortening over low heat, about 10 minutes, or until browned on all sides. Serves 4-6.

CARROTS WITH HONEY

¼ cup honey
¼ cup butter or margarine
½ teaspoon grated orange rind
1/8 teaspoon salt
12 medium-sized carrots, cooked

Combine honey, butter or margarine, orange rind and salt. Heat to boiling point, stirring constantly. Simmer 5 minutes. Pour honey mixture over carrots. Serves 4.

CANDIED CARROTS

12 medium-sized carrots, cooked
½ cup water
1 cup firmly packed brown sugar
3 tablespons melted butter or margarine
1/8 teaspoon salt

Arrange carrots in greased shallow baking pan. Combine remaining ingredients and cook over low heat until sugar melts, stirring constantly. Pour sugar mixture over carrots. Bake in moderate oven (350° F.) 20-25 minutes. Serves 4.

CHEESE CRUMBED CAULIFLOWER

1/3 cup butter
½ cup cracker crumbs
1 teaspoon grated onion
½ cup grated Swiss cheese
1/8 teaspoon salt
1 medium-sized cauliflower, cooked

Melt butter; add crumbs, onion, cheese and salt. Cook over low heat, stirring until cheese is melted. Pour over cauliflower. Serves 6.

COTTAGE CHEESE STUFFED BEETS

8 medium-sized beets, cooked
¼ cup chopped onion
1 tablespoon chili sauce
½ teaspoon lemon juice
½ cup cottage cheese
½ teaspoon salt
1/8 teaspoon pepper

Remove centers from beets, leaving a shell about inch thick. Chop beet pulp and add remaining ingredients. Mix lightly. Fill shells with cheese mixture. Place in greased shallow baking pan. Add enough water to cover bottom of pan. Bake in moderate oven (375° F.) about 20 minutes. Serves 4.

HARVARD BEETS

1/3 cup sugar
¼ teaspoon salt
1 tablespoon cornstarch
½ cup vinegar
1 tablespoon butter or margarine
1 tablespoon grated onion
3 cups diced cooked beets

Combine sugar, salt and cornstarch; gradually add vinegar and cook over low heat, stirring constantly, until thickened. Add remaining ingredients and cook, stirring frequently, 15 minutes. Serves 4.

BROCCOLI PARMESAN

1 package frozen chopped broccoli
2 tablespoons butter or margarine
1 small clove garlic, minced
1 tablespoon grated Parmesan cheese

Cook broccoli according to package directions; drain. Melt butter or margarine; add garlic and cook until lightly browned. Pour over broccoli and mix lightly. Sprinkle with Parmesan cheese. Serves 4.

BRAISED BRUSSELS SPROUTS

¼ cup chopped onion
3 tablespoons butter or margarine
¼ cup chicken stock
4 cups Brussels sprouts
½ teaspoon salt
2 tablespoons chopped chives

Cook onion in butter or margarine until tender. Add stock, Brussels sprouts and salt. Cook over low heat, stirring occasionally, 8-10 minutes or until liquid has evaporated and sprouts are tender. Sprinkle with chives. Serves 6.

BRUSSELS SPROUTS WITH CHESTNUTS

4 cups Brussels sprouts
¼ cup chopped onion
½ cup chopped, cooked chestnuts
½ cup chopped celery
1½ cups beef bouillon
2 tablespoons butter or margarine
½ teaspoon salt
1 tablespoon lemon juice

Arrange Brussels sprouts in greased 1½-quart casserole. Combine onion, chestnuts, celery and bouillon. Heat to boiling point and cook 10 minutes. Add remaining ingredients and mix well. Pour over Brussels sprouts. Bake in moderate oven (350° F.) 15-20 minutes or until sprouts are tender. Serves 6.

CABBAGE WITH SOUR CREAM

1 medium-sized head of cabbage, finely
   shredded
¼ cup melted butter or margarine
1 egg, slightly beaten
1 cup sour cream
1 tablespoon sugar
2 tablespoons lemon juice
½ teaspoon salt
1/8 teaspoon pepper

Cook cabbage in butter or margarine over low heat about 15 minutes or until tender. Combine remaining ingredients and mix well. Pour sour-cream mixture over cabbage and heat to serving temperature, stirring constantly. Serves 6.

CHINESE CABBAGE

1 medium-sized head Chinese cabbage, sliced
1 cup boiling water
½ teaspoon salt
¼ cup light cream
2 tablespoons butter or margarine
2 tablespoons minced parsley

Combine cabbage, boiling water and salt. Cook, covered, 7 minutes. Drain and add remaining ingredients. Heat to serving temperature. Serves 4.

CELERIAC HOLLANDAISE

4 celery roots
1 cup Hollandaise sauce (page 84)

Cut leaves and root fibers from celery roots. Pare and dice. Cook, covered, in boiling salted water 15-25 minutes or until tender. Serve with Hollandaise sauce. Serves 4-6.

WAX BEANS WITH DILL AND EGG

½ cup finely chopped onion
2 tablespoons melted butter or margarine
4 cups cooked, diced wax beans
½ teaspoon salt
1/8 teaspoon pepper
1 tablespoon chopped dill
1 hard-cooked egg, chopped

Cook onion in butter or margarine until lightly browned. Add remaining ingredients and heat to serving temperature, stirring frequently. Serves 6.

BRAISED CELERY

1 large bunch celery
¼ cup butter or margarine
¼ cup water
1 teaspoon salt
1/8 teaspoon pepper
¼ teaspoon nutmeg

Cut celery stalks in 2" lengths. Melt butter or margarine; add celery and cook until lightly browned. Add remaining ingredients, cover and cook over low heat 10-15 minutes or until celery is tender. Serves 6.

BAKED CELERY

3 medium-sized bunches celery
1 chicken bouillon cube
1 cup boiling water
¼ cup butter or margarine
½ teaspoon salt
1/8 teaspoon pepper

Cut celery stalks in 2" lengths and place in greased, shallow baking pan. Combine remaining ingredients and stir until bouillon cube is dissolved. Pour over celery. Cover and bake in moderate oven (350° F.) about 45 minutes or until celery is tender. Serves 4.

SWISS CHARD AND EGGS CHINESE

1 clove garlic, minced
2 tablespoons peanut oil
2 eggs, beaten
2 tablespoons milk
½ teaspoon salt
1/8 teaspoon pepper
3 cups cooked chopped Swiss chard

Cook garlic in peanut oil 1 minute. Combine remaining ingredients and add to garlic. Cook over low heat, stirring occasionally, until eggs are set. Serves 4.

BUTTERED SWISS CHARD

1 pound Swiss chard
½ teaspoon salt
1/8 teaspoon pepper
3 tablespoons melted butter or margarine

Wash Swiss chard thoroughly; cook, covered, with water that clings to leaves 10–12 minutes or until tender. Drain if necessary. Add remaining ingredients and mix lightly. Serves 4.

BACON, CORN AND TOMATOES

8 slices bacon
¼ cup chopped onion
¼ cup chopped green pepper
1 No. 303 can whole kernel corn, drained
1 No. 2 can tomatoes
1 teaspoon salt
¼ teaspoon sugar
1/8 teaspoon pepper

Cook bacon until crisp, reserving bacon dripping. Drain bacon on absorbent paper; crumble. Cook onion and green pepper in 3 tablespoons bacon drippings until onion is tender. Add corn, tomatoes, salt, sugar, pepper and bacon. Heat to serving temperature. Serves 6–8.

SOUTHERN CORN PUDDING

3 eggs, well beaten
2 cups cooked corn, cut from cob
2 tablespoons melted butter
2 cups milk
1 teaspoon salt
1/8 teaspoon pepper
½ teaspoon sugar
2 tablespoons fine dry bread crumbs

Combine eggs, corn, butter, milk, salt, pepper and sugar. Pour into greased 1½-quart baking dish. Sprinkle with crumbs. Bake in slow oven (325° F.) 40 minutes, or until firm. Serves 6.

CORN SCALLOP

1 No. 303 can whole kernel corn
Milk
2 tablespoons butter
2 tablespoons all-purpose flour
1 tablespoon chopped pimiento
2 tablespoons minced onion
1 teaspoon salt
1/8 teaspoon pepper
2 eggs, beaten
¼ cup buttered bread crumbs

Drain corn. Add enough milk to corn liquid to make one cup. Melt butter and blend in flour. Gradually add milk mixture and cook, stirring constantly, until thickened. Add pimiento, onion, salt and pepper. Add a little of hot mixture to eggs and mix well. Add egg mixture to hot mixture and mix well. Turn into greased 1-quart casserole. Sprinkle crumbs over top. Bake in moderate oven (350° F.) 45 minutes. Serves 4.

CORN FRITTERS

1 cup sifted all-purpose flour
1 teaspoon baking powder
½ teaspoon salt
2 cups grated fresh corn
2 eggs, separated
Fat

Sift flour, baking powder and salt together. Add grated fresh corn and mix well. Beat egg yolks well and stir into corn mixture. Beat egg whites until stiff and fold into batter. Drop by tablespoonfuls into deep hot fat (360° F.) and fry until browned on all sides. Drain on absorbent paper. Serves 4–6.

CORN CHEESE CASSEROLE

2 cups fresh corn
¼ cup light cream
2 tablespoons minced onion
2 tablespoons chopped green pepper
2 tablespoons chopped pimiento
¼ cup cooked crumbled bacon
1½ cups of soft bread crumbs
1 cup grated Cheddar cheese
2 tablespoons melted butter
1 teaspoon salt
1/8 teaspoon pepper

Combine all ingredients and mix lightly. Turn into greased 1½-quart casserole. Bake in moderate oven (350° F.) 40 minutes, or until lightly browned. Serves 6.

CORN CREOLE

1 green pepper, diced
1 small onion, diced
1 tablespoon melted butter
2 cups fresh corn
3 tomatoes, chopped
½ teaspoon salt
Dash cayenne pepper
1 teaspoon sugar

Cook pepper and onion in butter five minutes. Add remaining ingredients and cook, covered, ten minutes. Serves 4.

CORN AND ONION SCALLOP

1 No. 2½ can creamed style corn
1 cup small white onions, cooked
1 teaspoon salt
1/8 teaspoon pepper
1 cup buttered cracker crumbs

Combine corn, onion, salt and pepper. Turn into greased 1½-quart baking dish. Top with crumbs. Bake in moderate oven (350° F.) 25–30 minutes. Serves 6.

GERMAN RED CABBAGE

4 cups shredded, cooked red cabbage
2 tablespoons melted bacon drippings
2 tablespoons chopped onion
¼ cup vinegar
1 teaspoon sugar

Cook cabbage in bacon drippings, tossing lightly, until thoroughly heated. Add remaining ingredients and heat to serving temperature. Serves 6.

DANDELION GREEN BAKE

2 pounds dandelion greens, chopped
1/3 cup all-purpose flour
1/3 cup melted butter or margarine
1 cup milk
½ teaspoon salt
1/8 teaspoon pepper
½ cup grated Swiss cheese
½ cup cracker crumbs

Arrange greens in layers in greased 1½-quart baking dish, sprinkling flour between layers. Combine butter or margarine, milk, salt and pepper. Pour over greens. Combine cheese and crumbs. Sprinkle over top. Bake in moderate oven (350° F.) 35 minutes. Serves 6.

CHEESE EGGPLANT CASSEROLE

1 medium-sized eggplant
3 tablespoons melted shortening
¼ cup chopped onion
½ chopped green pepper
2 medium-sized tomatoes, sliced
1 teaspoon salt
1/8 teaspoon pepper
½ cup grated Cheddar cheese

Peel eggplant and cut in ½" slices. Brown eggplant slices in shortening on both sides. Arrange eggplant slices in greased 1-quart casserole. Top with onion, green pepper, tomato slices, salt and pepper. Cover and bake in moderate oven (350° F.) about 40 minutes. Uncover and sprinkle cheese over other ingredients. Continue baking 10 minutes, or until cheese is browned. Serves 4.

ARMENIAN EGGPLANT

1 large eggplant
2½ cups diced, cooked lamb
1 clove garlic, cut in half
¼ cup olive oil
2 tablespoons minced onion
¼ cup chopped green pepper
1 cup cooked tomatoes
1 cup cooked rice
2 tablespoons pinola nuts

½ teaspoon salt
1/8 teaspoon pepper
¼ cup water

Cook eggplant, covered, in boiling salted water 20 minutes. Drain. Cut eggplant in half lengthwise. Scoop out pulp, leaving a shell about ¼ inch thick. Cook lamb and garlic in olive oil until lamb is well browned. Remove garlic. Add onion, green pepper, tomatoes, rice, nuts, salt, pepper, water and eggplant. Mix well. Fill eggplant shells with lamb mixture. Bake in moderate oven (350° F.) 45 minutes. Serves 6.

OKRA WITH LEMON BUTTER

1 pound okra
¼ cup melted butter
½ teaspoon salt
2 tablespoons lemon juice

Cook okra, covered, in a small amount of boiling salted water 8-10 minutes or until tender. Combine remaining ingredients and heat to serving temperature. Drain okra. Pour lemon mixture over okra. Serves 4.

ONION AND CARROT SAUTÉ

4 medium-sized onions
4 medium-sized carrots
¼ cup melted butter or margarine
½ teaspoon salt
1/8 teaspoon pepper

Cut onions in ¼" slices. Cut carrots in 1/8" slices. Add onions and carrots to butter or margarine and cook, covered, over low heat 20 minutes, or until vegetables are tender. Stir occasionally. Season with salt and pepper. Serves 4.

BAKED ONIONS

4 medium-sized onions
1 tablespoon butter
½ cup beef bouillon
½ cup buttered bread crumbs

Peel onions and cut in half crosswise. Place in shallow baking pan. Dot with butter. Pour beef bouillon over onions. Cover and bake in moderate oven (350° F.) 40 minutes, or until tender. (Add more bouillon during baking period, if necessary.) Sprinkle crumbs over onions. Continue baking, uncovered, until lightly browned. Serves 4.

DUTCH ONION CASSEROLE

2 tablespoons butter
2 tablespoons all-purpose flour
1 cup milk
¼ cup butter
4 medium-sized onions, sliced
8 hard-cooked eggs, sliced
1 teaspoon salt
¼ teaspoon paprika
¼ cup buttered cracker crumbs

Melt the two tablespoons butter and blend in flour. Gradually add milk and cook, stirring constantly, until thickened. Melt the ¼ cup butter and add onions. Cook until onions are tender. Arrange onions and egg slices alternately in a greased 1½-quart casserole. Pour white sauce over onion-egg mixture. Sprinkle with salt and paprika. Top with crumbs. Bake in moderate oven, (350° F.) 20–30 minutes. Serves 6.

MORMON STEW

2 tablespoons butter or margarine
2 tablespoons all-purpose flour
3 medium-sized tomatoes, finely chopped
2 cups diced cooked eggplant
¼ cup chopped green pepper
2 tablespoons grated onion
1 cup diced cooked potatoes
½ cup diced cooked carrots
1 teaspoon sugar
1 teaspoon salt
1/8 teaspoon pepper
½ cup grated Cheddar cheese

Melt butter or margarine and blend in flour. Add tomatoes and cook over low heat, stirring constantly, until thickened. Add eggplant, green pepper, onion, potatoes, carrots, sugar, salt and pepper. Turn into greased 1½-quart baking dish. Sprinkle cheese over vegetable mixture. Bake in moderate oven (350° F.) 30–35 minutes. Serves 4–6.

ESTELLA'S KOHLRABI

4 medium-sized kohlrabi
2 tablespoons butter or margarine
2 tablespoons all-purpose ftour
1 teaspoon grated lemon rind
1 cup milk
½ teaspoon salt

Remove leaves from kohlrabi; wash and pare. Cut into ½" cubes. Cook, covered, in a small amount of boiling salted water 25 to 30 minutes or until tender. Drain. Melt butter or margarine; blend in flour. Gradually add milk. Add lemon rind and salt. Cook, stirring constantly, until thickened. Serve with kohlrabi. Serves 4.

DUTCH WILTED LETTUCE

1 head lettuce
8 slices bacon
½ cup vinegar
1 tablespoon sugar
¼ cup water
1 teaspoon salt
1 hard-cooked egg, sliced

Clean lettuce and separate leaves. Fry the bacon until crisp and remove from pan. Reserve drippings. Drain bacon on absorbent paper and crumble. Sprinkle half of bacon over lettuce. Add vinegar, sugar, water and salt to drippings. Heat to boiling point and pour over lettuce. Mix thoroughly. Sprinkle remaining bacon over top and garnish with hard-cooked egg slices. Serves 4-6.

CREAMED KALE AND ONIONS

2 pounds kale
3 tablespoons butter
3 tablespoons all-purpose Flour
1½ cups milk
¾ cup cooked small white pnlons
1 teaspoon salt
1/8 teaspoon pepper

Cook kale, covered, in a small amount of boiling water 10-15 minutes, or until tender; drain. Meanwhile, melt butter and blend in flour. Gradually add milk and cook, stirring constantly, until thickened. Add onions, salt and pepper. Heat to serving temperature. Serve onion sauce over kale. Serves 6.

MUSHROOM WITH ONION

1 pound small mushrooms, chopped
¼ cup chopped onion
¼ cup butter
½ cup sour cream
½ teaspoon salt
1/8 teaspoon pepper

Cook mushrooms and onion in butter until onion

is tender. Add remaining ingredients and cook, stirring occasionally, until thoroughly heated. Serves 4.

EGGPLANT PUFF

1 large eggplant
2 cups grated Cheddar cheese
2 cups soft bread crumbs
1 tablespoon chili sauce
2 tablespoons minced onion
½ teaspoon salt
2 eggs, separated

Cut eggplant in half lengthwise and scoop out pulp. Cook pulp, covered, in a small amount of boiling water 10 minutes, or until tender. Drain. Mash pulp. Combine eggplant pulp, cheese, crumbs, chili sauce, onion and salt. Beat egg yolks until thick and add to eggplant mixture. Beat egg whites until stiff and fold into eggplant mixture. Fill shells with eggplant mixture. Place in greased shallow baking pan. Bake in moderate oven (350° F.) about 40 minutes, or until firm. Serves 4.

GREEN BEAN-TOMATO BAKE

2 tablespoons minced onion
2 tablespoons chopped green pepper
2 tablespoons melted butter or margarine
3 cups cooked green beans
2 cups diced tomatoes
1 teaspoon salt
1/8 teaspoon pepper
¼ cup cracker crumbs
¼ cup grated American cheese

Cook onion and green pepper in butter or margarine until tender. Add beans, tomatoes, salt and pepper. Turn into greased 1½-quart baking dish. Top with crumbs and cheese. Bake in moderate oven (350° F.) 20-25 minutes. Serves 6.

GOLDEN MARRON BALLS

2 cups hot mashed chestnuts
¼ cup butter
2 eggs, slightly beaten
Salt and pepper to taste
¼ teaspoon sage
1 tablespoon minced onion
1 egg, slightly beaten
Dry bread crumbs

Combine chestnuts, butter, the 2 eggs, salt, pepper, sage and onion. Shape into croquettes.

Dip in the slightly beaten egg and roll in crumbs. Fry in deep hot fat (375° F.) until browned on all sides. Drain on absorbent paper. Serve with gravy or sauce, as desired. Serves 4.

PEPPERS WITH MUSHROOMS

6 medium-sized green peppers
1 cup chopped mushrooms
¼ cup melted butter
2 cups fine dry bread crumbs
2 tablespoons butter
2 tablespoons all-purpose flour
1 cup milk
1 teaspoon salt
1/8 teaspoon pepper

Remove stem ends, seeds and membrane from peppers. Cook in boiling salted water 5 minutes; drain. Combine mushrooms, the ¼ cup butter and crumbs. Melt the 2 tablespoons butter and blend in flour. Gradually add milk and cook, stirring constantly, until thickened. Add mushroom mixture, salt and pepper; mix lightly. Fill peppers with mushroom mixture. Place in shallow baking pan. Add enough water to cover bottom of pan. Bake in moderate oven (350° F.) 40–50 minutes, or until peppers are tender. Serves 6.

FRIED GREEN PEPPER RINGS

3 large green peppers
1 egg, slightly beaten
1 tablespoon water
½ cup dry bread crumbs
½ teaspoon salt

Remove stem end from peppers and cut into rings. Remove seeds and membrane. Combine egg and water. Combine crumbs and salt. Dip pepper rings in egg mixture and coat with crumb mixture. Fry in deep hot fat (375° F.) 3–4 minutes or until brown. Drain on absorbent paper. Serves 4–6.

ORIENTAL PEA SOUFFLÉ

¼ cup butter
¼ cup all-purpose flour
2 cups milk
3 eggs, separated
1 tablespoon grated onion
1 No. 303 can peas, drained
¼ cup chopped bean sprouts

½ teaspoon salt
1/8 teaspoon pepper

Melt butter and blend in flour. Gradually add milk and cook over low heat, stirring constantly, until thickened. Add a little of hot mixture to egg yolks and mix well. Stir into hot mixture and cook, stirring constantly, until thickened. Remove from heat; add onion, peas, bean sprouts, salt and pepper. Beat egg whites until stiff and fold into peas mixture. Turn into 1½-quart baking dish. Bake in moderate oven (350° F.) 40–50 minutes, or until firm. Serves 6.

SAUTÉED CUCUMBERS

4 medium-sized cucumbers
½ cup all-purpose flour, approx.
¼ cup melted butter or margarine
1 teaspoon salt
1/8 teaspoon pepper

Cut cucumbers into quarters; cook, covered, in small amount of boiling salted water 5 minutes. Drain. Coat with flour. Cook in butter or margarine until lightly browned. Sprinkle with salt and pepper. Serves 4–6.

PARSNIP SCALLOP

2 cups sliced cooked parsnips
3 tablespoons butter
3 tablespoons all-purpose flour
1½ cups milk
½ cup grated Cheddar cheese
¼ cup buttered cracker crumbs

Arrange parsnips in greased 1½-quart casserole. Melt butter and blend in flour. Gradually add milk and cook, stirring constantly, until thickened. Add cheese and stir until cheese melts. Pour cheese mixture over parsnips. Sprinkle crumbs over cheese. Bake in moderate oven (350° F.) 30 minutes. Serves 4.

MINTED PEAS DENVER

1 package frozen peas
2 tablespoons chopped mint
3 tablespoons butter or margarine
½ teaspoon salt
1/8 teaspoon pepper

Cook peas according to package directions; drain. Add remaining ingredients and stir until butter or margarine is melted. Serves 4.

FRENCH FRIED ONION RINGS

2 large sweet onions
2/3 cup milk
½ cup all-purpose flour
½ teaspoon salt
¼ teaspoon pepper
Deep hot fat

Peel onions and cut in crosswise slices ½ inch thick. Separate into rings. Pour milk over onions and let stand 30 minutes. Combine flour, salt and pepper. Coat onion rings with flour mixture. Cook in deep hot fat (365° F.) 1–2 minutes, or until lightly browned. Drain on absorbent paper. Serves 4.

STUFFED PEPPERS

6 medium-sized green peppers
1 pound ground meat
2 tablespoons melted butter
Salt and pepper to taste
1 cup cooked rice
1 8-ounce can tomato sauce

Remove stem ends from peppers; remove seeds and membrane. Brown beef in butter. Season with salt and pepper and add rice. Stuff peppers with meat mixture. Place peppers in greased baking dish. Pour tomato sauce over peppers. Bake in moderate oven (350° F.) 40 minutes. Serves 6.

MONTEREY STUFFED PIMIENTOS

1 can pimientos, drained
1 cup grated Swiss cheese
Fine dry bread crumbs
¼ cup melted butter

Fill pimientos with cheese; roll in crumbs. Cook in butter over low heat until browned on both sides. Serves 4.

BAKED POTATO CAKE

8 potatoes
1 tablespoon grated onion
3 eggs, beaten
1 cup milk, scalded
1/3 cup butter, melted
1 teaspoon salt

Peel and grate potatoes. Add remaining ingredients; mix well. Pour into a well-greased, shallow baking dish. Bake in a moderate oven (350° F.) 1 hour. Serves 6.

BAKED STUFFED POTATOES

6 medium-sized potatoes, baked
½ teaspoon salt
2 tablespoons chopped parsley
2 tablespoons butter or margarine
3 tablespoons light cream
1 teaspoon grated onion

Cut potatoes in half lengthwise and scoop out. Add remaining ingredients and beat until light and fluffy. Fill shells with potato mixture; bake in hot oven (400° F.) about 5 minutes, or until lightly browned. Serves 6.

POTATO CHEESE CASSEROLE

¼ cup butter
¼ cup all-purpose flour
2 cups milk
6 medium-sized potatoes, thinly sliced
1 teaspoon salt
1/8 teaspoon pepper
1 cup grated Cheddar cheese

Melt butter and blend in flour. Gradually add milk and cook, stirring constantly, until thickened. Add potatoes and heat to boiling point. Add salt and pepper. Alternate layers of potato mixture and cheese in greased 1½-quart casserole. Cover and bake in moderate oven (350° F.) 30 minutes. Uncover and continue baking 10 minutes or until potatoes are tender. Serves 6.

CREAMED POTATOES

3 cups diced raw potatoes
2 tablespoons chopped onion
½ cup light cream
2/3 cup milk
1 teaspoon salt
1/8 teaspoon pepper
2 tablespoons butter

Combine potatoes, onion, cream, milk, salt and pepper in top of double boiler. Cook, covered, over simmering water about 40 minutes, or until potatoes are tender. Add butter and stir until melted. Serves 4.

DUCHESS POTATOES

2 cups hot mashed potatoes
2 tablespoons butter
2 eggs, separated
½ teaspoon salt

Combine potatoes and butter. Beat egg yolks and add to potatoes. Season with salt. Force through pastry tube onto greased baking sheet, forming 1" balls. Or drop by teaspoonfuls onto greased baking sheets. Beat egg whites slightly and brush over potatoes. Bake in very hot oven (450° F.) 5–10 minutes, or until browned. Serves 6.

BASQUE POTATO HASH

4 medium-sized potatoes, peeled and sliced
¼ cup melted fat
4 eggs, slightly beaten
1 teaspoon salt
¼ teaspoon pepper
1 teaspoon chopped chives
2 tablespoons chopped parsley
¼ teaspoon thyme

Cook potatoes in fat over low heat until tender, turning occasionally. Pour eggs over potato mixture and mix lightly. Add remaining ingredients and cook over low heat until eggs are set, stirring occasionally. Serves 4.

OVEN FRENCH FRIES

6 medium-sized potatoes
¾ cup butter or margarine
½ teaspoon salt

Do not peel potatoes; cut into eighths. Place in shallow baking pan; dot with butter or margarine and sprinkle with salt. Bake in moderate oven (350° F.) about one hour or until tender. Stir occasionally during baking period. Serves 6.

STEAMED POTATOES AND ONIONS

6 medium-sized potatoes, thinly sliced
4 medium-sized onions, thinly sliced
1 teaspoon salt
1/8 teaspoon pepper
2 tablespoons chopped parsley
1/3 cup butter or margarine
1 cup boiling water

Alternate layers of potatoes and onions in greased 1½-quart casserole. Sprinkle salt, pepper and parsley over vegetables. Dot with butter or margarine. Pour water over ingredients. Bake in hot oven (400° F.) 40–50 minutes, or until potatoes are tender. Serves 6.

POTATO STEW CALAIS

6 large potatoes, cooked
1/3 cup butter
2 cups milk
2 tablespoons minced onion
1 teaspoon salt
1/8 teaspoon pepper

Cut potatoes into ½" cubes. Combine remaining ingredients and heat to boiling point. Add potatoes and cook over low heat, stirring occasionally, until slightly thickened. Serves 6.

POTATOES IN TOMATO SAUCE

4 cups thinly sliced potatoes
¼ cup chopped onion
2 cups tomato sauce
1 clove garlic, minced
¼ cup chopped green pepper
1 teaspoon salt
1/8 teaspoon pepper

Arrange potatoes and onion in greased 2-quart casserole. Combine remaining ingredients and pour over potato mixture. Cover and bake in moderate oven (350° F.) 1¼ hours, or until potatoes are tender. Serves 6.

SAVORY POTATO ROAST

6 medium-sized potatoes
½ cup all-purpose flour
¼ teaspoon salt
¼ teaspoon pepper
2 tablespoons butter
½ teaspoon thyme
1 teaspoon onion salt
1 bay leaf

Peel potatoes. Roll in flour. Sprinkle with salt and pepper. Place in greased shallow baking pan. Top with remaining ingredients. Cover and bake in hot oven (400° F.) 45–60 minutes. Remove bay leaf. Serves 6.

POTATO SCALLOP

4 cups thinly sliced potatoes
1 egg, beaten
1 1/3 cups light cream
1 teaspoon salt
¼ teaspoon black pepper
½ teaspoon nutmeg
2 tablespoons grated onion

Place potatoes in greased 1½-quart casserole. Combine remaining ingredients; pour over potatoes. Bake in hot oven (400° F.) 1 hour, or until potatoes are tender. Serves 6.

POTATO CURRY

2 cups cooked, diced potatoes
1 pint sour cream
2 teaspoons curry powder
¼ cup butter
1 teaspoon salt
½ teaspoon cloves
¼ teaspoon ginger
¼ cup beef bouillon

Combine all ingredients and heat to serving temperature, stirring frequently. Serves 4,

DUTCH POTATO PANCAKES

2 cups grated raw potatoes
¼ cup milk
1 egg, slightly beaten
½ teaspoon salt
1/8 teaspoon pepper
2 tablespoons all-purpose flour
2 tablespoons grated onion
3 tablespoons melted shortening

Combine potatoes, milk, egg, salt, pepper, flour and onion; mix well. Drop by tablespoonfuls into shortening. Brown well on both sides. Serves 4.

WESTERN STYLE POTATOES

¼ cup bacon drippings
4 cups thinly sliced potatoes
½ cup thinly sliced onions
1 teaspoon salt
1/8 teaspoon pepper

Melt bacon drippings over low heat. Add potatoes, onions, salt and pepper. Cover and cook about 15 minutes, or until browned on bottom. Turn and continue cooking, covered, 15 minutes, or until potatoes are tender. Serves 6.

RICED POTATOES

6 medium-sized cooked hot potatoes, cut in halves
1 tablespoon butter
1 teaspoon salt
1/8 teaspoon pepper

Force potatoes through ricer. Add butter, salt and pepper. Serves 4.

SOUTHERN BLACK-EYED PEAS

2 cups dried black-eyed peas
1½ teaspoons salt
1/8 teaspoon pepper
¼ cup bacon drippings
2 tablespoons molasses

Soak peas in water several hours; drain. Cover peas with cold water and add remaining ingredients. Cook, covered, 40–45 minutes, or until tender. Serves 4–6.

NEW ENGLAND BAKED PUMPKIN

1 3-pound pumpkin
½ cup melted butter
2 tablespoons chopped fresh ginger
1 teaspoon cinnamon
½ cup firmly packed brown sugar
¼ teaspoon salt

Cut pumpkin into serving pieces; remove seeds. Combine remaining ingredients. Place pumpkin in greased shallow baking pan. Top with sugar mixture. Bake in moderate oven (350° F.) about 1½ hours, or until tender. Baste occasionally during baking period. Serves 8.

PUMPKIN VEGETABLE SKILLET

4 cups diced pumpkin
¼ cup melted bacon drippings
½ cup onion slices
1 clove garlic, minced
½ cup chopped green pepper
1 cup chopped tomatoes
2 cups cut green beans
1 cup whole kernel corn
½ cup chicken stock
½ teaspoon chili powder
1 teaspoon salt
¼ teaspoon pepper

Cook pumpkin in bacon drippings 5 minutes. Add remaining ingredients and cook over low heat, covered, 30–35 minutes, or until vegetables are tender. Serves 6.

ESCAROLE WITH LEMON

2 pounds escarole
¼ cup melted butter or margarine
1 medium-sized lemon thinly sliced

Cook escarole, covered, in small amount of boiling salted water 10–12 minutes, or until tender. Drain and add butter or margarine. Top with lemon slices. Serves 4–6.

LEMON BUTTERED ONIONS

12 medium-sized onions, peeled
1/3 cup melted butter
2 tablespoons lemon juice
¼ teaspoon grated lemon rind
¼ teaspoon salt
1/8 teaspoon pepper

Cook onions, covered, in a small amount of boiling salted water, 30–40 minutes, or until tender. Drain. Combine remaining ingredients and heat to serving temperature. Pour over onions. Serves 4.

ONION RAISIN MEDLEY

2 pounds small white onions, peeled
¼ cup seedless golden raisins
¼ cup sugar
1 cup water
¼ cup lemon juice
½ cup tomato paste
3 tablespoons melted butter
1 teaspoon salt

Combine all ingredients. Cover and cook over low heat about 35 minutes, or until onions are tender. Serves 8.

CREAMY SPINACH AND EGG

1½ pounds spinach, cooked and chopped
2 hard-cooked eggs, chopped
2 tablespoons butter or margarine
½ cup heavy cream
1 teaspoon salt
1/8 teaspoon pepper

Combine all ingredients and heat to serving temperature, stirring occasionally. Serves 4.

RED RHUBARB PUDDING

2 cups diced rhubarb
1 cup raisins, chopped
¼ teaspoon cinnamon
¼ cup chopped candied fruits
1 teaspoon grated lemon rind
¼ cup sugar
2 tablespoons butter, melted
2 eggs
1¼ cups sifted all-purpose flour
1½ teaspoons baking powder
1/8 teaspoon salt
½ cup milk

Combine rhubarb, raisins, cinnamon, candied fruits and lemon rind. Turn into greased shallow baking dish. Cream sugar with butter until light. Add eggs and mix well. Sift flour, baking powder and salt together. Add sifted ingredients and milk alternately to sugar mixture. Mix well after each addition. Place batter over rhubarb mixture. Bake in moderate oven (350° F.) about 35–40 minutes. Serves 4.

LEMON BUTTER SALSIFY

1 tablespoon vinegar
1 quart cold water
1½ pounds salsify
1/3 cup melted butter or margarine
1½ tablespoons lemon juice
1 tablespoon chopped chives
½ teaspoon salt
1/8 teaspoon pepper

Combine vinegar and cold water. Wash and scrape salsify; slice and drop into vinegar-water mixture. Drain. Cook, covered, in a small amount of boiling salted water about 20 minutes or until tender. Drain. Combine remaining ingredients and heat to serving temperature, stirring occasionally. Pour lemon mixture over salsify. Serves 4.

FRIED SPINACH BALLS

2 cups cooked chopped spinach
1 tablespoon melted butter
2 tablespoons grated American cheese
½ teaspoon salt
⅛ teaspoon pepper
1 egg
1 cup fine dry bread crumbs
1 egg, slightly beaten
2 tablespoons water
Fine dry bread crumbs
Deep hot fat

Combine spinach, butter, cheese, salt, pepper, egg and the 1 cup bread crumbs. Mix well and chill 1 hour. Shape spinach mixture into 1" balls. Combine slightly beaten egg with water. Dip spinach balls in egg mixture and roll in bread crumbs. Fry in deep hot fat (365° F.) 3–4 minutes, or until well browned on all sides. Drain on absorbent paper. Serve with a tomato sauce, as desired. Serves 4.

WILTED SPINACH

4 slices bacon
3 cups chopped spinach
3 tablespoons all-purpose flour
1½ cups water
1 tablespoon brown sugar
3 tablespoons vinegar
½ teaspoon salt
⅛ teaspoon pepper
1 hard-cooked egg, chopped

Cook bacon until crisp. Reserve drippings. Drain bacon on absorbent paper and crumble. Combine bacon and spinach. Blend flour into drippings. Gradually add water and cook, stirring constantly, until thickened. Add sugar, vinegar, salt, pepper and egg; mix well. Add spinach mixture and heat to serving temperature, tossing lightly. Serves 4–6.

SPINACH RING WALLOON

3 cups cooked chopped spinach
½ cup fine dry bread crumbs
1 tablespoon minced onion
2 tablespoons chopped celery
⅛ teaspoon nutmeg
½ teaspoon salt
⅛ teaspoon pepper
2 tablespoons melted butter

3 eggs, well beaten
2 cups hot diced cooked carrots

Combine spinach, crumbs, onion, celery, nutmeg, salt, pepper, butter and eggs; mix well. Turn into well-greased 9" ring mold. Place in pan of hot water. Bake in moderate oven (350° F.) about 50 minutes, or until firm. Unmold and fill center with carrots. Serves 6.

SUMMER SQUASH PUDDING

1 pound small yellow squash
⅓ cup butter, melted
½ cup light cream
1 teaspoon salt
⅛ teaspoon pepper
¼ cup buttered cracker crumbs

Cut squash into quarters; cook in butter until lightly browned. Turn squash into greased 1-quart casserole. Pour cream over squash. Sprinkle with salt and pepper. Top with crumbs. Bake in moderate oven (350° F.) about 30 minutes, or until squash is tender. Serves 4.

SUMMER SQUASH SOUFFLÉ

1 tablespoon butter
1 tablespoon all-purpose flour
⅛ teaspoon salt
⅛ teaspoon pepper
½ cup milk
3 eggs, separated
1 cup mashed, cooked summer squash

Melt butter, stir in flour, salt and pepper. Remove from heat and gradually add milk. Cook 3 minutes over low heat, stirring constantly. Add beaten egg yolks. Stir. Add squash. Fold in stiffly beaten egg whites. Turn into ungreased casserole. Bake in slow oven (325° F.) 30–35 minutes. Serves 4.

BAKED ACORN SQUASH

2 medium-sized acorn squash
1 tablespoon minced chives
1 tablespoon minced celery
2 tablespoons melted butter or margarine
¾ cup grated American cheese
1¼ cups soft bread crumbs
½ teaspoon salt
⅛ teaspoon pepper

Cut squash in half lengthwise; remove seeds and stringy portion. Place cut side down in buttered baking pan. Bake in hot oven (400° F.) 25 minutes. Turn cut side up and continue baking 20-25 minutes or until tender. Scoop out pulp leaving a shell about ¼ inch thick. Mash pulp and add remaining ingredients. Stuff squash with bread-crumb mixture. Bake in moderate oven (350° F.) about 10-20 minutes, or until lightly browned. Serves 4.

ROSY RADISH SAUTÉ

2 medium-sized bunches radishes
2 tablespoons melted butter or margarine
1/3 cup light cream
½ teaspoon salt
1/8 teaspoon pepper

Cook radishes, covered, in small amount of boiling, salted water 10 minutes. Drain. Add radishes to butter or margarine and cook over low heat 10 minutes. Add remaining ingredients and heat to serving temperature. Serves 4-6.

SYRIAN BAKED EGGPLANT

1 medium-sized eggplant
¼ cup all-purpose flour (approx.)
3 tablespoons melted butter or margarine
1 teaspoon salt
1/8 teaspoon pepper
6 slices mild cheese

Peel eggplant and cut into slices ½ inch thick; coat eggplant slices with flour. Brown on both sides in butter or margarine. Sprinkle with salt and pepper. Alternate layers of eggplant and cheese in greased 2-quart casserole, ending with cheese. Bake in moderate oven (375° F.) about 20 minutes. Serves 4.

SUCCOTASH

2 cups cooked lima beans
2 cups cooked corn
2 tablespoons melted butter
½ cup light cream
½ teaspoon salt
1/8 teaspoon pepper
¼ teaspoon sugar

Combine all ingredients and heat to serving temperature. Serves 4.

TURNIPS WITH EGG SAUCE

3 tablespoons butter or margarine
3 tablespoons all-purpose flour
1½ cups milk
1½ teaspoon salt
1/8 teaspoon pepper
Dash cayenne pepper
2 hard-cooked eggs, chopped
4 cups diced, cooked yellow or white turnips

Melt butter or margarine; blend in flour. Gradually add milk and cook, stirring constantly, until thickened. Add remaining ingredients and heat to serving temperature, stirring constantly. Serves 6.

BAKED TOMATOES IN CREAM

6 medium-sized tomatoes
¼ cup chopped green pepper
¼ cup chopped pimiento
¼ cup chopped onion
1 teaspoon salt
1/8 teaspoon pepper
1/8 teaspoon oregano
2 tablespoons melted butter or margarine
1 cup light cream

Remove stem ends from tomatoes. Arrange tomatoes in greased shallow baking pan. Combine remaining ingredients and pour over tomatoes. Bake in moderate oven (350° F.) about 45 minutes, or until tomatoes are tender. Baste with cream mixture occasionally during baking period. Serves 6.

COUNTRY FRIED TOMATOES

6 medium-sized tomatoes
Flour
3 tablespoons melted butter
2 tablespoons all-purpose flour
1 cup light cream
Salt and pepper

Cut tomatoes into ½" slices. Dip in flour. Cook in butter until lightly browned on both sides. Remove tomatoes. Add 2 tablespoons flour to butter and stir until browned. Gradually add cream and cook, stirring constantly, until thickened. Season with salt and pepper. Add tomato slices and heat to serving temperature. Serves 6.

STEWED TOMATOES WITH ONIONS

1 cup sliced onions
2 cups chopped fresh tomatoes
½ teaspoon salt
1/8 teaspoon pepper
½ cup dry bread cubes
1 tablespoon butter or margarine

Combine onions, tomatoes, salt and pepper. Cover and cook over low heat 25–30 minutes, or until onions are tender. Add remaining ingredients. Stir until butter or margarine melts. Serves 4.

TOMATO-CORN FARM STYLE

8 medium-sized tomatoes
¼ cup butter
1 teaspoon salt
1/8 teaspoon pepper
½ teaspoon sugar
1 No. 303 can whole kernel corn

Remove stem ends from tomatoes. Cut tomatoes into quarters. Combine tomatoes, butter, salt, pepper and sugar. Cook, covered, over low heat 30 minutes. Add corn and heat to serving temperature. Serves 6–8.

BROILED OLIVE TOMATOES

4 medium-sized tomatoes
½ cup chopped stuffed olives
3 tablespoons butter or margarine
Pepper

Remove stem ends from tomatoes. Cut tomatoes into crosswise halves. Top with olives and dot with butter or margarine. Sprinkle lightly with pepper. Broil 3 or 4 inches from source of heat 10–15 minutes, or until tomatoes are tender. Serves 4.

FRIED SWEET POTATOES

4 cups thinly sliced sweet potatoes
½ cup thinly sliced onions
¼ cup melted fat
1 teaspoon salt
1/8 teaspoon pepper

Cook sweet potatoes and onions in fat, covered, 15 minutes. Turn and add salt and pepper. Continue cooking, covered, 15minutes or until potatoes are tender. Serves 4–6.

OLD-FASHIONED SWEET POTATO PONE

½ cup all-purpose flour
½ teaspoon cinnamon
¼ teaspoon freshly grated nutmeg
¾ teaspoon salt
4 cups grated, raw sweet potatoes
1 egg
¾ cup corn syrup
3 tablespoons melted butter
1 cup milk

Sift flour and seasonings. Add remaining ingredients. Pour into greased 1½-quart baking dish. Bake in slow oven (325° F.) for 2½ hours, stirring occasionally during first hour. Serves 8.

DE SOTO PARISH SWEET POTATOES

3 cups cubed cooked sweet potatoes
½ cup chopped green pepper
½ cup chopped onions
1 tablespoon chopped pimiento
1/8 teaspoon salt
1/3 cup melted bacon drippings

Combine sweet potatoes, green pepper, onions, pimiento and salt; mix lightly. Cook vegetable mixture in bacon drippings over medium heat until browned. Serves 4.

SWEET POTATOES WITH APPLES

3 sweet potatoes
3 apples
3 tablespoons butter
1 teaspoon salt
½ cup firmly packed brown sugar

Peel and cut sweet potatoes into ¼" slices. Peel, core and slice apples. Melt butter; add potatoes and apples. Season with salt, and sprinkle with sugar. Cook, covered, over low heat about 30 minutes or until tender, turning occasionally. Serves 6.

CANDIED SWEET POTATOES

4 medium-sized cooked, peeled sweet
  potatoes
1 cup firmly packed brown sugar
3 tablespoons butter
2 tablespoons cornstarch
1 cup water
¼ teaspoon salt
½ teaspoon nutmeg

Cut sweet potatoes in half lengthwise. Arrange sweet potatoes in greased shallow baking pan. Combine remaining ingredients and cook, stirring constantly, over low heat until thickened. Pour sugar mixture over sweet potatoes. Bake in moderate oven (350° F.) 30 minutes. Baste occasionally during baking period. Serves 4.

COMPANY BAKED YAMS

6 medium-sized yams, cooked and peeled
1 No. 2 can crushed pineapple
1 cup firmly packed brown sugar
1 tablespoon butter
½ teaspoon salt
½ cup chopped pecans
8 marshmallows

Cut yams in half lengthwise. Arrange yams in greased 8" x 8" pan. Combine pineapple, sugar, butter, salt and pecans; heat to boiling point, stirring constantly. Simmer 5 minutes. Pour pineapple mixture over yams. Top with marshmallows. Bake in moderate oven (350° F.) 30 minutes. Baste occasionally during baking period. Serves 6.

YAM AND PRUNE CASSEROLE

4 medium-sized yams, cooked and peeled
1 cup cooked prunes
½ cup firmly packed brown sugar
1 teaspoon salt
2 tablespoons orange juice
2 tablespoons lemon juice
½ teaspoon nutmeg
¼ cup melted butter

Cut yams into ¼" slices. Arrange yams and prunes alternately in greased 1½-quart casserole. Sprinkle each layer with sugar. Combine remaining ingredients and pour over yam mixture. Bake in moderate oven (350° F.) 40 minutes. Serves 6.

BAKED TURNIP WITH PARSLEY

4 cups cooked, mashed white or yellow turnip
3 tablespoons melted butter or margarine
3 tablespoons chopped parsley
½ teaspoon salt
1 egg, well beaten
½ cup grated American cheese

Combine turnip, butter or margarine, parsley and salt. Turn into greased 1½-quart baking dish. Pour egg over turnip mixture. Top with cheese. Bake in hot oven (400° F.) 20–25 minutes. Serves 4.

ZUCCHINI WITH TOMATO

3 medium-sized zucchini
2 tablespoons minced onion
2 tablespoons melted butter or margarine
1 No. 2 can tomatoes
1 teaspoon salt
⅛ teaspoon pepper

Cut zucchini into ½" slices, cook, covered, in small amount boiling salted water about 5 minutes or until tender. Drain. Cook onion in butter or margarine until tender; add tomatoes, salt and pepper. Simmer 5 minutes. Add zucchini and heat to serving temperature. Serves 6.

LOMPOC ZUCCHINI WITH MUSHROOMS

1 pound zucchini
1 pound mushrooms, sliced
¼ cup melted butter or margarine
3 tablespoons all-purpose flour
1 cup light cream
1 teaspoon salt
⅛ teaspoon pepper

Cut zucchini into 1" slices. Cook, covered, in a small amount of boiling salted water until tender; drain. Cook mushrooms in butter or margarine until tender. Remove mushrooms. Blend flour into butter or margarine. Gradually add cream and cook, stirring constantly, until thickened. Add salt, pepper, mushrooms and zucchini, heat to serving temperature, stirring occasionally. Serves 4.

Fruit

HOT APPLE SAUCE

3 medium-sized apples
1½ cups water
1 tablespoon vinegar
½ cup firmly packed brown sugar
1½ tablespoons cornstarch
1 teaspoon dry mustard
¼ teaspoon cinnamon
¼ teaspoon salt
3 tablespoons butter

Pare and core apples; cut into thin slices. Heat water to boiling point; add vinegar and apples and cook 1 minute. Remove apples. Combine sugar, cornstarch, mustard, cinnamon and salt. Gradually add to water and mixture and cook over low heat, stirring constantly, until thickened. Add butter and apples. Heat to serving temperature, stirring occasionally. Serve with ham and beef, as desired. Makes about 2 cups.

GLAZED APPLE RINGS

4 large tart apples
1½ cups water
1 cup sugar
2 tablespoons cinnamon candies
1/8 teaspoon salt

Core apples and cut into ½" slices. Combine remaining ingredients and heat to boiling point. Add apple slices and simmer about 10 minutes, or until apples are tender. Serve with meat. Serves 6.

BAKED APPLE SURPRISE

6 medium-sized tart apples
1/3 cup chopped pecans
1/3 cup sugar
2 tablespoons butter or margarine
1 cup orange juice

Core apples and place in greased shallow baking pan. Combine pecans and sugar. Fill apple centers with pecan mixture. Dot with butter or margarine. Pour orange juice over apples. Bake in moderate oven (350° F.) 35-40 minutes, or until apples are tender. Baste apples with orange juice occasionally during baking period. Serves 6.

APPLE CRISP

6 cups sliced tart apples
1 cup sifted all-purpose flour
½ cup firmly packed brown sugar
1 teaspoon cinnamon
½ teaspoon nutmeg
1/3 cup butter

Arrange apples in greased 2-quart casserole. Combine flour, sugar, cinnamon and nutmeg. Cut in butter. Sprinkle sugar mixture over apples. Bake in moderate oven (350° F.) about 30 minutes, or until apples are tender. Serve with cream as desired. Serves 6.

BANANAS GLACÉ

¼ cup butter
6 bananas, peeled
¼ cup currant jelly
1 tablespoon orange juice
½ cup apricot nectar

Melt butter; add bananas. Cook until bananas are lightly browned. Add remaining ingredients. Continue cooking until bananas are tender. Baste often with sauce. Serves 6.

MINCEMEAT STUFFED APPLES

6 medium-sized tart apples
1 cup mincemeat
2 tablespoons butter
1 cup sugar
1½ cups water
1 tablespoon brandy

Core apples and arrange in greased shallow baking pan. Fill apple centers with mincemeat. Dot with butter. Combine sugar, water and brandy; pour over apples. Bake in moderate oven (350° F.) 30-45 minutes, or until apples are tender. Serves 6.

BLUEBERRY SLUMP

4 cups blueberries
3 cups water
2 cups sugar
1½ cups sifted all-purpose flour
1/8 teaspoon salt
1½ teaspoons baking powder
½ cup light cream

Combine berries, water and sugar. Cook over low heat until berries are soft. Sift flour, salt and baking powder together. Add cream and mix lightly. Drop by tablespoonfuls into blueberry mixture. Cover and cook 15 minutes. Serves 6.

GLAZED ORANGES

4 seedless oranges
½ cup sugar
1/3 cup water
2 tablespoons light corn syrup
4 whole cloves

Peel and section oranges. Combine remaining ingredients and heat to boiling point. Add orange sections and simmer 5 minutes. Serves 4.

SPICY BANANA BAKE

6 firm bananas
¼ cup melted butter
¼ cup lemon juice
½ cup sugar
½ teaspoon cinnamon
½ teaspoon nutmeg

Peel bananas and cut in half lengthwise. Arrange bananas in greased shallow baking pan. Combine remaining ingredients and pour evenly over bananas. Bake in moderate oven (350° F.) 15 minutes, or until bananas are tender. Serves 6.

COLD FRUIT COUP

2 pounds sweet cherries, pitted
2 cups sugar
3 quarts water
2 teaspoons grated lemon rind
¾ pint sherry

Combine cherries, sugar and water. Cook over low heat until mixture boils, stirring frequently. Cool. Add lemon rind and sherry. Chill thoroughly. Serves 6.

FRIED PEARS OREGON

1 cup sifted all-purpose flour
1 teaspoon baking powder
¼ teaspoon salt
1 tablespoon sugar
3 eggs, well beaten
1 cup milk
6 large pears, cored and peeled
Fat
¼ cup confectioners' sugar

Sift flour, baking powder, salt and the 1 tablespoon sugar together. Add eggs and milk to sifted ingredients; stir until smooth. Dip pears into egg mixture. Fry in deep hot fat (350° F.) 2–3 minutes, or until browned on all sides. Drain on absorbent paper. Sprinkle with confectioners' sugar. Serves 6.

SAUTEED PEACHES

6 medium-sized peaches
¼ cup firmly packed brown sugar
2 tablespoons butter

Peel peaches; cut in half and remove pits. Sprinkle peaches with sugar. Melt butter; add peaches and cook over low heat 10 minutes, or until peaches are tender. Serves 6.

QUICK SPICED PEACHES

1 No. 2½ can peach halves
1 cup firmly packed brown sugar
½ cup vinegar
2 3" sticks cinnamon
1½ teaspoons whole cloves

Drain peaches and reserve syrup. Combine peach syrup, sugar, vinegar, cinnamon and cloves. Simmer 5 minutes. Add peaches and simmer 5 minutes. Chill 24 hours. Serve with meat or poultry. Serves 8.

STEWED PEACHES

¾ cup sugar
1 cup water
12 fresh peaches, peeled

Combine sugar and water. Heat to boiling point. Add peaches and simmer about 20 minutes, or until tender. Chill thoroughly. Serves 6.

PEARS IN WINE

4 fresh pears
¾ cup sugar
½ cup sherry or port wine
1 tablespoon butter

Cut pears in half and remove cores. Place cut side down on greased shallow baking pan. Combine remaining ingredients and heat to boiling point. Pour wine mixture over pears and make in moderate oven (350° F.) 15 minutes. Turn pears and baste with sauce. Continue baking 15 minutes. Serves 4.

DELUXE BLUEBERRY FRUIT CUP

1 cup blueberries
1 cup diced peaches
½ cup diced pears
1 cup strawberries
½ cup water
½ cup light corn syrup
1 tablespoon lemon juice
1 teaspoon grated lemon rind
¼ teaspoon cinnamon
¼ teaspoon nutmeg

Combine fruits and mix lightly. Combine remaining ingredients. Heat to boiling point and simmer 10 minutes. Cool. Add syrup to fruits and mix lightly. Chill thoroughly. Serves 6.

BAKED PEACHES

1 tablespoon grated orange rind
¼ cup sugar
¼ cup orange juice
6 fresh peaches
¼ cup melted butter
2 cups crushed corn flakes

Combine orange rind, sugar and juice. Peel peaches; cut in half, removing pits. Dip peach halves in orange mixture, then butter and roll in corn flakes. Place peaches in greased 7" x 11" baking pan. Bake in moderate oven (350° F.) about 30 minutes, or until peaches are tender. Serves 6.

CRANBERRY-ORANGE COMPOTE

2 cups raw cranberries
1 cup orange sections
5 whole cloves
2 cups diced fresh pears
1 cup light corn syrup

Combine all ingredients and turn into greased 1½-quart baking dish. Bake in moderate oven (350° F.) 30 minutes, or until pears are tender. Serves 6.

HONEY GINGER PEARS

¼ cup honey
¼ cup sugar
½ teaspoon ginger
1 tablespoon grated lemon rind
1 tablespoon lemon juice
½ cup water
8 pears

Combine honey, sugar, ginger, lemon rind, lemon juice and water. Heat to boiling point and cook 5 minutes. Arrange pears in greased shallow baking pan. Pour lemon mixture over pears. Cover and bake in moderate oven (350° F.) 30 minutes, or until pears are tender. Serves 8.

PRUNES IN CLARET

1 cup claret wine
¾ cup water
2 dozen dried prunes
1/3 cup sugar
¼ teaspoon vanilla

Combine wine and water; add prunes and let stand several hours. Cook 25 minutes, or until prunes are tender. Add sugar and continue cooking 5 minutes. Stir in vanilla. Chill. Serves 6.

GINGER PRUNES CATHAY

3 cups dried prunes
5 cups water
3 lemons, thinly sliced
2 cups sugar
1/3 cup sliced preserved ginger

Combine all ingredients, and cook over low heat, covered, 1¼ hours. Chill thoroughly before serving. Serves 6-8.

SHERRY GRAPEFRUIT BROIL

2 grapefruits, cut in half
¼ cup firmly packed brown sugar
½ teaspoon nutmeg
¼ teaspoon cinnamon
1 tablespoon butter or margarine
¼ cup sherry

Section grapefruits. Combine sugar and spices. Sprinkle sugar mixture over grapefruit sections. Dot with butter or margarine. Broil 3 or 4 inches from source of heat about 5 minutes, or until lightly browned. Pour sherry over grapefruit. Serve hot. Serves 4.

ISABEL'S MELON RINGS

Peel 1 medium-sized cantaloupe, remove seeds and cut into 1-inch slices. Arrange cantaloupe rings on serving plates. Fill centers with diced pineapple, using about 1 cup. Centers may be filled with fruit sherbet, if desired. Serves 4.

ORANGE AND GRAPEFRUIT CUP

½ cup diced orange sections
1 cup diced grapefruit sections
¼ cup chopped maraschino cherries
2 tablespoons lime juice

Combine all ingredients and chill. Serve with Custard Sauce, if desired. Serves 4.

STRAWBERRY-MELON BALL CUP

1 package frozen crushed strawberries
1 package frozen melon balls
¼ cup chopped mint

Thaw strawberries and melon balls. Arrange in serving dishes. Top with mint. Serves 8.

Salads

FRUIT SALADS

APPLE-ONION SALAD

2 cups diced apples
2 tablespoons chopped onion
¼ cup salad oil
¼ cup vinegar
½ teaspoon salt
Salad greens

Combine apples, onion, oil, vinegar and salt. Mix lightly and arrange on greens. Serve immediately. Serves 4.

WALDORF SALAD

4 unpeeled red apples, cubed
3 tablespoons lemon juice
2 cups diced celery
½ cup chopped walnuts
Mayonnaise
Salad greens

Combine apples, lemon juice, celery and walnuts with enough mayonnaise to moisten. Arrange on greens. Serves 4.

GELATIN AND FROZEN SALADS

APPLE-STRAWBERRY DESSERT SALAD

2 packages strawberry-flavored gelatin
3 ½ cups hot apple juice
¼ cup lemon juice
2 cups diced apples
1 cup chopped celery
½ cup chopped pecans
½ cup salad dressing
Salad greens

Dissolve gelatin in apple juice. Add lemon juice. Pour into ring mold and chill until firm. Combine apples, celery, pecans and salad dressing. Unmold gelatin; fill center with apple mixture. Garnish with greens. Serves 6–8.

FROZEN DATE AND HONEY SALAD

¼ cup honey
1 8-ounce package cream cheese
1 cup canned crushed pineapple
2 tablespoons chopped pecans
½ cup chopped dates
½ cup heavy cream, whipped

Combine honey and cheese. Beat until well blended. Add pineapple, pecans and dates. Fold in cream. Turn into refrigerator tray. Freeze until firm. Serve with salad greens, if desired. Serves 6.

MOLDED FRUIT SALAD

1 envelope unflavored gelatin
1/3 cup cold water
1/3 cup boiling water
1/3 cup lemon juice
1 cup ginger ale
½ cup chopped pecans
½ cup blueberries
½ cup diced peaches
Salad greens

Soften gelatin in cold water. Add boiling water and stir until dissolved. Add lemon juice and ginger ale. Chill until slighdy thickened. Fold in pecans, blueberries and peaches. Turn into 1-quart mold and chill until firm. Unmold and garnish with greens. Serve with French dressing, as desired. Serves 4–6.

RIO GRANDE LIME SALAD

1 package lime-flavored gelatin
1 cup boiling water
1 No. 2 can crushed pineapple
1 cup cottage cheese
2 tablespoons chopped pimiento
1 8-ounce package cream cheese
2 tablespoons mayonnaise
2 tablespoons lemon juice
Salad greens

Combine gelatin and water; stir until gelatin is dissolved. Chill until slightly thickened. Fold in pineapple, cottage cheese and pimiento. Turn into 8" x 8" pan and chill until firm. Combine cream cheese, mayonnaise and lemon juice. Beat until light and fluffy. Cut lime mixture into squares and arrange on greens. Top with cream-cheese mixture. Serves 6–8.

MINTED APPLE SALAD

2 cups diced apples
¼ cup lemon juice
2 cups diced celery
Salad dressing
¼ teaspoon salt
1 tablespoon finely chopped mint
Salad greens

Combine apples, lemon juice, celery and enough salad dressing to moisten. Add salt and mint; toss lightly. Arrange on greens. Serves 6.

CRANBERRY-ORANGE SALAD

2 cups cranberries
1 orange, quartered
1 cup sugar
2 large apples, cored and diced
2 tablespoons lemon juice

Grind cranberries and orange. Add sugar and chill. Add apples and lemon juice; mix well. Serve with salad greens, if desired. Serves 6.

BOG CRANBERRY-PEAR SALAD

1 8-ounce package cream cheese with chives
¼ cup cranberry sauce
¼ cup chopped pecans
1 No. 2 can pear halves, well drained

Combine cheese, cranberry sauce and pecans. Beat until thoroughly blended. Top pear halves with cheese mixture. Serve with salad greens, if desired. Serves 4.

HOLIDAY SALAD

1 package lemon-flavored gelatin
2 cups cranberries, ground
½ cup drained canned crushed pineapple
1 cup diced apples
½ cup orange sections
¼ teaspoon salt
Salad greens
Salad dressing

Prepare gelatin according to package directions. Chill until slightly thickened. Fold in cranberries, pineapple, apples, orange sections and salt. Pour into 8" x 8" pan and chill until firm. Cut salad into squares and arrange on greens. Top with salad dressing. Serves 6.

APPLE RING SALAD

2 red apples, cored and sliced
¼ cup lemon juice
1 8-ounce package cream cheese
2 tablespoons light cream
½ cup chopped dates
2 tablespoons chopped walnuts
Salad greens
French dressing

Brush apple slices with lemon juice. Combine cheese, cream, dates, and walnuts. Arrange apple slices on greens. Top with cheese mixture. Serve with French dressing. Serves 4.

FRUIT SALAD BOWL

1 small head lettuce
2 cups watermelon balls
2 cups cantaloupe balls
1 cup white grapes
French dressing

Separate lettuce into leaves; line salad bowl with lettuce leaves. Arrange fruits over lettuce; add enough French dressing to moisten. Serves 4.

EGG-SHRIMP ASPIC

2 packages unflavored gelatin
1 cup cold water
2 10½ ounce cans (2½ cups) consommé
3 tablespoons lemon juice
¼ cup sherry
1 pound cooked shrimp
8 eggs, poached
Mayonnaise

Soften gelatin in water. Heat consommé to boiling point; add gelatin and stir until dissolved. Add lemon juice and sherry; chill until slightly thickened. Arrange shrimp in 8 individual molds. Add enough gelatin mixture to cover shrimp. Add eggs. Pour remaining gelatin mixture over eggs. Chill until firm. Serve with mayonnaise. Serves 8.

GULF SHRIMP SALAD MOLD

1 package lemon-flavored gelatin
1 ¾ cups boiling water
1 cup cooked chopped shrimp
1 cup diced celery
½ cup chopped stuffed olives
¼ cup chopped sweet pickles
¼ teaspoon salt
Salad greens
Salad dressing

Add gelatin to water and stir until dissolved. Chill until slightly thickened. Add shrimp, celery, olives, pickles and salt. Turn into 1½-quart mold and chill until firm. Unmold and garnish with greens. Serve with dressing. Serves 4–6.

TOMATO-AVOCADO MOLD

1 envelope unflavored gelatin
¼ cup cold water
1 ¾ cups tomato juice
1 bay leaf
3 whole cloves
¼ cup minced onions
½ teaspoon salt
1/8 teaspoon pepper
1 cup diced avocado
1 cup diced celery Salad greens

Soften gelatin in cold water. Combine tomato juice, bay leaf, cloves, onions, salt and pepper. Simmer 5 minutes; strain. Add gelatin and stir until dissolved. Chill until slightly thickened. Fold in avocado and celery. Turn into 1½-quart mold and chill until firm. Unmold and garnish with greens. Serve with French dressing, as desired. Serves 6.

DILL TOMATO ASPIC

1 envelope unflavored gelatin
¼ cup cold water
1 8-ounce can tomato sauce
¾ cup water
¼ teaspoon dill seeds
2 tablespoons vinegar

1 teaspoon horseradish
½ teaspoon salt
1/8 teaspoon pepper
½ teaspoon sugar

Soften gelatin in cold water. Combine tomato sauce and water; heat to boiling point. Add gelatin and stir until dissolved. Add remaining ingredients and mix well. Turn into 2-cup mold. Chill until firm. Unmold and garnish with salad greens, as desired. Serves 4.

STRAWBERRY-FRUIT SALAD

1 pint strawberries, cleaned
1 cup honeydew melon balls
1 grapefruit, peeled and sectioned
1 cup canned pineapple chunks
Mayonnaise

Combine fruits with enough mayonnaise to moisten; serve on salad greens, if desired. Serves 6.

MEAT, FISH, AND CHEESE SALADS

GOURMET SWISS CHEESE SALAD

½ pound Swiss cheese, diced
6 hard-cooked eggs, chopped
½ cup sour cream
1 tablespoon prepared mustard
2 teaspoons chopped sweet pickle
½ teaspoon salt
¼ teaspoon pepper
1 teaspoon chopped chives

Combine all ingredients and mix lightly. Serve with lettuce, romaine or chicory, as desired. Serves 6.

HOT CHICKEN SALAD DELAWARE

3 cups diced, cooked chicken
1 cup diced celery
1 tablespoon grated onion
½ cup chopped almonds
1 tablespoon lemon juice
1 teaspoon grated lemon rind
1 cup grated Cheddar cheese
½ teaspoon salt

1/8 teaspoon pepper
Mayonnaise
1 cup crushed potato chips

Combine chicken, celery, onion, almonds, lemon juice, lemon rind, cheese, salt and pepper. Add enough mayonnaise to moisten; turn into greased individual baking dishes. Top with potato chips. Bake in moderate oven (350° F.) 25-30 minutes, or until lightly browned. Serves 4-6.

CRAB MEAT SALAD À LA REINE

4 cups cooked flaked crab meat
1 tablespoon chopped pimiento
1/4 cup chopped green pepper
I tablespoon grated onion
1 teaspoon salt
1/8 teaspoon pepper
3 hard-cooked eggs, chopped
French dressing
Salad greens

Combine crab meat, pimiento, green pepper, onion, salt, pepper and eggs; mix lightly. Add enough French dressing to moisten. Arrange on greens. Serves 6.

CHOPPED HERRING SALAD PARISIENNE

2 cups grated cabbage
2/3 cup grated carrot
2 tablespoons grated onion
1/4 cup chopped green pepper
1/4 cup chopped marinated herring
2 tablespoons lemon juice
1/2 cup sour cream
1/4 teaspoon sugar

Combine all ingredients; mix lightly. Serve with salad greens, if desired. Serves 4.

HAM AND POTATO SALAD

2 cups diced, cooked ham
2 cups diced, cooked potatoes
1 cup chopped celery
1/4 cup chopped green pepper
4 hard-cooked eggs, chopped
1/2 cup salad dressing
2 tablespoons prepared mustard
1 tablespoon vinegar
1 teaspoon salt
1/8 teaspoon pepper

Combine all ingredients; mix lightly. Serve with salad greens, if desired. Serves 6.

CHICKEN-APPLE SALAD NEW YORK

2 cups diced cooked chicken
1 cup diced apple
2 tablespoons lemon juice
1/4 cup chopped celery
1/4 cup chopped green pepper
1 teaspoon salt
Salad dressing
Salad greens

Combine chicken, apple, lemon juice, celery, green pepper and salt; mix lightly. Add enough salad dressing to moisten. Arrange chicken mixture on greens. Serves 4.

CHICKEN SALAD CAPRI

2 cups cooked, cubed chicken
1 cup French dressing
3 cups shredded lettuce
6 poached eggs, chilled
1/2 cup mayonnaise
2 cups cooked chilled asparagus tips

Combine chicken and French dressing; let stand 1 hour. Arrange lettuce on serving plates. Arrange chicken mixture over lettuce and cover with eggs. Top with mayonnaise. Surround eggs with asparagus tips. Serves 6.

VEGETABLE SALADS

ASPARAGUS SALAD BOWL

1 1/2 pounds fresh asparagus, cooked
3 hard-cooked eggs, chopped
1 cup thin cucumber slices
3 tomatoes, cut in wedges
1/2 cup chopped green pepper
1/2 cup onion rings
1 medium-sized head lettuce, broken in bite-size pieces

Cut asparagus in 1" pieces. Add remaining ingredients and toss lightly. Serve with French dressing or mayonnaise, as desired. Serves 6-8.

LAMB AND CELERY SALAD

2½ cups diced cooked lamb
3 tablespoons chili sauce
2 tablespoons chopped dill pickle
1 hard-cooked egg, chopped
1½ cups chopped celery
½ cup chopped water cress
1 teaspoon salt
1/8 teaspoon pepper
Mayonnaise

Combine lamb, chili sauce, pickle, egg, celery, water cress, salt and pepper; mix lightly. Add enough mayonnaise to moisten. Serve with salad greens, as desired. Serves 6.

SALMON SALAD ALASKA

2 cups cooked flaked salmon
¾ cup chopped celery
1 cup cooked peas
3 hard-cooked eggs, chopped
2 teaspoons capers
1 cup mayonnaise
1 teaspoon salt
1/8 teaspoon pepper

Combine all ingredients; mix lightly. Chill thoroughly. Arrange salmon mixture on salad greens, as desired. Serves 4.

SARDINE-PEA SALAD

½ cup mashed sardines
1 tablespoon lemon juice
1/3 cup salad dressing
1 cup cooked peas
½ cup chopped celery
1 tablespoon chopped onion
2 hard-cooked eggs, chopped
¼ teaspoon salt
1/8 teaspoon pepper

Combine all ingredients and mix lightly. Serve on salad greens, if desired. Serves 4.

VEAL PEPPER SALAD

2 cups diced, cooked veal
1 cup chopped green pepper
1½ cups chopped celery
3 hard-cooked eggs, chopped
1/3 cup chopped dill pickles
Salad dressing

Combine veal, pepper, celery, eggs and pickles. Add enough salad dressing to moisten. Serve with salad greens, if desired. Serves 6.

VEGETABLE MEAT SALAD

2 cups shredded cabbage
1 cup cooked diced green beans
1 cup grated carrots
¼ cup onion rings
1 cup thin luncheon meat strips
1 cup thin Cheddar or American cheese strips
1 cup French dressing
Salt and pepper to taste
Salad greens

Combine vegetables, meat, cheese and French dressing. Season with salt and pepper. Serve on greens. Serves 6.

ASPARAGUS-ALMOND SALAD

16 cooked asparagus spears
4 green pepper rings
Salad greens
½ cup toasted slivered almonds
½ cup French dressing

Arrange asparagus and green pepper rings on greens. Combine almonds and French dressing; pour dressing over salad. Serves 4.

AVOCADO ROMAINE SALAD

1 head romaine
1 head lettuce
1 tomato, cut in wedges
1 avocado, peeled and sliced
2 tablespoons sweet pickle relish
¼ cup onion rings
French dressing

Tear romaine and lettuce in bite-size pieces. Combine romaine, lettuce, tomato, avocado, pickle relish, onion rings and enough French dressing to moisten. Serves 6.

BEAN AND BACON SALAD IOWA

2 cups cooked, diced green beans
¼ cup cooked, crumbled bacon
1 cup chopped celery
2 tablespoons chopped green pepper
½ cup onion rings
Mayonnaise

Combine beans, bacon, celery, green pepper and onion rings; mix lightly. Add enough mayonnaise to moisten. Serve on salad greens, if desired. Serves 6.

BEET AND CUCUMBER SALAD

1 cup sliced cucumber
½ cup diced, cooked beets
1 teaspoon salt
2 tablespoons vinegar
2 tablespoons minced onion
¾ cup sour cream

Sprinkle cucumber and beets with salt and let stand 1 hour. Add remaining ingredients and mix lightly. Serve with salad greens, if desired. Serves 4,

SHRIMP SALAD

2 cups diced, cooked shrimp
½ cup chopped stuffed olives
1/3 cup chopped sweet pickles
2 tablespoons chopped onion
French dressing

Combine shrimp, olives, pickles and onion. Add enough French dressing to moisten. Serve with salad greens, if desired. Serves 4.

PICKLED BEET SALAD

1 cup diced, cooked beets
¼ cup sweet pickle relish
½ cup diced cucumber
1/8 teaspoon salt
French dressing

Combine beets, pickle relish, cucumber and salt. Add enough French dressing to moisten. Serve on salad greens, if desired. Serves 4.

CABBAGE-CARROT SALAD

1 cup grated carrots
2 cups shredded cabbage
¼ cup chopped sweet pickles
1½ cups shredded turnip
Mayonnaise
Salt and pepper to taste
Salad greens

Combine carrots, cabbage, pickles, turnip and enough mayonnaise to moisten. Season with salt and pepper. Serve on salad greens. Serves 4.

OLD-FASHIONED COLESLAW

2/3 cup heavy cream
¼ cup vinegar
½ teaspoon salt
1/8 teaspoon pepper
3 cups shredded cabbage

Beat cream until stiff gradually adding vinegar. Combine cream mixture with salt, pepper and cabbage. Mix lightly. Chill thoroughly. Serves 4.

CABBAGE-CARROT SLAW

3 cups grated cabbage
¼ cup prepared mustard
2 tablespoons light cream
2 tablespoons lemon juice
1 teaspoon salt
1 cup grated carrots
¼ cup raisins

Combine all ingredients; mix lightly. Serves 4.

RED CABBAGE SALAD

4 cups grated red cabbage
1 large apple, cored and diced
1 cup chopped celery
1 cup heavy cream, whipped
1 tablespoon lemon juice
1 teaspoon grated lemon rind
1 teaspoon salt
1 tablespoon sugar
½ cup chopped walnuts

Combine all ingredients and mix lightly. Serves 4-6.

CARROT-RAISIN SALAD

2 cups grated carrots
½ cup raisins
2 tablespoons salad oil
1 tablespoon vinegar
1 tablespoon honey
1/8 teaspoon salt
1/8 teaspoon pepper
Lettuce
¼ cup mayonnaise

Combine carrots, raisins, oil, vinegar, honey, salt and pepper; mix lightly. Arrange carrot mixture on lettuce. Top with mayonnaise. Serves 4.

BLUE CHEESE TOSSED SALAD

1 small head lettuce
3 tomatoes, cut in wedges
1 cup sliced cucumber
½ cup diced celery
½ cup sliced radishes
½ cup crumbled blue cheese
French dressing

Break lettuce into bite-size pieces. Combine vegetables and cheese in salad bowl. Add enough French dressing to moisten. Toss lightly. Serves 4–6.

MIDWEST CORN AND BEAN SALAD

1 No. 2 can whole kernel corn, drained
1 No. 2 can cut green beans, drained
½ cup chopped celery
1 cup sliced radishes
2 talespoons catsup
½ cup mayonnaise

Combine corn, beans, celery and radishes. Blend catsup with mayonnaise and add to vegetable mixture. Mix lightly. Serve with salad greens, if desired. Serves 6.

COTTAGE CHEESE-STUFFED TOMATO SALAD

6 medium-sized tomatoes
2 cups cottage cheese
½ cup chopped green pepper
1 teaspoon salt
1/8 teaspoon pepper
Salad greens
1/3 cup mayonnaise

Remove stem ends from tomatoes; cut each tomato into quarters without cutting all the way through. Combine cottage cheese, green pepper, salt and pepper. Fill tomato centers with cheese mixture. Arrange tomatoes on greens. Top cheese mixture with mayonnaise. Serves 6.

HOT CHICORY SALAD

4 strips bacon, diced
2 tablespoons white vinegar
1 tablespoon garlic salt
Salt and pepper to taste
½ pound chicory

Cook bacon until crisp; add vinegar, garlic salt, salt and pepper. Pour over chicory. Serves 4.

HOT POTATO SALAD

6 medium sized unpeeled potatoes
4 slices bacon, diced
¼ cup minced onion
1 egg, beaten
½ cup vinegar
1 teaspoon salt
1/8 teaspoon pepper

Cook potatoes until tender. Drain, peel and slice. Cook bacon with onion until onion is tender. Remove bacon and onion; reserve drippings. Gradually add drippings to egg, stirring constantly. Add vinegar, salt and pepper. Combine potatoes, bacon, onion and egg mixture. Heat to serving temperature. Serves 6.

MIXED VEGETABLE SALAD

1 cup cucumber slices
1 cup cooked peas
1 cup cooked diced carrots
¼ cup chopped green pepper
2 tomatoes, diced
¼ cup onion rings
1 teaspoon salt
Salad greens
1 cup mayonnaise
2 tablespoons chili sauce

Combine vegetables and salt; mix lightly. Arrange vegetable mixture on greens. Combine mayonnaise and chili sauce. Top vegetables with mayonnaise mixture. Serves 4–6.

MARINATED TOMATO SALAD

4 large tomatoes
½ cup French dressing
¼ cup chopped chives
2 tablespoons chopped parsley
½ teaspoon salt
¼ teaspoon pepper

Peel and slice tomatoes; pour French dressing over tomatoes and let stand 1 hour. Sprinkle remaining ingredients over tomato mixture. Garnish with greens, if desired. Serves 6.

TOMATO-PEPPER SALAD WITH BACON DRESSING

1 cup chopped green peppers
2 cups diced tomatoes
¼ cup chopped onion
3 cups shredded lettuce
¼ teaspoon salt
4 slices bacon
1 teaspoon chili powder
1/3 cup vinegar

Combine peppers, tomatoes, onion, lettuce and salt. Cook bacon until crisp and crumble. Add chili powder and vinegar to bacon drippings and heat to boiling point. Add bacon and vinegar mixture to vegetable mixture and toss lightly. Serves 6.

VEGETABLE SALAD BOWL

2 cups sliced cucumbers
1 cup sliced radishes
1/3 cup chopped onions
1 small bunch water cress
1 cup chopped celery
1 cup shredded cabbage
1 teaspoon salt French dressing

Combine vegetables and salt with enough French dressing to moisten. Serves 4-6.

HOT DUTCH POTATO SALAD

6 medium-sized potatoes, cooked and cubed
2 hard-cooked eggs, chopped
4 slices bacon
1 egg, beaten
1/3 cup minced onions
¼ cup vinegar
1 teaspoon salt

Combine potatoes and eggs. Cook bacon until crisp and crumble. Reserve bacon drippings. Add a little of drippings to egg and mix well. Stir into remaining drippings. Add onions, vinegar and salt. Cook, stirring constantly, until thickened. Add to potato mixture. Add bacon and toss lightly. Serves 4.

MARINATED LIMA BEAN SALAD

2 cups cooked lima beans
1/3 cup sour cream
1 clove garlic, minced
2 tablespoons chopped parsley
1 tablespoon vinegar
2 tablespoons salad oil
½ teaspoon sugar
1 teaspoon salt
1 tablespoon grated onion

Combine all ingredients. Mix lightly but thoroughly. Chill several hours. Serve on salad greens, as desired. Serves 6.

SOUR CREAM POTATO SALAD

4 cups diced cooked potatoes
½ cup diced celery
2 tablespoons grated onion
1 teaspoon celery seed
1 teaspoon salt
¼ teaspoon pepper
2 hard-cooked eggs, chopped
½ cup sour cream
2 tablespoons lemon juice
1 tablespoon prepared mustard

Combine potatoes, celery, onion, celery seed, salt and pepper. Mix lightly. Combine remaining ingredients and mix well. Add sour cream mixture to vegetable mixture and mix lightly. Serve with salad greens, as desired. Serves 4-6.

CUCUMBER-SOUR CREAM SALAD

2 large cucumbers
1½ cups sour cream
¼ cup chopped pecans
2 tablespoons grated onion
1 teaspoon lemon juice
½ teaspoon salt
Salad greens

Cut cucumbers into thin slices. Combine sour cream, pecans, onion, lemon juice and salt. Mix well and add to cucumber slices. Arrange on greens. Serves 4-6.

COUNTRY DANDELION GREEN SALAD

2 cups chopped, cooked dandelion greens
¼ cup sliced scallions
¼ cup grated cucumber
½ cup grated carrot
French dressing

Combine greens, scallions, cucumber and carrot. Add enough French dressing to moisten. Serve with salad greens, if desired. Serves 4.

ENDIVE-SOUR CREAM SALAD

1 medium-sized bunch endive
½ cup sour cream
2 tablespoons lemon juice
2 tablespoons horseradish
¼ teaspoon salt

Separate endive into leaves. Combine remaining ingredients and mix well; pour over endive. Serves 6.

CAULIFLOWER SALAD

1 small head cauliflower
1 apple, cored and diced
2 tablespoons lemon juice
¼ cup chopped onion
½ cup chopped parsley
½ cup chopped celery
½ teaspoon salt
1/8 teaspoon pepper
¼ cup vinegar
¼ cup salad oil

Separate cauliflower into small flowerets. Add remaining ingredients and mix lightly. Serves 6.

SPINACH AND EGG SALAD

1 pound fresh spinach, chopped
2 tablespoons chopped onions
2 tablespoons chopped green pepper
2 hard-cooked eggs, chopped
¾ cup French dressing
¼ teaspoon salt

Combine all ingredients; mix lightly. Serves 4–6.

Salad Dressings

UNCOOKED

CERISE CHIFFONADE DRESSING

1 cup French dressing
1 tablespoon chopped parsley
1 tablespoon grated onion
1 hard-cooked egg, chopped
¼ cup cooked chopped beets

Combine all ingredients and shake well. Makes about 1½ cups.

CHIFFONADE DRESSING

1 cup French dressing
2 tablespoons chopped sweet pickles
2 tablespoons grated onion
1/8 teaspoon salt
1/8 teaspoon pepper
2 tablespoons vinegar

Combine all ingredients and shake until thoroughly blended. Serve with salad greens as desired. Makes about 1¼ cups.

WHIPPED CREAM DRESSING

1 cup salad dressing
2 tablespoons lime juice
2 teaspoons sugar
1 cup heavy cream, whipped

Combine salad dressing, lime juice and sugar; mix well. Fold in cream. Serve with fruit salads, as desired. Makes about 2cups.

CREAMY EGG DRESSING

2 hard-cooked eggs, chopped
2 tablespoons vinegar
1½ cups sour cream
½ teaspoon salt
1/8 teaspoon pepper
Dash cayenne pepper

Combine all ingredients and mix well. Serve with meat, fish and vegetable salads, as desired. Makes about 1¾ cups.

CALIFORNIA SALAD DRESSING

2 medium-sized avocados, sieved
2 tablespoons lemon juice
1 teaspoon grated lemon rind
2 tablespoons onion juice
½ teaspoon salt
1/8 teaspoon pepper

Combine all ingredients and mix welL Serve with meat and vegetable salads as desired. Makes about 1¾ cups.

CHILI SAUCE DRESSING

1 cup chili sauce
¼ cup sugar
¾ cup vinegar
1 cup salad oil
½ teaspoon salt

Combine all ingredients and shake until thoroughly blended. Serve with green and vegetable salads, as desired. Makes about 3 cups.

ANCHOVY-CHIVE DRESSING

8 anchovy fillets, chopped
1 tablespoon minced onion
2 tablespoons minced parsley
2½ cups salad dressing
¼ cup vinegar
¼ cup chopped chives

Combine all ingredients and mix well. Serve with meat and vegetable salads, as desired. Makes about 3 cups.

CREAMY CUCUMBER DRESSING

1 **cup diced cucumbers**
¾ **cup sour cream**
2 **tablespoons vinegar**
½ **teaspoon salt**
1/8 **teaspoon paprika**

Combine all ingredients and mix well. Serve with meat, fish, poultry and vegetable salads, as desired. Makes about 1½ cups.

HORSERADISH DRESSING

¾ **cup salad oil**
1 **teaspoon salt**
1 **teaspoon sugar**
3 **tablespoons horseradish**
1 **tablespoon chopped chives**
1 **teaspoon paprika**
1/3 **cup vinegar**
2 **teaspoons dry mustard**
1/8 **teaspoon pepper**
1 **teaspoon Worcestershire sauce**

Combine all ingredients and shake until thoroughly blended. Serve with meat, fish, poultry and vegetable salads, as desired. Makes about 1¼ cups.

LOW CALORIE DRESSING

1 **cup tomato juice**
1 **teaspoon Worcestershire sauce**
1 **tablespoon onion juice**
1 **tablespoon lemon juice**
½ **teaspoon salt**
1/8 **teaspoon pepper**

Combine all ingredients and shake well. Makes about 1 cup.

MAYONNAISE

1 **egg**
¼ **teaspoon salt**
1/8 **teaspoon white pepper**
1/8 **teaspoon paprika**
1 **tablespoon lemon juice**
1 **cup salad oil**

Combine egg, salt, pepper and paprika; beat well. Add lemon juice and beat well. Add oil, a few drops at a time, beating constantly. Makes about 1¼ cups.

POPPY SEED-ONION DRESSING

1/3 **cup sugar**
½ **teaspoon salt**
1 **teaspoon dry mustard**
1½ **teaspoons poppy seeds**
½ **teaspoon celery seed**
1 **tablespoon onion juice**
1 **cup salad oil**
¼ **cup white vinegar**

Combine sugar, salt, mustard, poppy seeds, celery seed and onion juice; mix well. Add oil, a few drops at a time, beating constantly. Add vinegar and mix well. Serve with fruit and vegetable salads, as desired. Makes about 1½ cups.

PINEAPPLE-LEMON DRESSING

1/3 **cup pineapple juice**
2 **tablespoons lemon juice**
½ **cup salad oil**
1 **teaspoon grated lemon rind**
1 **teaspoon sugar**
¼ **teaspoon salt**
½ **teaspoon paprika**

Combine all ingredients and shake until well blended. Serve with fruit salads, as desired. Makes about 1 cup.

SEA FOOD DRESSING

½ **cup mayonnaise**
½ **cup chili sauce**
½ **cup chopped tomatoes**
1 **tablespoon lemon juice**
¼ **cup chopped green pepper**
1 **tablespoon onion juice**
¼ **teaspoon salt**
1/8 **teaspoon pepper**

Combine all ingredients and mix well. Serve with fish salads, as desired. Makes about 1¾ cups.

RUSSIAN DRESSING

1 **cup mayonnaise**
2 **tablespoons chili sauce**
1 **tablespoon sweet pickle relish**
1/8 **teaspoon salt**
½ **teaspoon sugar**

Combine all ingredients and mix until well blended. Serve with meat, fish, poultry and vegetable salads, as desired. Makes about 1¼ cups.

FRENCH DRESSING

¼ cup vinegar
½ cup salad oil
¼ teaspoon paprika
1 teaspoon salt
1/8 teaspoon pepper

Combine all ingredients and shake until well blended. Serve with fruit and vegetable salads, as desired. Makes about ¾ cup.

THOUSAND ISLAND DRESSING

1 cup mayonnaise
1/3 cup chili sauce
1 tablespoon catsup
1 tablespoon minced green pepper
2 tablespoons chopped pimiento
1 tablespoon grated onion
½ teaspoon paprika

Combine all ingredients and mix well. Serve with meat, fish, poultry and vegetable salads, as desired. Makes about 1½ cups.

TOMATO DRESSING

½ cup tomato juice
2 tablespoons salad oil
3 tablespoons lemon juice
1 teaspoon salt
1 teaspoon dry mustard
1 tablespoon grated onion
1 tablespoon Worcestershire sauce

Combine all ingredients and shake until well blended. Serve with green, vegetable and meat salads, as desired. Makes about ¾ cup.

WINE DRESSING

½ cup dry white wine
¼ cup white vinegar
¾ cup salad oil
1 teaspoon salt
1/8 teaspoon pepper
1 teaspoon onion juice

Combine all ingredients and shake until well blended. Serve with meat, fish and vegetable salads, as desired. Makes about 1½ cups.

SOUR CREAM DRESSING

1 cup sour cream
2 tablespoons vinegar
1 tablespoon sugar
¼ teaspoon salt

Beat until thoroughly blended. Chill well. Makes about 1¼ cups.

TART CREAM DRESSING

1 cup heavy cream
¼ cup lemon juice
½ teaspoon salt
1/8 teaspoon white pepper

Combine all ingredients and beat until thoroughly blended. Serve with fruit or vegetable salads, as desired. Makes about 1¼ cups.

COOKED DRESSINGS

BOILED SALAD DRESSING

1 tablespoon sugar
1 tablespoon all-purpose flour
1 teaspoon dry mustard
3 eggs, slightly beaten
½ cup vinegar
½ cup water
Dash Tabasco
½ teaspoon salt
2 tablespoons butter or margarine

Combine sugar, flour and mustard; mix well. Add eggs, vinegar, water, Tabasco and salt. Cook over boiling water, stirring constantly, until thickened. Remove from heat and add butter or margarine. Stir until butter or margarine melts. Serve with meat, fish and vegetable salads, as desired. Makes about 1½ cups.

MUSTARD DRESSING

1 tablespoon sugar
1 tablespoon all-purpose flour
1 teaspoon dry mustard
½ teaspoon salt
2 eggs, slightly beaten
¾ cup light cream
½ cup vinegar
½ cup water
1 tablespoon onion juice

Combine sugar, flour, mustard and salt; mix well. Combine eggs and cream; add sugar mixture and mix well. Stir in remaining ingredients. Cook over boiling water, stirring constantly, until thickened. Serve with meat, fish and vegetable salads, as desired. Makes about 2 cups.

HOT BACON DRESSING

4 slices bacon, diced
2 teaspoons grated onion
1/3 cup vinegar
2 teaspoons sugar
½ teaspoon salt
1/8 teaspoon pepper

Cook bacon until crisp. Add remaining ingredients and heat to boiling point, stirring occasionally. Pour over salad greens, as desired. Makes about ¾ cup.

FRUIT SALAD DRESSING

2 eggs
2 tablespoons lemon juice
1/8 teaspoon dry mustard
¼ cup milk
1 cup heavy cream, whipped

Beat eggs with lemon juice and mustard. Add milk and cook over very low heat until thickened, stirring constantly. Cool thoroughly. Fold in cream. Makes about 1½ cups.

COOKED SOUR CREAM DRESSING

3 eggs, slightly beaten
1 cup sour cream
1 cup sugar
¾ cup vinegar
½ teaspoon salt
1/8 teaspoon pepper
1 teaspoon dry mustard
1 teaspoon horseradish

Combine all ingredients and cook over boiling water, stirring until ingredients are well blended. Continue cooking, stirring occasionally, until thickened. Serve with meat, fish, poultry and vegetable salads, as desired. Makes about 3 cups.

SWEET AND SOUR DRESSING

3 eggs, slightly beaten
¾ cup sugar
2 tablespoons all-purpose flour
¼ cup orange juice
1 tablespoon vinegar
1 cup water
2 tablespoons butter

Combine all ingredients and cook over low heat, stirring constantly, until thickened. Serve with fruit salads, as desired. Makes about 2½ cups.

Desserts

FROZEN DESSERTS

ICE CREAM APPLESAUCE PARFAIT

2 cups applesauce
1 pint vanilla ice cream
½ cup chopped walnuts
½ cup heavy cream, whipped

Arrange applesauce, ice cream and nuts alternately in layers in serving glasses. Top with whipped cream. Serves 6–8.

CRANBERRY FLUFF

1 1-pound can cranberry sauce
2 tablespoons sugar
1 tablespoon grated orange rind
1 cup heavy cream, whipped
½ teaspoon almond extract

Beat cranberry sauce with sugar and orange rind until light. Fold cream and almond extract into cranberry mixture. Turn into refrigerator tray and freeze until firm. Stir occasionally during freezing period. Serves 6.

APRICOT-ALMOND SHERBET

2 egg whites
½ cup sugar
½ cup light corn syrup
¼ teaspoon salt
2 tablespoons lemon juice
2 teaspoons grated lemon rind
1 cup apricot puree
1 cup light cream
¼ cup chopped almonds

Beat egg whites until frothy. Gradually add sugar, beating constantly. Continue beating until stiff. Gradually add syrup and salt, beating constantly. Combine remaining ingredients and fold into egg-white mixture. Turn into refrigerator tray and freeze until frozen 1 inch from sides of tray. Turn into chilled bowl and beat until smooth. Turn into refrigerator tray and freeze until firm. Serves 6.

AVOCADO-WALNUT ICE CREAM

1 cup milk
1 cup light cream
½ cup sugar
3 egg yolks, well beaten
¾ cup avocado pulp
¼ cup chopped walnuts

Combine milk, cream and sugar; heat to boiling point, stirring constantly. Pour cream mixture over egg yolks, stirring constantly. Add remaining ingredients and mix well. Cool and turn into refrigerator trays. Freeze until firm. Turn into chilled bowl and beat until smooth. Turn into refrigerator trays and freeze until firm. Serves 10–12.

ICEBOX BANANA WHIP

6 bananas, mashed
¼ cup lemon juice
½ cup orange juice
½ cup sugar
2 egg whites, beaten stiff

Combine bananas, juices and sugar. Turn into refrigerator tray. Freeze until mushy. Fold in egg whites. Freeze until firm. Serves 6.

TOASTED ALMOND ICE CREAM

1 cup toasted almonds
2½ cups milk, scalded
1 cup sugar
1 teaspoon vanilla
1 teaspoon almond extract
1 cup heavy cream, whipped

Grind almonds. Combine milk and sugar; stir until sugar is dissolved. Add almonds, vanilla and almond extract; mix well. Cool thoroughly. Fold in cream. Turn into refrigerator tray and freeze until frozen 1 inch from sides of tray. Beat well.

Turn into refrigerator tray and freeze until firm. Serves 6.

FIG RUM FREEZE

2 cups milk
2 cups light cream
6 eggs, separated
1 cup sugar
3 tablespoons rum
4 cups fresh figs, peeled and chopped

Scald milk and cream together. Beat egg yolks with sugar until light. Beat egg whites until stiff. Pour milk mixture over sugar and egg yolks, stirring constantly. Fold in egg whites. Add rum. Add figs. Freeze until firm. Serves 6.

BLUE BAY GINGER FREEZE

¼ pound preserved ginger, chopped
3 cups light cream
½ cup sugar
1 tablespoon ginger syrup

Combine all ingredients. Turn into refrigerator tray. Freeze until firm. Serves 6–8.

CREAMY LEMON SHERBET

1½ cups sugar
¾ cup lemon juice
1 teaspoon grated lemon rind
3 cups milk
1 cup heavy cream
1/8 teaspoon salt

Combine sugar and lemon juice; stir until sugar dissolves. Add remaining ingredients and mix well. Turn into refrigerator trays and freeze until frozen 1 inch from sides of tray. Turn into chilled bowl and beat until smooth. Turn into refrigerator trays and freeze until firm. Serves 6–8.

OLD-FASHIONED MINT FREEZE

1 envelope unflavored gelatin
4 cups milk
2 squares unsweetened chocolate
1 tablespoon all-purpose flour
1½ cups sugar
1/8 teaspoon salt
3 egg yolks, slightly beaten
3 egg whites, stiffly beaten
2 cups heavy cream, whipped
1 teaspoon vanilla

½ teaspoon mint extract
¼ cup crushed peppermint stick candy

Stir gelatin into cold milk to soften. Add chocolate and heat to dissolve gelatin and melt chocolate. Stir until smooth. Mix flour, sugar and salt; add to milk mixture, stirring constantly until mixture begins to thicken. Add a little of hot mixture to egg yolks, return to hot mixture, cook 1 minute, stirring. Chill until slightly thickened, beat until light. Fold in egg whites, cream, vanilla, mint extract and candy. Pour into refrigerator tray. Freeze 1 hour. Beat until smooth. Freeze until firm. Serves 6–8.

CALIFORNIA ORANGE SHERBET

1 cup milk
1 cup sugar
1 teaspoon grated orange rind
½ cup orange juice
1 cup heavy cream, whipped

Combine milk and sugar. Heat to boiling point, stirring until sugar melts. Remove from heat and add orange rind and orange juice. Cool thoroughly. Fold in cream. Turn into refrigerator tray and freeze until mushy. Stir well. Continue freezing until firm. Serves 6.

ORANGE-LIME SHERBET

1 tablespoon unflavored gelatin
¼ cup cold water
1 cup water
1½ cups sugar
1 tablespoon grated orange rind
1 teaspoon grated lemon rind
1 ¾ cups orange juice
¼ cup lime juice
¼ cup lemon juice

Soften gelatin in cold water. Combine water and sugar. Heat to boiling point, stirring until sugar melts. Add gelatin and stir until dissolved. Cool thoroughly. Add remaining ingredients and turn into refrigerator tray. Freeze until frozen 1 inch from sides of tray. Turn into chilled bowl and beat until smooth. Turn into refrigerator tray and freeze until firm. Serves 10–12.

BUTTER PECAN ICE CREAM

2/3 **cup condensed milk**
1 **tablespoon melted butter**
½ **cup water**
1 **teaspoon vanilla**
1½ **cups heavy cream, whipped**
¾ **cup toasted chopped pecans**

Combine milk and butter; mix well. Add water and vanilla; mix well. Chill thoroughly. Fold in cream. Turn into rerefrigerator tray and freeze until frozen 1 inch from sides of tray. Beat until smooth. Fold in pecans. Turn into refrigerator tray and freeze until firm. Serves 6.

GRAPE MOUSSE

1 **envelope unflavored gelatin**
1 **cup grape juice**
1 **tablespoon lemon juice**
½ **cup sugar**
½ **teaspoon vanilla**
1 **teaspoon grated orange rind**
1½ **cups heavy cream, whipped**

Soften gelatin in ¼ cup grape juice; dissolve over hot water. Add remaining grape juice, lemon juice, sugar, vanilla and orange rind. Chill until slightly thickened. Fold in cream. Turn into refrigerator tray and freeze until firm. Serves 8–10.

TROPICAL MOUSSE

1½ **cups sieved avocado**
1/8 **teaspoon salt**
1/3 **cup sugar**
1 **teaspoon lime juice**
1 **teaspoon grated lime rind**
2 **egg whites, stiffly beaten**
1 **cup heavy cream, whipped**

Combine avocado, salt, sugar, lime juice and rind; mix well. Fold in egg whites and cream. Turn into refrigerator tray and freeze until firm. Serves 4–6.

STRAWBERRY CREAM FREEZE

1 **cup heavy cream**
1 **pint vanilla ice cream**
1½ **quarts sweetened strawberries**
3 **tablespoons Cointreau**

Whip cream until stiff. Soften ice cream slightly and fold into cream. Combine berries and Cointreau. Fold into cream mixture. Freeze until firm. Serves 6–8.

FROZEN STRAWBERRY CREAM

1 **quart strawberries**
¾ **cup sugar**
1/8 **teaspoon salt**
¼ **teaspoon vanilla**
1 **cup heavy cream, whipped**

Crush strawberries. Combine berries with remaining ingredients. Turn into refrigerator tray and freeze until frozen 1 inch from sides of tray. Turn into chilled bowl and beat until smooth. Turn into refrigerator tray and freeze until firm. Serves 4–6.

STRAWBERRY ICE

3 **cups strawberries**
½ **pound marshmallows**
2 **tablespoons lemon juice**
½ **teaspoon grated lemon rind**
1/8 **teaspoon salt**

Crush berries; reserve ¼ cup juice. Combine strawberry juice and marshmallows; cook over low heat until marshmallows are melted. Cool thoroughly. Fold in remaining ingredients. Turn into refrigerator tray and freeze until frozen 1 inch from sides of tray. Turn into chilled bowl and beat until smooth. Turn into refrigerator tray and freeze until firm. Serves 6.

FROZEN TUTTI-FRUTTI

1 **cup mixed candied fruits, chopped**
½ **cup brandy**
2 **eggs, slightly beaten**
1 **cup sugar**
1/8 **teaspoon salt**
½ **teaspoon vanilla**
2½ **cups milk**
1 **cup heavy cream, whipped**

Combine fruits and brandy; let stand 1 hour. Combine eggs, sugar, salt, vanilla and milk. Cook over low heat, stirring constantly, until thickened. Cool. Fold fruits and cream into milk mixture. Turn into refrigerator tray and freeze until frozen 1 inch from sides of tray. Beat well. Turn into refrigerator tray and freeze until firm. Serves 6–8.

SPICED BANANA DESSERT

4 ripe bananas, mashed
½ cup sugar
1/8 teaspoon salt
½ cup apricot nectar
1 teaspoon grated lemon rind
2 tablespoons sherry
1 cup heavy cream, whipped
¼ teaspoon nutmeg
1 teaspoon ginger
¼ teaspoon vanilla

Combine all ingredients and mix lightly. Turn into refrigerator trays. Freeze until firm. Serves 6.

CHOCOLATE MINT MALLOW

16 marshmallows, cut in quarters
1 cup milk
1/8 teaspoon salt
½ teaspoon mint extract
1 cup heavy cream, whipped
¼ cup chopped pecans
½ cup semi-sweet chocolate pieces

Melt marshmallows in milk over hot water. Add salt. Chill until slightly thickened. Add mint extract. Fold in cream, nuts and chocolate pieces. Pour into refrigerator tray and freeze until firm. Serves 6.

PINK PIE PLANT MOUSSE

1 cup cooked and mashed rhubarb
2/3 cup sugar
1 cup heavy cream, whipped
1 teaspoon lemon extract

Combine rhubarb and sugar, mix well. Fold into cream. Add lemon extract Pour into refrigerator tray. Freeze until firm. Serves 6–8.

CINNAMON-CHOCOLATE ICE CREAM

1 1-ounce square unsweetened chocolate
2/3 cup condensed milk
¾ teaspoon cinnamon
½ teaspoon nutmeg
2/3 cup water
¼ teaspoon vanilla
½ cup heavy cream, whipped

Melt chocolate over very low heat. Add milk, cinnamon and nutmeg; cook, stirring constantly, over low heat 5 minutes. Add water and mix well. Cool thoroughly. Fold in vanilla and cream. Turn

into refrigerator tray and freeze until frozen 1 inch from sides of tray. Turn into chilled bowl and beat until smooth. Turn into refrigerator tray and freeze until firm. Serves 6.

WARM DESSERTS

MEXICAN COFFEE PUDDING

2 eggs
¼ cup sugar
1 teaspoon cocoa
1/8 teaspoon salt
1 cup milk
1 cup cold strong coffee

Beat eggs slightly. Add sugar, cocoa, salt, milk and coffee. Pour into greased custard cups. Place in pan with hot water about 1 inch deep. Bake in moderate oven (350° F.) about 1 hour, or until firm. Serves 4.

RASPBERRY BREAD PUDDING

2½ cups small dry bread cubes
4 cups scalded milk
2 eggs
2 eggs, separated
1/3 cup sugar
¼ teaspoon salt
1 teaspoon vanilla
¼ cup melted butter
½ cup raspberry jam
¼ cup sugar

Combine bread cubes and milk. Beat 2 eggs and 2 egg yolks slightly; add the 1/3 cup sugar, salt, vanilla and butter. Mix well. Combine egg mixture with bread-cube mixture. Turn into greased 2-quart baking dish. Bake in moderate oven (350° F.) 25 minutes. Remove from oven and spread evenly with jam. Beat egg whites until foamy. Gradually add the ¼ cup sugar, beating constantly. Continue beating until stiff. Pile meringue over jam. Continue baking 15 minutes. Serves 8.

APPLE BROWN BETTY

¼ cup butter, melted
2 cups soft bread crumbs
3 cups diced apples
2/3 cup firmly packed brown sugar
¼ teaspoon salt
½ teaspoon nutmeg
1 teaspoon cinnamon
½ teaspoon grated lemon rind
2 tablespoons lemon juice
1/3 cup water

Combine butter and crumbs. Combine apples, sugar, salt, nutmeg, cinnamon, and lemon rind. Arrange alternate layers of crumb mixture and apple mixture in greased 1½-quart baking dish, ending with crumb mixture. Combine lemon juice and water; pour over other ingredients. Bake in moderate oven (350° F.). Serve with Hard Sauce (page 134), if desired. Serves 6.

RED CHERRY COBBLER

3 cups pitted sour cherries
1 cup sugar
1 cup water
1 tablespoon cornstarch
1 tablespoon butter
¾ teaspoon cinnamon
2 cups sifted all-purpose flour
3 teaspoons baking powder
1 teaspoon salt
2 tablespoons sugar
1/3 cup shortening
¾ cup milk

Combine cherries, sugar and water; heat to boiling point. Moisten cornstarch with water and add to cherry mixture. Cook, stirring constantly, five minutes. Pour cherry mixture into greased 2-quart baking dish. Dot with butter and sprinkle with cinnamon. Sift flour with baking powder, salt and sugar. Cut in shortening. Add milk and mix lightly. Arrange dough over cherry mixture. Bake in hot oven (400° F.) 25-30 minutes. Serves 6-8.

BRANDIED CHESTNUTS

1¼ cups sugar
½ cup water
¼ teaspoon vanilla
1 pound chestnuts, peeled
1/3 cup brandy

Combine 1 cup of the sugar, water and vanilla. Cook over low heat, stirring until sugar dissolves. Add chestnuts and cook until tender; drain. Arrange chestnuts on serving platter. Sprinkle with remaining ¼ cup sugar. Pour brandy over chestnuts; light. Serves 6.

CHOCOLATE SOUFFLÉ

1½ tablespoons butter or margarine
1½ tablespoons all-purpose flour
½ cup milk
2 squares unsweetened chocolate, melted
3 eggs, separated
1/3 cup sugar
¼ teaspoon vanilla
¼ teaspoon cream of tartar

Melt butter or margarine. Blend in flour. Gradually add milk and cook over low heat, stirring constantly, until thickened. Add chocolate and mix well. Beat egg yolks until thick. Beat in sugar; add vanilla. Gradually add chocolate mixture and mix well. Beat egg whites with cream of tartar until stiff and fold into chocolate mixture. Turn into ungreased 1½-quart baking dish. Place in pan of hot water. Bake in moderate oven (350° F.) 45-50 minutes, or until firm. Serve immediately. Serves 4-6.

COTTAGE PUDDING

1¾ cups sifted cake flour
2½ teaspoons baking powder
¼ teaspoon salt
¼ cup butter or margarine
¾ cup sugar
1 egg
1 teaspoon vanilla
2/3 cup milk

Sift flour, baking powder and salt together. Cream butter or margarine and sugar until light and fluffy. Add egg and vanilla; mix well. Add sifted ingredients alternately with milk, beating well after each addition. Turn into greased 8" x 8" baking pan. Bake in moderate oven (350° F.) 40 minutes or until done. Serve with whipped cream or fruit sauce such as Orange Sauce (page 135), if desired. Serves 6.

LEMON-CHEESE PUDDING

2 tablespoons butter or margarine
¾ cup sugar
1 tablespoon grated lemon rind
3 eggs, separated
1 cup creamed cottage cheese
2 tablespoons all-purpose flour
1/8 teaspoon salt
1/3 cup lemon juice

Cream butter or margarine, sugar and lemon rind together until light and fluffy. Beat egg yolks and cheese together well. Add lemon-rind mixture and mix well. Add flour, salt and lemon juice; mix well. Beat egg whites until stiff and fold into lemon mixture. Turn into 6 greased baking cups. Place in pan of hot wrater. Bake in moderate oven (350° F.) 30–35 minutes. Serves 6.

RICE CREAM PUDDING

1 cup cooked rice
1 cup sugar
¼ cup raisins
½ cup well-drained canned, crushed
    pineapple
1 teaspoon grated lemon rind
6 egg yolks
1/8 teaspoon salt
4 cups milk
¼ teaspoon nutmeg
½ teaspoon vanilla
¼ teaspoon cinnamon
2 egg whites
1/8 teaspoon cream of tartar
¼ cup sugar

Combine rice, the 1 cup sugar, raisins, pineapple, lemon rind, egg yolks, salt, milk, nutmeg, vanilla and cinnamon; beat well. Turn into greased 2-quart baking dish. Bake in moderate oven (350° F.) 30 minutes. Remove from oven. Beat egg whites with cream of tartar until frothy. Gradually add the ¼ cup sugar, beating constantly, until stiff. Pile meringue over rice mixture. Bake in moderate oven (350° F.) 12–15 minutes, or until lightly browned. Serves 6.

APPLE-PECAN POLONAISE

6 medium-size apples
1 cup water
¼ cup white wine
3 tablespoons sugar
2 teaspoons grated orange rind
¼ cup chopped pecans
1 envelope unflavored gelatin
½ cup cold water

Pare apples. Add the 1 cup water, wine, sugar and orange rind. Cover and simmer about 25 minutes, or until apples are tender. Remove apples and arrange in serving dishes. Sprinkle with pecans. Soften gelatin in the ½ cup water. Heat apple liquid to boiling point. Add gelatin and stir until dissolved. Chill until slightly thickened. Pour over apples. Chill several hours. Serves 6.

CARAMEL PUDDING

½ cup firmly packed brown sugar
2 tablespoons melted butter or margarine
2 cups milk, scalded
½ cup cold milk
¼ cup all-purpose flour
¼ teaspoon salt
2 eggs, well beaten
½ teaspoon vanilla

Combine sugar and butter or margarine. Cook over low heat, stirring constantly, 5 minutes. Add scalded milk and stir until sugar dissolves. Combine cold milk, flour and salt. Add flour mixture to sugar mixture and cook over very low heat, stirring constantly, 15 minutes. Add a little of hot mixture to eggs and mix well. Add to hot mixture and cook, stirring constantly, 2 minutes. Add vanilla. Chill. Serves 4.

PINEAPPLE-CHEESE PUDDING

1 cup creamed cottage cheese
½ cup heavy cream, whipped
¼ cup sugar
¾ cup drained, canned crushed pineapple
¼ teaspoon vanilla
½ cup shredded toasted coconut

Combine all ingredients and mix lightly. Serves 4.

COLD DESSERTS

CHOCOLATE ANGEL DESSERT

1 10" angel food cake
6 tablespoons cocoa
6 tablespoons sugar
¼ teaspoon salt
2 cups heavy cream
½ cup chopped pecans
1 tablespoon chopped maraschino cherries

Cut slice 1 inch thick from top of cake. Remove center from cake leaving shell 1" thick. Combine cocoa, sugar, salt and cream. Chill 1 hour. Beat cream mixture until stiff. Add pecans and cherries. Fill cake with 1/3 of cream mixture. Place top on cake and frost with remaining mixture, stirring constantly, until ture. Chill 2 hours. Serves 8–10.

FRENCH CREAM LADYFINGERS

¼ cup all-purpose flour
1/3 cup sugar
½ cup light cream
1 cup milk, scalded
1 egg, slightly beaten
1 teaspoon vanilla
12 ladyfingers, split

Combine flour and sugar; gradually add cream and mix until smooth. Add sugar mixture gradually to milk and cook over hot water, stirring occasionally, 15 minutes. Add a little of hot mixture to egg and mix well. Add to hot mixture and cook, stirring constantly, 2 minutes. Remove from heat and add vanilla. Cool thoroughly. Line serving dishes with ladyfingers. Add cream mixture. Serves 6.

EGG NOG MOLD

1 envelope unflavored gelatin
¼ cup cold water
1¼ cups prepared egg nog
1 cup heavy cream, whipped
½ teaspoon vanilla
½ cup chopped nuts

Soften gelatin in water; dissolve over boiling water. Add egg nog and mix well. Chill until slightly thickened. Fold in remaining ingredients. Turn into 1-quart mold and chill until firm. Serves 4–6.

MOLDED MARSHMALLOW DESSERT

½ pound marshmallows
½ cup milk
¼ cup chopped walnuts
1 medium-sized banana, diced
2 tablespoons lemon juice
1½ cups heavy cream, whipped

Combine marshshmallows and milk. Cook over low heat, stirring constantly, until marshmallows are melted. Add walnuts. Combine banana and lemon juice. Combine marshmallow mixture and banana mixture. Fold cream into marshmallow mixture. Turn into 1-quart mold. Chill until firm. Serves 4–6.

LEMON SNOW

1 envelope unflavored gelatin
½ cup cold water
¾ cup boiling water
¾ cup sugar
1/8 teaspoon salt
1½ teaspoons grated lemon rind
¼ cup lemon juice
2 egg whites

Soften gelatin in ½ cup cold water. Add boiling water, sugar and salt and stir until dissolved. Add lemon rind and lemon juice. Chill until slightly thickened. Add egg whites; beat until mixture begins to hold shape. Turn into a 1½-quart mold; chill until firm. Serve with Custard Sauce (page 134). Serves 6.

TAPIOCA PUDDING

¼ cup sugar
1/3 cup quick-cooking tapioca
1/8 teaspoon salt
2 eggs, separated
4 cups milk, scalded
¾ teaspoon vanilla

Combine sugar, tapioca, salt and egg yolks. Gradually add 1 cup of the milk; add remaining 3 cups milk. Cook over hot water, stirring constantly, until thickened. Beat egg whites until stiff. Fold a little of hot mixture into egg whites. Fold egg-white mixture into tapioca mixture. Add vanilla. Chill. Serves 6–8.

MARSHMALLOW CHOCOLATE PUDDING

1 envelope unflavored gelatin
¼ cup milk
1 egg, separated
1¾ cups milk
2 squares unsweetened chocolate, grated
½ cup sugar
⅛ teaspoon salt
1½ cups quartered marshmallows
¼ cup chopped walnuts
½ cup heavy cream, whipped

Stir gelatin into the ¼ cup milk to soften. Beat egg yolk; add the 1¾ cups milk, chocolate, sugar and salt. Cook over low heat, stirring constantly, until slightly thickened. Add gelatin and stir until dissolved. Chill until slightly thickened. Fold in remaining ingredients. Chill until firm. Serves 6–8.

CHOCOLATE MOUSSE

6 ounces semi-sweet chocolate
3 tablespoons black coffee
½ cup butter
⅛ teaspoon salt
⅛ teaspoon cinnamon
6 eggs, separated
½ cup heavy cream
¼ cup confectioners' sugar

Melt chocolate with coffee over low heat. Add butter, salt and cinnamon. Beat egg yolks until light and stir into chocolate mixture. Cool. Beat cream and add sugar. Beat egg whites until stiff. Fold cream and egg whites into chocolate mixture. Chill. Serves 6.

MOCHA DESSERT

½ pound sweet chocolate
¼ cup strong coffee
5 eggs, separated
½ teaspoon vanilla

Grate chocolate; add coffee and cook over low heat, stirring constantly until chocolate melts. Beat egg yolks until thick. Gradually add egg yolks to chocolate mixture and cook over low heat, stirring constantly, until thickened. Cool. Beat egg whites until stiff. Fold egg whites and vanilla into chocolate mixture. Turn into serving dishes and chill. Serves 6.

MOCHA MERINGUE

3 egg whites
¼ teaspoon cream of tartar
⅛ teaspoon salt
¾ cup sugar
¼ teaspoon cinnamon
2 6-ounce packages semi-sweet chocolate morsels
1 tablespoon instant coffee
¼ cup boiling water
½ teaspoon vanilla
1 cup heavy cream, whipped

Beat egg whites until foamy; add cream of tartar and salt; beat until stiff. Gradually add sugar; beat until very stiff. Fold in cinnamon. Cover baking sheet with heavy brown paper. Pile about 2/3 of meringue on paper into a 7" round. Make a depression in the center leaving an inch around sides. Spoon remaining meringue in mounds around edge. Bake in very slow oven (275° F.) 1 hour. Cool. Meanwhile melt chocolate morsels over hot water. Combine instant coffee and boiling water; stir into chocolate. Add vanilla; beat until smooth. Cool thoroughly. Fold in cream; turn into meringue shell. Chill. Serves 8.

ZABAGLIONE

6 egg yolks
¼ cup sugar
½ cup Marsala wine

Beat egg yolks and sugar until very light. Gradually add wine, beating constantly. Cook over hot water until mixture coats spoon. Chill thoroughly. Serves 4.

SARATOGA SHORTCAKE

1 cup sifted cake flour
½ teaspoon salt
5 eggs, separated
1 teaspoon grated lemon rind
1 cup sugar
2 cups crushed sweetened strawberries

Sift flour with ¼ teaspoon of the salt. Beat egg yolks until very thick, add lemon rind. Beat egg whites with remaining ¼ teaspoon salt until stiff but not dry. Gradually add sugar, beating until stiff. Fold in egg yolk mixture. Sift flour gradually over egg white mixture and fold into batter. Turn into 2 ungreased 9" layer cake pans. Bake in slow over (325° F.) 30–35 minutes. Cool in pans on rack; remove from pans. Spread strawberries between layers. Serve with Custard Sauce (page 134). Serves 6–8.

MERINGUE GLACES

2 cups sugar
¾ cup water
5 egg whites
¼ teaspoon salt
1/8 teaspoon cream of tartar
¾ teaspoon vanilla
¼ teaspoon almond extract

Cook sugar and water to 238° F. Beat egg whites until stiff, add salt and cream of tartar. Pour syrup over egg whites gradually, beating constantly. Beat until cool. Fold in vanilla and almond extract. Shape meringues into cups with pastry tube on wet unglazed paper. Bake in slow oven (275° F.) 1 hour. Cool and fill with ice cream. Top with a Chocolate or Fruit Sauce. Makes about 12.

CURRANT JELLY RICE PUDDING

2 cups milk
2 cups light cream
½ cup uncooked rice
3 tablespoons sugar
¼ teaspoon salt
¼ teaspoon nutmeg
1/8 teaspoon cinnamon
¼ cup currant jelly

Combine milk, cream, rice, sugar, salt and spices. Turn into greased 1½-quart baking dish. Dot with jelly. Bake in slow oven (300° F.) 2½ hours, or until rice is tender. Stir frequently during baking period. Cool thoroughly. Serves 4–6.

SHERRY DESSERT MOLDS

2 envelopes unflavored gelatin
½ cup cold water
1¼ cups boiling water
¾ cup sugar
1 teaspoon grated orange rind
2 tablespoons lemon juice
1 cup sherry wine

Soften gelatin in cold water. Add boiling water and stir until gelatin is dissolved. Add sugar, orange rind and lemon juice; mix well. Cool thoroughly. Add sherry and mix well. Turn into 6 individual molds. Chill until firm. Serves 6.

RAISIN RICE PUDDING

½ cup rice
1 cup milk
1 teaspoon grated lemon rind
¼ cup raisins
1 egg yolk, beaten
Sugar

Cook rice according to package directions. Add milk, lemon rind and raisins. Cook over low heat 15 minutes. Remove from heat. Add a little of the hot mixture to egg and mix well. Add to hot mixture and cook, stirring constantly, 2 minutes. Remove from heat and season to taste with sugar. Chill. Serves 4–6.

Dessert Sauces

FRESH PEACH SAUCE

6 medium-sized fresh peaches
¾ cup sugar
¼ teaspoon almond extract
1 teaspoon lemon juice

Peel peaches and mash. Fold in remaining ingredients. Serve on ice cream. Makes about 2 cups.

PINEAPPLE SAUCE

1½ cups canned crushed pineapple
1 cup sugar
½ cup water
Few drops mint extract

Combine pineapple, sugar and water. Cook over low heat, stirring occasionally 10 minutes. Cool. Stir in mint extract. Serve on ice cream, unfrosted cake, banana splits. Makes about 2½ cups.

FLUFFY PUDDING SAUCE

1 egg, separated
¾ cup confectioners' sugar
1/8 teaspoon salt
½ cup heavy cream, whipped
2 tablespoons Sherry

Beat egg white until stiff. Gradually add sugar, continuing to beat. Beat in salt and egg yolk; fold in cream and Sherry. Chill thoroughly. Serve on pudding. Makes about 1½ cups.

RASPBERRY SAUCE

1 cup raspberry jam
3 tablespoons hot water
1 tablespoon lemon juice
¼ teaspoon grated lemon rind
1/8 teaspoon salt

Combine all ingredients and cook over low heat, stirring constantly until jam melts. Serve on ice cream, pancakes and waffles. Makes about 1¼ cups.

ST. CROIX RUM SAUCE SUPREME

2 eggs
1 cup confectioners' sugar
1 cup heavy cream, whipped
1 tablespoon rum
½ teaspoon nutmeg

Beat eggs until thick. Gradually add sugar, beating constantly. Fold in cream, rum and nutmeg. Makes about 2½ cups.

CUSTARD SAUCE

2 eggs, slightly beaten
2½ tablespoons sugar
1/8 teaspoon salt
2 cups milk
½ teaspoon vanilla

Combine eggs, sugar and salt in top of double boiler. Gradually stir in milk. Cook over hot water, stirring constantly, until thickened. Add vanilla and cool. Serve on Lemon Snow (page 131); Orange and Grapefruit Cup (page 111); Cake. Makes about 2 cups.

HARD SAUCE

1/3 cup butter
1 cup sifted confectioners' sugar
1 tablespoon cream
½ teaspoon vanilla

Cream butter with sugar until light and fluffy. Add cream and vanilla and beat well. Serve with apple pie, Apple Brown Betty (page 129). Makes about 1¼ cups.

HONEY-ORANGE HARD SAUCE

½ cup butter
½ cup honey
1 tablespoon orange juice
½ teaspoon grated orange rind

Combine all ingredients and beat until light. Chill. Serve with apple pie, bread pudding. Makes about 1 cup.

MIDNIGHT SUPPER SAUCE

½ cup butter or margarine
1/3 cup firmly packed brown sugar
1 tablespoon orange juice
1 teaspoon grated orange rind

Combine all ingredients and cook over low heat, stirring constantly, until sugar melts. Serve with pancakes and waffles, as desired. Makes about 2/3 cup.

CARAMEL SAUCE

1 cup sugar
1 cup boiling water
1 teaspoon vanilla

Melt sugar over low heat, stirring constantly. Remove from heat and gradually stir in water. Cook over low heat 10 minutes. Add vanilla and mix well. Makes about 2 cups.

SHERRY CHEESE SAUCE

1 8-ounce package cream cheese
3 tablespoons sherry
2 tablespoons confectioners' sugar
1/8 teaspoon salt
¼ teaspoon vanilla

Soften cheese. Add remaining ingredients and beat until light and fluffy. Serve with fruit salad. Makes about 1 cup.

CHERRY SAUCE

1½ cups sugar
2 tablespoons all-purpose flour
¼ teaspoon salt
¾ cup sour cherry juice
¼ cup boiling water
1 tablespoon butter or margarine
1 cup canned sour cherries, drained
1 tablespoon lemon juice

Combine sugar, flour and salt. Add cherry juice and water. Cook over low heat, stirring constantly, 5 minutes. Add remaining ingredients and mix well. Serve on ice cream, cake, bread pudding. Makes about 2 cups.

SPEEDY CHOCOLATE SAUCE

2 squares unsweetened chocolate
1 1/3 cups sweetened condensed milk
¼ teaspoon vanilla
1/8 teaspoon salt

Melt chocolate over hot water; add remaining ingredients and beat well. Serve on ice cream. Makes about 1 1/3 cups.

NUTMEG SAUCE

1 cup sugar
2 tablespoons all-purpose flour
2 cups boiling water
1½ tablespoons butter or margarine
1 teaspoon nutmeg
1/8 teaspoon salt

Combine sugar and flour. Gradually add water and cook, stirring constantly until thickened. Add butter or margarine and cook five minutes, stirring occasionally. Add nutmeg and salt. Makes about 2½ cups.

ORANGE SAUCE

½ cup sugar
1 tablespoon cornstarch
1 cup orange juice
1 tablespoon butter
1 tablespoon grated orange rind
1/8 teaspoon nutmeg
1/8 teaspoon salt

Combine sugar and cornstarch; gradually add orange juice and cook, stirring constantly, until thickened. Add remaining ingredients and mix well. Serve on Cottage Pudding (page 129); bread puddings. Makes about 1¼ cups.

APRICOT CREAM SAUCE

1 cup heavy cream
¼ cup sugar
1 teaspoon vanilla
½ cup apricot jam
1 tablespoon lemon juice

Beat cream until stiff. Fold in remaining ingredients. Chill thoroughly. Serve with angel food cake, gingerbread. Makes about 1½ cups.

BRANDY SAUCE

1 egg, separated
¾ cup confectioners' sugar
1/8 teaspoon salt
½ cup heavy cream, whipped
¼ cup brandy

Beat egg white until stiff, gradually adding sugar. Beat in salt and egg yolk. Fold in cream and brandy. Serve with Chocolate Soufflé (page 129), if desired. Makes about 1½ cups.

RICH BUTTERSCOTCH SAUCE

1½ cups firmly packed brown sugar
2/3 cup light corn syrup
1/3 cup water
2/3 cup evaporated milk

Combine sugar, syrup and water. Cook over low heat, stirring constantly until sugar melts. Continue cooking to softball stage (235° F. on candy thermometer). Cool thoroughly. Gradually add milk and mix well. Serve on ice cream. Makes about 2 cups.

CIDER SAUCE

¼ cup butter or margarine
1 cup confectioners' sugar
¼ cup cider
2 eggs, separated
½ cup evaporated milk

Cream butter or margarine and sugar until light and fluffy. Add cider and beat well. Beat egg yolks until thick and lemon colored. Add to cider mixture; mix well. Gradually add evaporated milk. Cook over low heat, stirring constantly, until thickened. Beat egg whites until stiff. Gradually add hot mixture, beating constantly. Serve with gingerbread. Makes about 1¼ cups.

SHERRY SAUCE

1 cup sugar
1 tablespoon all-purpose flour
2 cups boiling water
2 tablespoons butter
¼ cup Sherry

Combine sugar and flour. Gradually add water and cook, stirring constantly until thickened. Remove from heat and add butter and Sherry. Beat well. Serve on steamed pudding, fruit cake. Makes about 3 cups.

STRAWBERRY SAUCE

1 cup sugar
½ cup water
2 cups crushed strawberries

Combine sugar and water and cook over low heat, stirring until sugar is dissolved. Simmer 10 minutes. Add strawberries and cook 1 minute. Chill. Serve on ice cream, pound cake. Makes about 2½ cups.

Pie

APPLE CRUMB PIE

6 large tart apples
1 unbaked 9" pastry shell
3 tablespoons granulated sugar
1 teaspoon cinnamon
¼ teaspoon nutmeg
½ cup firmly packed brown sugar
½ cup all-purpose flour
¼ cup butter or margarine

Pare and core apples; cut into thin slices. Arrange apple slices in pastry shell. Combine granulated sugar and spices. Sprinkle spice mixture over apples. Combine brown sugar and flour. Cut in butter or margarine. Sprinkle brown sugar mixture over apple mixture. Bake in hot oven (400° F) 40 minutes. Makes one 9" pie.

ANGEL PIE

4 eggs, separated
¼ teaspoon salt
¼ teaspoon cream of tartar
1 cup sugar
¾ cup sugar
¼ cup lemon juice
1 teaspoon grated lemon rind
1 cup heavy cream, whipped
Toasted shredded coconut

Beat egg whites until frothy, add salt and cream of tartar. Beat until stiff but not dry. Beat in the 1 cup sugar adding about 2 tablespoons at a time and beating very thoroughly after each addition; continue beating until satiny smooth. Spread over bottom and sides of well-buttered 9" pie pan. Bake in slow oven (300° F.) about 1 hour; cool. Beat egg yolks until thick. Gradually beat in the ¾ cup sugar. Add lemon juice and lemon rind. Cook over very low heat, stirring constantly, until thickened. Cool and turn into meringue shell. Spread cream over lemon mixture. Top with coconut. Chill. Makes one 9" pie.

BUTTERMILK PIE

1 cup sugar
3 tablespoons all-purpose flour
½ teaspoon salt
3 egg yolks
2 cups buttermilk
4 tablespoons butter
3 egg whites
1 9" pastry shell

Combine the sugar, flour, and salt, blending thoroughly. Beat egg yolks slightly, add the buttermilk and butter which has been melted, then cooled. Add gradually to dry ingredients and blend thoroughly. Fold in stiffly beaten egg whites gently but thoroughly. Pour into pastry shell and bake in a moderate over (375° F.) 45 minutes, or until a silver knife inserted in the center comes out clean. Makes one 9" pie.

CATSKILL MOUNTAIN APPLE PIE

1 recipe pastry for double-crust 9" pie
8 large tart apples
¾ cup sugar
1/8 teaspoon salt
½ teaspoon cinnamon
½ teaspoon nutmeg
1 tablespoon lemon juice
2 tablespoons butter or margarine

Roll ½ of pastry out on lightly floured surface to 1/8-inch thickness. Line 9" pie pan with pastry. Pare and core apples; cut into thin slices. Arrange apples over pastry. Combine sugar, salt, spices and lemon juice. Sprinkle sugar mixture over apples. Dot with butter or margarine. Roll remaining pastry out to 1/8-inch thickness. Place over apple mixture. Seal edges and prick top. Bake in hot oven (400° F.) about 45 minutes. Makes one 9" pie.

BANANA-CHOCOLATE PIE

1½ squares unsweetened chocolate
2 cups milk
¾ cup sugar
5 tablespoons all-purpose flour
¼ teaspoon salt
2 egg yolks
2 teaspoons butter or margarine
1 teaspoon vanilla
2 medium-sized bananas, sliced
1 baked 9" pastry shell

Combine chocolate and milk. Cook over low heat, stirring constantly, until chocolate is melted. Combine sugar, flour and salt. Stir into chocolate mixture. Cook over low heat, stirring constantly, until thickened. Cook 5 minutes, stirring occasionally. Add a little of hot mixture to egg yolks and mix well. Stir into hot mixture and cook, stirring constantly, 1 minute. Add butter or margarine and vanilla and mix well. Cool thoroughly. Arrange banana slices over bottom of pastry shell. Pour chocolate mixture over bananas. Serve with whipped cream, if desired. Makes one 9" pie.

APPLESAUCE-WALNUT PIE

2 eggs
1/3 cup sugar
1 cup light cream
1 cup applesauce
1 teaspoon vanilla
1/8 teaspoon salt
1 cup chopped walnuts
1 9" unbaked pastry shell

Beat eggs slightly. Add sugar, cream, applesauce, vanilla and salt. Sprinkle walnuts over bottom of shell. Add applesauce mixture. Bake in hot oven (400° F.) 45 minutes. Makes one 9" pie.

DUTCH APPLE PIE

6 medium-sized apples, pared and thinly sliced
1 9" unbaked pastry shell
½ cup sifted all-purpose flour
1 cup sugar
1 teaspoon cinnamon
¼ teaspoon nutmeg
½ cup sour cream
½ teaspoon vanilla
1 tablespoon butter or margarine

Arrange apples in pastry shell. Combine flour, sugar and spices; sprinkle over apples. Combine sour cream and vanilla. Pour sour cream mixture over apple mixture. Dot with butter or margarine. Bake in moderate oven (350° F.) 35 minutes. Cover and bake 15–20 minutes, or until apples are tender. Make one 9" pie.

SPICY SCHNITZ PIE

½ pound dried apples
2 cups cold water
¼ cup lemon juice
1 tablespoon grated lemon rind
1 teaspoon cinnamon
1 teaspoon nutmeg
1/8 teaspoon salt
1 cup sugar
1 recipe pastry for 2-crust 9" pie

Combine apples and water. Cook, covered, over low heat until tender. Add lemon juice, rind, cinnamon, nutmeg, salt and sugar; mix well. Cool. Line pie pan with pastry. Pour apple mixture over pastry. Cover with remaining pastry. Prick top of pastry. Bake in hot oven (400° F.) 40 to 45 minutes. Makes one 9" pie.

BANANA CREAM PIE

2/3 cup sugar
1/3 cup all-purpose flour
1/8 teaspoon salt
2 eggs, well beaten
2 cups milk, scalded
½ teaspoon vanilla
3 medium-sized bananas, sliced
1 baked 9" pastry shell
1 cup heavy cream, whipped

Combine sugar, flour, salt and eggs. Gradually add milk. Cook over low heat, stirring constandy, until thickened. Cool thoroughly. Add vanilla and mix well. Arrange banana slices over bottom of pastry shell. Pour milk mixture over bananas. Top with whipped cream to serve. Makes one 9" pie.

CHOCOLATE CHIFFON PIE

2 1-ounce squares unsweetened chocolate, grated
½ cup boiling water
1 envelope unflavored gelatin
¼ cup cold water
3 eggs, separated

½ cup sugar
1/8 teaspoon salt
½ teaspoon vanilla
½ cup sugar
1 10" baked pastry shell

Combine chocolate and boiling water. Stir until chocolate melts. Soften gelatin in cold water. Add to chocolate mixture and stir until gelatin dissolves. Beat egg yolks with ½ cup sugar until light. Add gelatin mixture. Add salt and vanilla; cool thoroughly. Beat egg whites until foamy. Gradually add ½ cup sugar, beating constantly until stiff. Fold into chocolate mixture; pour into pastry shell. Chill until firm. Serve with whipped cream, if desired. Makes one 10" pie.

FRUIT COCKTAIL PIE

1 cup sugar
1 cup chopped Brazil nuts
1/8 teaspoon salt
1 teaspoon grated lemon rind
½ teaspoon cinnamon
½ teaspoon vanilla
¾ cup crumbled soda crackers
3 egg whites, stiffly beaten
½ cup heavy cream, whipped
1 cup drained canned fruit cocktail

Combine sugar, Brazil nuts, salt, lemon rind, cinnamon, vanilla and crackers. Fold egg whites into cracker mixture. Spread cracker mixture over bottom and sides of well greased 8" pie pan. Bake in moderate oven (350° F.) 25-30 minutes. Cool thoroughly. Combine cream and fruit cocktail. Top pie with fruit mixture. Makes one 8" pie.

GOOSEBERRY PIE

3 cups gooseberries
1 cup sugar
½ cup water
½ cup sugar
2 tablespoons all-purpose flour
½ teaspoon salt
1 tablespoon lemon juice
1/8 teaspoon nutmeg
1 recipe pastry for double-crust 9" pie

Combine gooseberries, the 1 cup sugar, and water. Cook over low heat, stirring occasionally until berries are tender. Combine the ½ cup sugar, flour, salt, lemon and nutmeg. Add to gooseberry mixture and mix well. Cool

thoroughly. Roll ½ of pastry out on lighdy floured surface to 1/8-inch thickness. Line 9" pie pan with pastry. Pour gooseberry mixture over pastry. Roll remaining pastry out to 1/8-inch thickness. Place over gooseberry mixture. Seal edges and prick top. Bake in hot oven (400° F.) 35-40 minutes. Makes one 9" pie.

BOG CRANBERRY AND RAISIN PIE

2½ cups chopped cranberries
1 cup raisins
1 cup sugar
1½ tablespoons all-purpose flour
1/8 teaspoon salt
1 recipe pastry for 9" double-crust pie
1½ tablespoons butter or margarine

Combine cranberries, raisins, sugar, flour and salt. Roll out ½ of pastry on lightly floured surface to 1/8-inch thickness. Line 9" pie pan with pastry; pour cranberry mixture over pastry. Dot with butter or margarine. Roll remaining pastry out to 1/8-inch thickness. Place over cranberry mixture. Seal edges and prick top. Bake in hot oven (400° F.) about 40 minutes. Makes one 9" pie.

OPEN GOOSEBERRY TART

4 cups gooseberries
1 9" unbaked pastry shell
¾ cup sugar
1 egg yolk
¼ cup sour cream
1/8 teaspoon nutmeg
1/8 teaspoon cinnamon

Turn berries into pastry shell. Sprinkle with sugar. Bake in moderate oven (350° F.) 20 minutes. Combine remaining ingredients and spread over berry mixture. Bake in moderate oven (350° F.) 20 minutes. Makes one 9" pie.

GRAPE PIE

1 cup seedless white grapes
1 baked 9" pastry shell
4 eggs, separated
1 can sweetened condensed milk
½ cup lemon juice
1/8 teaspoon salt
½ cup sugar

Arrange grapes evenly over bottom of pastry shell. Beat egg yolks until thick; add milk and mix well. Stir in lemon juice and salt. Pour lemon mixture over grapes. Beat egg whites until foamy; gradually add sugar, beating constantly until stiff. Pile meringue over filling. Bake in slow oven (325° F.) about 15 minutes, or until lightly browned. Makes one 9" pie.

GRAPEFRUIT PIE

4 cups grapefruit sections
1 cup firmly packed brown sugar
2 tablespoons all-purpose flour
½ teaspoon cinnamon
1 teaspoon nutmeg
1 recipe pastry for double-crust 9" pie
1 tablespoon butter or margarine

Combine grapefruit sections, sugar, flour and spices. Mix well. Roll ½ of pastry out on lightly floured surface to 1/8-inch thickness. Line 9" pan with pastry. Arrange grapefruit mixture over pastry. Dot with butter or margarine. Roll remaining pastry out to 1/8-inch thickness. Place over grapefruit mixture; seal edges and prick top. Bake in hot oven (400° F.) 35–40 minutes. Makes one 9" pie.

LEMON MERINGUE PIE

1½ cups sugar
2 tablespoons cornstarch
¼ cup all-purpose flour
1/8 teaspoon salt
2 cups boiling water
3 eggs, separated
1 teaspoon grated lemon rind
1/3 cup lemon juice
1½ tablespoons butter or margarine
1 baked 9 pastry shell
6 tablespoons sugar

Combine the 1½ cups sugar, cornstarch, flour and salt. Gradually add boiling water and cook over low heat, stirring constantly, until mixture thickens. Beat egg yolks slightly; add lemon rind and lemon juice. Add to cornstarch mixture and cook over low heat, stirring constantly, 2 minutes. Add butter or margarine and mix well. Cool slightly and turn into pastry shell. Beat egg whites until foamy. Gradually add 6 tablespoons sugar, beating constantly until stiff. Pile meringue over lemon mixture. Bake in moderate oven (350° F.) 12–15 minutes. Makes one 9" pie.

TWO-CRUST LEMON PIE

1 cup sugar
½ cup all-purpose flour
2 tablespoons cornstarch
¼ teaspoon salt
2 ¼ cups boiling water
3 eggs
½ cup sugar
½ cup lemon juice
2 teaspoons grated lemon rind
1 recipe pastry for double-crust 9" pie

Combine the 1 cup sugar, flour, cornstarch and salt. Gradually add boiling water and cook over low heat, stirring constantly, until thickened. Beat eggs with ½ cup sugar. Pour cornstarch mixture gradually over egg mixture, stirring constantly. Add lemon juice and lemon rind. Cool thoroughly. Roll ½ of pastry out on lightly floured surface. Line 9" pie pan with pastry. Pour lemon mixture over pastry. Roll remaining pastry out to 1/8-inch thickness. Place over lemon mixture. Seal edges and prick top. Bake in hot oven (400° F.) 35–40 minutes. Makes one 9" pie.

LIME MERINGUE PIE

7 tablespoons cornstarch
1/8 teaspoon salt
1½ cups sugar
2½ cups water
4 eggs, separated
2 tablespoons lemon juice
1 teaspoon grated lemon rind
½ cup lime juice
¼ cup sugar
Green food coloring
1 baked 9" pastry shell
¼ teaspoon cream of tartar
½ cup sugar

In saucepan combine cornstarch, salt and the 1½ cups sugar. Stir in water; mix until blended. Cook over low heat, stirring constantly, until thickened. Beat egg yolks slightly. Add lemon juice, lemon rind, lime juice and the ¼ cup sugar. Gradually add egg yolk mixture to cornstarch mixture and cook over low heat, stirring constantly, 2 minutes. Add enough green coloring to make mixture light green. Cool thoroughly. Pour into pastry shell. Beat egg whites until foamy. Gradually add cream of tartar and ½ cup sugar, beating constantly until stiff. Pile meringue over lime filling. Bake in hot oven (400° F.) 10 minutes. Cool thoroughly. Makes one 9" pie.

LEMON SPONGE PIE

4 eggs, separated
½ cup sugar
1/3 cup lemon juice
1 teaspoon grated lemon rind
1 tablespoon butter or margarine
2 tablespoons all-purpose flour
2 tablespoons water
1 baked 9" pastry shell

Beat egg yolks slightly; add sugar, lemon juice, lemon rind, butter or margarine, flour and water. Cook over low heat, stirring constantly, until thickened. Cool thoroughly. Beat egg whites until stiff and fold into lemon mixture. Turn into pastry shell. Broil 3 or 4 inches from source of heat 4–5 minutes or until lightly browned. Makes one 9" pie.

OPELOUSAS PECAN PIE

1/3 cup butter or margarine
2/3 cup firmly packed brown sugar
1/8 teaspoon salt
¾ cup dark corn syrup
3 eggs, well beaten
1¼ cups pecan halves
½ teaspoon vanilla
1 unbaked 8" pastry shell

Cream butter and sugar together until light and fluffy. Add salt, syrup, eggs, pecan halves and vanilla. Mix well. Turn into pastry shell. Bake in hot oven (400° F.) about 40 minutes or until firm. Makes one 8" pie.

DIXIE PERSIMMON PIE

2 cups persimmon pulp
½ cup sugar
¼ teaspoon cinnamon
1 tablespoon orange juice
1 baked 8" pastry shell
½ cup heavy cream, whipped

Combine persimmon pulp, sugar, cinnamon and orange juice. Turn into pastry shell. Spread with whipped cream. Makes one 8" pie.

FRIED GEORGIA PEACH PIES

1 recipe pastry for double-crust pie
2 cups sweetened mashed peaches
1 teaspoon grated orange rind
Fat for frying
Confectioners' sugar

Roll pastry out on lightly floured surface to 1/8-inch thickness. Cut into circles about 5 inches in diameter. Place peach mixture on pastry. Sprinkle with orange rind. Moisten edges and fold to make semicircles. Seal edges and prick tops. Fry in deep hot fat (375° F.) until light brown on all sides. Drain on absorbent paper. Sprinkle with confectioners' sugar. Serves 6.

DE SOTO PECAN PIE

3 eggs, separated
¾ cup sugar
1 tablespoon cornstarch
1/8 teaspoon salt
½ cup chopped pecans
1 cup sour cream
1 8" unbaked pastry shell
6 tablespoons sugar

Beat egg yolks well. Combine the ¾ cup sugar, cornstarch and salt. Add egg yolks and mix well. Add pecans and sour cream; mix well. Pour into pastry shell and bake in moderate oven (350° F.) 45 minutes or until set. Remove from oven. Cool. Beat egg whites until foamy. Gradually add the 6 tablespoons sugar, beating constantly until stiff. Pile meringue over pecan mixture. Bake in moderate oven (350° F.) 12–15 minutes. Makes one 8" pie.

MINCEMEAT PIE

¼ cup butter or margarine
½ cup sugar
½ cup molasses
½ teaspoon salt
2 eggs, unbeaten
1 cup prepared mincemeat
½ cup seedless raisins
½ cup chopped nuts
2 tablespoons minced orange rind
1 recipe pastry

Cream together butter and sugar and blend in molasses and salt. Add eggs one at a time, beating thoroughly after each addition. Add mincemeat, raisins, chopped nuts and orange rind. Prepare pastry, and roll out one round of dough to fit a 9" pie. Roll out remaining dough and cut into strips ¾ of an inch wide. Line pan with pastry, pour in filling and shape pastry strips into lattice on top. Bake in a hot oven (400° F.) 30 to 40 minutes. Makes one 9" pie.

NESSELRODE PIE

3 eggs, separated
1½ cups milk
1/8 teaspoon salt
2/3 cup sugar
1 envelope unflavored gelatin
¼ cup cold water
1½ tablespoons rum flavoring
½ cup chopped marashino cherries
1 baked 9" pastry shell
2 tablespoons grated sweet chocolate

Beat egg yolks slightly. Add milk, salt and 1/3 cup of the sugar. Cook over hot water, stirring constantly, until mixture thickens. Soften gelatin in water. Add to egg yolk mixture and stir until dissolved. Chill until slightly thickened. Beat egg whites until foamy. Gradually add remaining 1/3 cup sugar, beating constandy until stiff. Fold egg white mixture, rum flavoring and cherries into gelatin mixture. Turn into pastry shell. Sprinkle chocolate over filling. Chill until firm. Makes one 9" pie.

CREAMY MOCHA PIE

1 tablespoon cocoa
¾ cup sugar
5 tablespoons cornstarch
¼ teaspoon salt
1 cup evaporated milk
1 cup strong coffee
1 egg, slightly beaten
½ teaspoon vanilla
1 baked 9" pastry shell
½ cup heavy cream, whipped

Combine cocoa, sugar, cornstarch and salt. Combine milk and coffee and heat. Add to cornstarch mixture gradually, stirring constantly. Cook over boiling water until thickened, stirring frequently. Add a little of hot mixture to egg and mix well. Stir egg into hot mixture and cook 2 minutes, stirring constantly. Cool. Add vanilla. Turn into pastry shell. Spread with whipped cream. Makes one 9" pie.

ORANGE CUSTARD PIE

2 egg yolks
1 cup sour cream
1/3 cup orange juice
1 cup sugar
2 tablespoons all-purpose flour
½ teaspoon cloves
¼ teaspoon nutmeg
¼ cup raisins
1 tablespoon grated orange rind
1 unbaked 8" pastry shell

Beat egg yolks slightly; add sour cream, orange juice, sugar, flour, cloves, nutmeg, raisins and orange rind. Mix well. Turn sour cream mixture into pastry shell. Bake in moderate oven (350° F.) 45 minutes. Makes one 8" pie.

ORANGE FLUFF PIE

½ pound marshmallows
1 cup orange juice
1 tablespoon lemon juice
1 tablespoon lime juice
½ cup heavy cream, whipped
1 9" graham cracker shell
1 orange, sliced

Melt marshmallows over low heat. Fold in fruit juices. Cool thoroughly. Fold in cream. Chill until slightly thickened. Turn cream mixture into shell. Chill until firm. Garnish with orange slices. Makes one 9" pie.

LITTLE PLANTATION PIES

¾ cup rice
3 cups milk
¼ teaspoon salt
4 egg yolks
1 cup sugar
½ teaspoon ginger
1 teaspoon vanilla
¼ cup rum
1 cup heavy cream, whipped
8 individual baked tart shells

Wash rice. Heat milk, add salt and rice, and cook over low heat until rice is tender, stirring occasionally. Beat egg yolks; add sugar. Add rice. Cook over low heat 1 minute, stirring constantly. Cool. Fold in ginger, vanilla, rum and cream. Pour into shells. Makes 8 tarts.

DEEP-DISH PLUM PIE

4 cups diced plums
1 cup sugar
¼ cup all-purpose flour
¼ teaspoon salt
1 tablespoon butter or margarine
½ recipe pastry for double-crust 9" pie

Arrange plums in 9" pie pan. Combine sugar, flour and salt. Sprinkle flour mixture over plums. Dot with butter or margarine. Roll pastry out on lightly floured surface to 1/8-inch thickness. Moisten rim of pie pan. Place pastry over plum mixture. Seal edges and prick top. Bake in hot oven (400° F.) 35–40 minutes. Makes one 9" pie.

SWEET POTATO PIE

2 cups cooked, mashed sweet potatoes
3 eggs, slightly beaten
¼ cup firmly packed brown sugar
¼ teaspoon salt
1/8 teaspoon cinnamon
¼ teaspoon ginger
½ teaspoon allspice
½ cup light cream
¼ cup orange juice
1 tablespoon melted butter or margarine
1 unbaked 9" pastry shell

Combine sweet potatoes, eggs, sugar, salt, spices, cream, orange juice and butter or margarine. Turn into pastry shell; bake in hot oven (400° F.) about 45 minutes or until firm. Makes one 9" pie.

HARVEST PUMPKIN PIE

1½ cups cooked, mashed pumpkin
2 eggs, well beaten
¾ cup firmly packed brown sugar
¼ teaspoon ginger
1 teaspoon cinnamon
½ teaspoon nutmeg
¼ teaspoon salt
1½ cups milk
1 9" unbaked pastry shell

Combine pumpkin, eggs, sugar, spices, salt and milk. Mix well and pour into pastry shell. Bake in hot oven (400° F.) about 35 minutes or until firm. Makes one 9" pie.

CUSTARD PIE

4 eggs, slightly beaten
¾ cup sugar
¼ teaspoon salt
3 cups milk
½ teaspoon vanilla
1 unbaked 9" pastry shell

Combine eggs, sugar, salt, milk and vanilla. Mix well. Pour into pastry shell. Bake in hot oven (400° F.) 30–35 minutes or until firm. Makes one 9" pie.

LOUISIANA STRAWBERRY PIE

1 quart strawberries
1 cup sugar
1/3 cup quick cooking tapioca
1/8 teaspoon salt
1 package pie crust mix
1½ tablespoons butter or margarine

Wash and hull strawberries. Combine strawberries, sugar, tapioca and salt. Prepare pie crust mix according to package directions. Roll ½ of pastry out on lightly floured surface to 1/8-inch thickness. Line 9" pie pan with pastry. Pour strawberry mixture over pastry. Dot with butter or margarine. Roll remaining pastry out to 1/8-inch thickness. Arrange over strawberry mixture. Seal edges and prick top. Bake in hot oven (400° F.) 40–45 minutes. Makes one 9" pie.

STRAWBERRY CHIFFON PIE

1 envelope unflavored gelatin
¼ cup cold water
½ cup boiling water
¾ cup sugar
1 cup strawberry pulp
½ cup shredded coconut
1/8 teaspoon salt
2 egg whites
¼ cup sugar
½ cup heavy cream, whipped
1 baked 9" pastry shell

Soften gelatin in cold water; add boiling water and stir until dissolved. Cool. Add the ¾ cup sugar, strawberry pulp, coconut and salt. Chill until mixture begins to thicken. Beat egg whites until foamy. Gradually add the ¼ cup sugar, beating constantly until stiff. Fold egg white mixture and cream into strawberry mixture. Turn into pastry shell. Chill until firm. Serve with whipped cream, if desired. Makes one 9" pie.

GLAZED STRAWBERRY PIE

¼ cup cornstarch
1¼ cups sugar
½ cup cold water
1 cup boiling water
⅛ teaspoon salt
2 tablespoons lemon juice
Red food coloring
1 quart strawberries
1 baked 9" pastry shell

Combine cornstarch and sugar. Add cold water and mix well. Add boiling water and cook over low heat, stirring constantly, until mixture is thickened. Add salt, lemon juice and enough food coloring to make mixture a light red. Add strawberries and mix lightly. Cool thoroughly. Turn into pastry shell. Garnish with whipped cream, if desired. Makes one 9" pie.

DIXIE RAISIN PIE

1 cup seeded raisins
1 cup sour cream
¾ cup sugar
¼ teaspoon salt
2 tablespoons lime juice
½ teaspoon ginger
¼ teaspoon allspice
¼ teaspoon nutmeg
2 eggs, well beaten
1 recipe pastry for double-crust 9" pie

Combine raisins, cream, sugar, salt, lime juice, spices and eggs. Mix well. Roll ½ of pastry out on lightly floured surface to ⅛-inch thickness. Line 9" pie pan with pastry. Add raisin mixture. Roll remaining pastry to ⅛-inch thickness. Arrange over raisin mixture. Seal edges; prick top. Bake in hot oven (400° F.) 35–40 minutes. Makes one 9" pie.

TREE OF MUSIC PIE

1 recipe pastry for double-crust 9" pie
3 cups elderberries
½ cup sugar
⅛ teaspoon salt
2 tablespoons all-purpose flour
1 tablespoon butter or margarine

Roll ½ of pastry out on lightly floured surface to ⅛-inch thickness. Line 9" pie pan with pastry. Arrange elderberries over pastry. Combine sugar, salt and flour; sprinkle over elderberries. Dot with butter or margarine. Roll remaining pastry out to ⅛-inch thickness. Cut into strips ¼-inch wide. Arrange pastry strips over elderberry mixture, lattice fashion. Bake in hot oven (400° F.) about 35 minutes. Makes one 9" pie.

THREE FRUIT PIE

1 recipe pastry for double-crust 9" pie
2 cups fresh strawberries
1 cup diced fresh rhubarb
1 cup diced fresh pineapple
¾ cup sugar
2½ tablespoons minute tapioca
1 teaspoon grated lemon rind

Roll one-half of pastry out on lightly floured surface to ⅛-inch thickness. Line 9" pie pan with pastry. Combine fruits, sugar, tapioca and lemon rind. Arrange over pastry. Roll remaining pastry out to ⅛-inch thickness and arrange over fruit. Seal edges and prick top. Bake in hot oven (400° F.) 45–50 minutes. Makes one 9" pie.

RASPBERRY-CHEESE PIE

1 cup sugar
¼ cup cornstarch
⅛ teaspoon salt
½ cup water
2 cups raspberries
1 9" graham cracker shell
1 8-ounce package cream cheese, softened
1 cup heavy cream, whipped

Combine sugar, cornstarch and salt. Gradually add water and cook, stirring constantly, until thickened. Add raspberries and mix lightly. Cool thoroughly. Dot bottom of graham cracker shell with cream cheese. Pour raspberry mixture over cheese. Chill thoroughly. Top with cream to serve. Makes one 9" pie.

RHUBARB CUSTARD PIE

1 package frozen rhubarb
2 eggs
¾ cup sugar
2 tablespoons all-purpose flour
1 recipe pastry for double-crust 9" pie
1½ tablespoons butter or margarine

Thaw rhubarb; beat eggs slightly and add sugar and flour. Add rhubarb and mix well. Roll ½ of pastry out on lightly floured surface to ⅛-inch thickness. Line 9" pie pan with pastry. Pour rhubarb mixture over pastry. Dot with butter or margarine. Roll remaining pastry out to 1/8-inch thickness. Place over rhubarb mixture. Seal edges and prick top. Bake in moderate oven (375° F.) 50–60 minutes. Makes one 9" pie.

SHOO FLY PIE

¾ **cup dark molasses**
¾ **cup boiling water**
½ **teaspoon baking soda**
1½ **cups sifted all-purpose flour**
½ **cup brown sugar, firmly packed**
¼ **cup butter or margarine**
1 **unbaked 9" or 10" pastry shell**

Combine molasses, water and baking soda. Combine flour and sugar; cut in butter or margarine. In pastry shell, alternate layers of molasses mixture and flour mixture starting with molasses layer and ending with flour layer. Bake in moderate oven (375° F.) about 30 minutes. Makes one 9" or 10" pie.

RASPBERRY CREAM PIE

1 **package raspberry flavored gelatin**
1¼ **cups boiling water**
¾ **cup sugar**
1½ **cups raspberries**
½ **cup heavy cream, whipped**
1 **baked 8" pastry shell**

Dissolve gelatin in water. Add sugar and raspberries. Chill until slightly thickened. Fold in cream. Pour into pastry shell and chill until firm. Makes one 8" pie.

Cookies

ROLLED COOKIES

PINWHEEL COOKIES

2 cups sifted all-purpose flour
½ teaspoon baking powder
¼ teaspoon salt
½ teaspoon cinnamon
¼ teaspoon cloves
½ cup shortening
1 cup firmly packed brown sugar
1 egg
1 teaspoon vanilla
1 8-ounce package figs, finely chopped
½ cup granulated sugar
½ cup water
1 teaspoon grated orange rind
¼ cup chopped nuts

Sift flour, baking powder, salt and spices together. Cream shortening and brown sugar together until light and fluffy. Add egg and vanilla and mix well. Gradually add sifted ingredients and mix well. Roll out on lightly floured surface into a rectangle ¼" thick. Combine figs, granulated sugar, water and orange rind. Cook over medium heat, stirring constantly until thickened. Cool thoroughly. Add nuts. Spread fig mixture over dough and roll up jelly roll fashion. Wrap in waxed paper and chill thoroughly. Cut into slices ¼" thick. Place on greased baking sheets. Bake in moderate oven (375° F.) about 12 minutes. Makes 36–48.

ALMOND CRESCENTS ESPAÑA

½ cup butter or margarine
½ cup sugar
1/8 teaspoon salt
2 egg yolks
1/3 cup finely chopped blanched almonds
1 cup sifted all-purpose flour
1 egg white
1 teaspoon water

Cream butter or margarine and sugar together until light and fluffy. Add salt and egg yolks; beat well. Add almonds and mix well. Gradually blend in flour and mix thoroughly. Chill thoroughly. Roll out on lightly floured surface to 1/8-inch thickness. Cut with floured crescent-shaped cutter. Place on greased baking sheets. Beat egg white with water until frothy. Brush egg-white mixture over cookies. Bake in moderate oven (375° F.) 10–12 minutes. Makes about 18.

MOLASSES CHRISTMAS SNAPS

½ cup shortening
½ cup peanut butter
2/3 cup sugar
½ cup molasses
1/3 cup pineapple juice
3 cups sifted all-purpose flour
1 teaspoon baking soda
1½ teaspoons cinnamon
¼ teaspoon nutmeg
¼ teaspoon salt

Cream shortening, peanut butter and sugar together until light and fluffy. Add molasses and pineapple juice; beat well. Sift flour, baking soda, cinnamon, nutmeg and salt together. Add to molasses mixture and mix well. Roll out to 1/8-inch thickness on lightly floured surface. Cut with floured cutter; place on greased baking sheets. Bake in moderate oven (350° F.) 10–12 minutes. Makes about 48.

VIENNESE CARAWAY SEED COOKIES

1 cup shortening
1 cup sugar
2 eggs
1 tablespoon light cream
1 tablespoon grated lemon rind
1 teaspoon caraway seeds
3 cups sifted cake flour
¼ teaspoon salt
¼ teaspoon baking soda
½ teaspoon ginger

Cream shortening and sugar until light and fluffy. Add eggs; beat well. Add cream, lemon rind and caraway seeds. Mix well. Sift remaining ingredients together and blend into creamed mixture. Chill several hours. Roll dough out on lightly floured surface to ¼-inch thickness. Cut with floured cutter and place on greased baking sheets. Bake in hot oven (400° F.) 10-12 minutes. Makes about 40.

TRUE GINGER SNAPS

1 cup shortening
1 cup molasses
1 egg
½ teaspoon lemon extract
4½ cups sifted all-purpose flour
4 teaspoons ginger
1 teaspoon baking soda
½ teaspoon salt

Melt shortening and cool. Add molasses, egg and lemon extract. Beat well. Sift flour, ginger, baking soda and salt together. Add to molasses mixture and mix thoroughly. Chill. Roll out on lightly floured surface to 1/8-inch thickness. Cut with floured cutter and place on greased baking sheets. Bake in moderate oven (375° F.) about 12 minutes. Makes about 48.

CHINESE ALMOND COOKIES

1¼ cups sifted cake flour
1/3 cup sugar
1/8 teaspoon salt
1 teaspoon baking powder
½ cup shortening
1 egg
1 teaspoon almond flavoring
Blanched almonds

Sift flour, sugar, salt and baking powder together. Cut in shortening. Add egg and almond flavoring.

Mix well. Knead until smooth on lightly floured surface. Chill 1 hour. Roll out to ¼-inch thickness on lightly floured surface. Cut with 2" cutter. Place on greased baking sheets. Top each cooky with an almond. Bake in moderate oven (350° F.) about 20 minutes. Makes about 18.

ABERDEEN SHORTBREAD

2 cups butter or margarine
1 cup sugar
3 cups sifted all-purpose flour

Cream butter or margarine until light and fluffy. Gradually add sugar and beat well. Gradually add flour and mix until dough is smooth. Roll out on lightly floured surface to ¼-inch thickness. Cut with floured cutter. Place on ungreased baking sheets. Pierce cookies well with tines of fork. Bake in moderate oven (350°) 15-20 minutes. Makes about 48.

KRINGLES

2 cups sifted all-purpose flour
2 teaspoons baking powder
¼ teaspoon salt
½ cup butter or margarine
1 cup granulated sugar
1 egg, well beaten
2 teaspoons caraway seeds
3 tablespoons brandy
1/3 cup confectioners' sugar

Sift flour, baking powder and salt together. Cream butter or margarine and granulated sugar until light and fluffy. Add egg, caraway seeds and brandy; beat well. Gradually add sifted ingredients and blend thoroughly. Chill. Roll out on lightly floured surface to 1/8-inch thickness. Cut with floured cutter. Place on ungreased baking sheets and sprinkle with confectioners' sugar. Bake in moderate oven (375° F.) 12-15 minutes. Makes about 48.

SUGAR COOKIES

1½ cups sifted all-purpose flour
½ teaspoon baking powder
¼ teaspoon salt
½ teaspoon baking soda
½ cup sugar
½ cup butter or margarine
1 egg
2 tablespoons milk
1 teaspoon vanilla

Sift flour, baking powder, salt, baking soda and sugar together. Cut in butter or margarine until mixture resembles coarse meal. Add egg, milk and vanilla; mix well. Roll out on lightly floured surface to 1/16"inch thickness. Cut as desired. Place on ungreased baking sheets. Bake in hot oven (400° F.) about 8 minutes. Makes about 60.

RASPBERRY JAMBOREES

1 cup butter or margarine
1 8-ounce package cream cheese
1½ cups sifted all-purpose flour
1/8 teaspoon salt
½ cup raspberry jam (approx.)

Cream butter or margarine, and cheese. Gradually add flour and salt. Chill several hours. Roll out on lightly floured surface to 1/8-inch thickness. Cut in 4" squares. Place 1 teaspoon jam in center. Fold corners over to center. Place on greased baking sheets. Bake in hot oven (400° F.) 10 minutes. Makes about 24.

DROP COOKIES

ENGLISH BRANDY SNAPS

¾ cup butter or margarine
¾ cup sugar
½ cup molasses
1½ cups sifted all-purpose flour
2½ teaspoons ginger

Combine butter or margarine, sugar and molasses. Cook over low heat, stirring constantly, until ingredients are well blended. Remove from heat. Add flour and ginger. Beat until smooth. Drop by teaspoonfuls onto greased baking sheets 2 inches apart. Bake in slow oven (300° F.) 10-12 minutes. Let stand a minute, then quickly remove cookies from sheet and roll into cone shapes. Makes about 48.

SOUTH PACIFIC ALMOND COOKIES

1 cup sifted all-purpose flour
1 teaspoon baking powder
¼ teaspoon salt
½ cup butter or margarine

2/3 cup sugar
2 egg whites
¼ teaspoon vanilla
¼ teaspoon almond extract
2/3 cup shredded coconut

Sift flour, baking powder and salt together. Cream butter or margarine and sugar together until light and fluffy. Add egg whites, vanilla and almond extract. Beat well. Add coconut and mix well. Blend in sifted ingredients and mix until thoroughly blended. Drop by teaspoonfuls onto greased baking sheets. Bake in moderate oven (375° F.) 12 minutes. Makes about 36.

APPLESAUCE DROPS

1¾ cups sifted all-purpose flour
1 teaspoon baking powder
½ teaspoon salt
½ teaspoon cinnamon
½ teaspoon cloves
½ teaspoon nutmeg
¾ cup shortening
1 cup sugar
1 egg
1 cup applesauce
2/3 cup raisins
1 cup corn flakes

Sift flour, baking powder, salt and spices together. Cream shortening and sugar until light and fluffy. Add egg and beat well. Add sifted ingredients and applesauce alternately to creamed mixture, beating well after each addition. Fold in raisins and corn flakes. Drop by teaspoonfuls 2 inches apart onto greased baking sheets. Bake in hot oven (400° F.) 12-15 minutes. Makes about 48.

BANANA COOKIES

2¼ cups sifted all-purpose flour
1 cup sugar
2 teaspoons baking powder
¼ teaspoon baking soda
¼ teaspoon salt
2/3 cup shortening
2 eggs
1 cup mashed banana
1 teaspoon vanilla
¼ teaspoon nutmeg
1 tablespoon sugar

Sift flour, the one cup sugar, baking powder, baking soda and salt together. Cut in shortening.

Add eggs, bananas and vanilla. Beat well. Drop by teaspoonfuls 2 inches apart onto ungreased baking sheets. Combine nutmeg and the one tablespoon sugar. Top each cookie with nutmeg mixture. Bake in hot oven (400° F.) 10–12 minutes. Remove from baking sheets immediately. Makes about 36.

CHOCOLATE MACAROON DROPS

¼ teaspoon salt
2 egg whites
1 cup sifted confectioners' sugar
¼ teaspoon vanilla
¾ cup shredded coconut
2 cups corn flakes
1 6-ounce package semi-sweet chocolate
  morsels

Add salt to egg whites and beat until frothy. Add sugar gradually and beat until stiff and shiny. Beat in vanilla. Fold in coconut, corn flakes and chocolate morsels. Drop by teaspoonfuls onto well-greased baking sheets. Bake in moderate oven (350° F.) 20 minutes. Makes about 2½ dozen cookies.

CHOCOLATE CHIP COOKIES

½ cup shortening
½ cup granulated sugar
¼ cup firmly packed brown sugar
1 egg, well beaten
1 cup sifted all-purpose flour
¼ teaspoon salt
½ teaspoon baking soda
1 package semi-sweet chocolate pieces
½ cup chopped nuts
1 teaspoon vanilla

Cream shortening and sugars together until light and fluffy. Add egg and beat well. Sift flour, salt and baking soda together. Blend sifted ingredients into creamed mixture. Add remaining ingredients and mix well. Drop by teaspoonfuls onto greased baking sheets 2 inches apart. Bake in moderate oven (350° F.) 10–12 minutes. Makes about 48.

CHOCOLATE COCONUT FLIPS

2 squares unsweetened chocolate
¼ cup water
¾ cup sugar
1½ cups shredded coconut
1 tablespoon all-purpose flour
1/8 teaspoon salt
½ teaspoon vanilla
3 egg whites, stiffly beaten

Combine chocolate and water. Cook over low heat, stirring constantly, until mixture is smooth. Remove from heat and add sugar and coconut; mix well. Stir in flour, salt and vanilla. Fold in egg whites. Drop by teaspoonfuls 2 inches apart onto greased baking sheets. Bake in moderate oven (350° F.) 12–15 minutes. Makes about 24.

CHOCOLATE DROPS

½ cup butter or margarine
¾ cup sugar
1 square unsweetened chocolate, melted
1 egg, slightly beaten
1 teaspoon vanilla
1¼ cups sifted cake flour
½ teaspoon baking powder
1/8 teaspoon salt

Cream butter or margarine and sugar until light and fluffy. Add chocolate, egg and vanilla. Beat well. Sift remaining ingredients together and blend into chocolate mixture. Drop by teaspoonfuls 2 inches apart onto greased baking sheets. Bake in moderate oven (375° F.) about 15 minutes. Makes about 24.

HERMITS

2 cups sifted cake flour
2 teaspoons baking powder
1/8 teaspoon salt
½ teaspoon nutmeg
1 teaspoon cinnamon
½ teaspoon mace
1/8 cup shortening
½ cup granulated sugar
½ cup firmly packed brown sugar
2 eggs, well beaten
1 cup raisins
¾ cup chopped walnuts

Sift flour, baking powder, salt and spices together. Cream shortening, granulated sugar and brown sugar until light and fluffy. Add eggs and beat well. Add raisins and walnuts; mix well. Gradually add sifted ingredients, blending well. Drop by teaspoonfuls onto greased baking sheets. Bake in moderate oven (350° F.) about 15 minutes. Makes about 24.

CHOCOLATE MOLASSES COOKIES

1 cup shortening
1 cup firmly packed brown sugar
3 eggs
½ cup molasses
2½ cups sifted all-purpose flour
3 teaspoons baking powder
¼ teaspoon salt
1½ teaspoons cinnamon
¼ teaspoon nutmeg
¼ teaspoon baking soda
½ cup milk
1 cup shredded coconut
1 cup semi-sweet chocolate pieces

Cream together shortening and sugar; add eggs, 1 at a time, beating after each addition. Add molasses and beat well. Sift flour, baking powder, salt, cinnamon, nutmeg and baking soda together. Add sifted ingredients alternately with milk, beating well after each addition. Add coconut and chocolate. Drop by teaspoonfuls onto greased baking sheets. Bake in hot oven (400° F.) about 10 minutes. Makes about 48.

COCONUT-ORANGE DROPS

1 cup butter
½ cup sugar
1 egg
1 teaspoon grated orange rind
2 cups sifted all-purpose flour
1/8 teaspoon salt
¾ cup shredded coconut

Cream butter with sugar until light and fluffy. Add egg and beat well. Add rind and mix well. Sift flour and salt together. Gradually add sifted ingredients to creamed mixture, beating well after each addition. Add coconut and mix well. Drop by teaspoonfuls onto ungreased baking sheets. Bake in moderate slow oven (325° F.) 12–15 minutes. Makes 60.

OLD-TIME GINGER COOKIES

1 cup shortening
1 cup sugar
1 egg
2 cups molasses
2 tablespoons vinegar
7 cups sifted all-purpose flour
2 tablespoons ginger
1 teaspoon allspice
½ teaspoon cloves
¼ teaspoon nutmeg
4 teaspoons baking soda
½ teaspoon salt
1 cup boiling water

Cream shortening and sugar together until light and fluffy. Add egg and beat well. Add molasses and vinegar; mix well. Sift flour, spices, baking soda and salt together. Add to creamed mixture and mix well. Add water and mix well. Drop by teaspoonfuls onto greased baking sheets. Bake in moderate oven (350° F.) 8–10 minutes. Makes about 96.

SOUR CREAM NUTMEG COOKIES

2 cups sifted all-purpose flour
1 teaspoon nutmeg
½ teaspoon baking soda
2 teaspoons baking powder
¼ teaspoon salt
½ cup shortening
1 cup sugar
1 egg
½ cup sour cream
½ cup chopped walnuts

Sift flour, nutmeg, baking soda, baking powder and salt together. Cream shortening and sugar until light and fluffy. Add egg and beat well. Add sour cream and sifted ingredients alternately, beating well after each addition. Add walnuts. Drop by teaspoonfuls 2 inches apart onto well-greased baking sheets. Bake in moderate oven (375° F.) 10–12 minutes. Makes about 36.

LONDON LACE COOKIES

1 cup sifted all-purpose flour
1 cup finely chopped walnuts
½ cup light corn syrup
½ cup butter or margarine
2/3 cup firmly packed brown sugar

Combine flour and nuts. Combine syrup, butter or margarine and sugar. Cook over medium heat, stirring constantly, until mixture boils. Remove from heat and add flour mixture, and mix well. Drop by teaspoonfuls 3 inches apart onto greased baking sheets. Bake in slow oven (325° F.) 8–10 minutes. Cool 1 minute. Remove from baking sheet and roll around handle of wooden spoon to shape into cone. Makes about 60.

MARMALADE MUNCHES

3 cups sifted cake flour
½ teaspoon baking soda
¼ teaspoon salt
½ cup shortening
1 cup sugar
2 eggs, well beaten
2/3 cup orange marmalade

Sift flour, baking soda and salt together. Cream shortening with sugar until light and fluffy. Add eggs and beat well. Gradually blend in sifted ingredients. Add marmalade and mix well. Drop by teaspoonfuls 2 inches apart onto greased baking sheets. Bake in moderate oven (350° F.) 10–12 minutes. Remove from baking sheets immediately. Makes about 42.

SPICY NUT DROPS

¾ cup butter or margarine
¾ cup molasses
2 eggs
2 ¼ cups sifted all-purpose flour
3 teaspoons baking powder
¼ teaspoon salt
½ teaspoon nutmeg
1 teaspoon cinnamon
¼ teaspoon cloves
½ teaspoon baking soda
½ cup milk
½ cup chopped pecans

Melt butter or margarine. Add molasses and eggs and beat well. Sift flour, baking powder, salt, spices and baking soda together. Add sifted ingredients alternately with milk to molasses mixture, beating well after each addition. Add pecans. Drop by teaspoonfuls onto greased baking sheets. Bake in hot oven (400° F.) about 10 minutes. Makes about 48.

GOOBER COOKIES

1 egg, well beaten
¾ cup firmly packed brown sugar
1¼ cups sifted all-purpose flour
½ teaspoon baking soda
¼ teaspoon salt
½ cup cooking oil
1 teaspoon vanilla
¾ cup chopped peanuts

Combine egg and sugar and beat well. Sift flour, baking soda and salt together. Add sifted

ingredients alternately with oil to egg mixture, beating well after each addition. Add vanilla and peanuts; mix well. Drop by teaspoonfuls onto greased baking sheets. Bake in moderate oven (375° F.) 8–10 minutes. Makes about 36.

PECAN NUT KISSES

2 egg whites
1¼ cups firmly packed brown sugar
1/8 teaspoon salt
1 teaspoon vanilla
1¼ cups finely chopped pecans

Beat egg whites until frothy. Gradually add sugar, beating constantly until stiff. Fold in remaining ingredients. Drop by teaspoonfuls onto greased baking sheets. Bake in moderate oven (350° F.) 12–15 minutes. Makes about 24.

PINEAPPLE DROPS

½ cup shortening
1 cup firmly packed brown sugar
1 egg
¾ cup canned crushed pineapple, not drained
2 cups sifted all-purpose flour
¼ teaspoon baking soda
1 teaspoon baking powder
1/8 teaspoon salt
½ cup chopped pecans
½ teaspoon vanilla

Cream shortening with sugar until light and fluffy. Add egg and beat well. Add pineapple and mix well. Sift flour, baking soda, baking powder and salt together. Add sifted ingredients gradually to creamed mixture, beating well after each addition. Add pecans and vanilla; beat well. Drop by teaspoonfuls onto greased baking sheets. Bake in moderate oven (375° F.) 12–15 minutes. Makes about 48.

CARAMEL PECAN COOKIES

1½ cups sifted all-purpose flour
¼ teaspoon salt
½ cup shortening
½ cup firmly packed brown sugar
½ cup light corn syrup
1 egg
½ teaspoon vanilla
Pecan halves

Sift flour and salt together; cream shortening and sugar together until light and fluffy. Add syrup and beat well. Add egg and vanilla; beat well. Gradually blend in sifted ingredients. Drop by teaspoonfuls onto greased baking sheets. Top with pecan halves. Bake in hot oven (400° F.) 8–10 minutes. Makes about 48.

SCOTCH OATMEAL COOKIES

1¾ cups sifted all-purpose flour
½ teaspoon baking soda
½ teaspoon salt
½ teaspoon cinnamon
¼ teaspoon nutmeg
¼ teaspoon cloves
¾ cup shortening
½ cup granulated sugar
1 cup firmly packed brown sugar
1 egg
½ cup buttermilk
¼ cup light corn syrup
½ teaspoon vanilla
2 cups rolled oats
1 cup chopped nuts
½ cup raisins

Sift flour, baking soda, salt and spices together. Cream shortening and sugars until light and fluffy. Add egg and beat well. Combine buttermilk, syrup and vanilla. Add buttermilk mixture and sifted ingredients alternately to creamed mixture, beating well after each addition. Add oats, nuts and raisins; mix well. Drop by tablespoonfuls 2 inches apart onto greased baking sheets. Bake in moderate oven (375° F.) about 15 minutes. Makes about 48.

PEANUT COCONUT COOKIES

½ cup peanut butter
1 teaspoon orange juice
1/8 teaspoon salt
1 1/3 cups sweetened condensed milk
1½ cups shredded coconut
½ cup chopped dates
½ cup chopped peanuts

Combine peanut butter, orange juice and salt. Mix well. Add remaining ingredients and mix until thoroughly blended. Drop by teaspoonfuls onto greased baking sheets. Bake in moderate oven (375° F.) 10–12 minutes. Makes about 24.

MOLDED COOKIES

MALUCCA CINNAMON ROUNDS

½ cup butter or margarine
1 cup sugar
1 egg, well beaten
½ teaspoon vanilla
1¼ cups sifted all-purpose flour
1 teaspoon baking powder
¼ teaspoon salt
½ cup chopped peanuts
2½ teaspoons cinnamon

Cream butter or margarine and sugar together until light and fluffy. Add egg and vanilla; mix well. Sift flour, baking powder and salt together. Blend sifted ingredients into creamed mixture. Combine peanuts and cinnamon. Shape dough into balls about ½" in diameter. Roll each ball in peanut mixture. Place 2 inches apart on greased baking sheets. Bake in moderate oven (375° F.) about 15 minutes. Remove from baking sheets immediately. Makes about 24.

CORNMEAL COOKIES

3 cups sifted all-purpose flour
1 teaspoon baking powder
½ teaspoon salt
1 cup yellow cornmeal
1 cup butter
1½ cups sugar
2 eggs
¼ cup pineapple juice
½ teaspoon grated lemon rind
1 tablespoon orange juice

Sift flour, baking powder and salt together. Add cornmeal and mix lightly. Cream butter with sugar until fluffy, add eggs and beat well. Add pineapple juice, lemon rind and orange juice. Blend in cornmeal mixture. Shape dough into 1" balls and place on greased baking sheets. Flatten with tines of fork. Bake in moderate oven (375° F.) 12–15 minutes. Makes about 60.

BRAZIL NUT COOKIES

1¾ cups sifted all-purpose flour
½ teaspoon baking powder
¼ teaspoon salt
½ cup shortening

¾ cup sugar
1/3 cup ground Brazil nuts
2 eggs, well beaten
½ teaspoon vanilla

Sift flour, baking powder and salt together. Cream shortening and sugar together until light and fluffy. Add nuts, eggs and vanilla. Beat well. Add sifted ingredients and mix thoroughly. Chill. Shape into small balls and place on greased baking sheets. Bake in hot oven (400° F.) 12–15 minutes. Makes about 36.

LADY FINGERS

½ cup sifted cake flour
1/8 teaspoon salt
1/3 cup confectioners' sugar
3 eggs, separated
1/3 cup confectioners' sugar
¼ teaspoon vanilla

Sift flour, salt and 1/3 cup confectioners' sugar. Beat egg whites until foamy. Gradually add remaining 1/3 cup sugar and beat until stiff. Beat egg yolks until thick and lemon colored. Fold egg yolks and vanilla into egg-white mixture. Gradually fold flour mixture into egg-white mixture. Press through pastry bag onto ungreased baking sheets in 4" x 1" strips. Bake in moderate oven (350° F.) about 12 minutes. Makes about 24.

PEANUT BUTTER PLOPS

½ cup shortening
½ cup peanut butter
1½ cups firmly packed brown sugar
½ cup granulated sugar
1 teaspoon vanilla
1 egg
1½ cups sifted all-purpose flour
1 teaspoon baking soda
½ teaspoon salt

Cream shortening, peanut butter and sugars together until light and fluffy. Add vanilla and egg; beat well. Sift flour, baking soda and salt together. Blend into creamed mixture. Shape into 1" balls. Place on greased baking sheets 2 inches apart. Flatten with tines of fork. Bake in moderate oven (375° F.) 10–12 minutes. Makes about 48.

PENNSYLVANIA DUTCH PFEFFERNUSSE

4½ cups sifted all-purpose flour
¼ teaspoon baking soda
1 teaspoon cloves
½ teaspoon nutmeg
¼ teaspoon cinnamon
½ teaspoon salt
¼ teaspoon black pepper
1½ teaspoons anise seed
4 eggs, slightly beaten
2 cups firmly packed brown sugar
Confectioners' sugar

Sift flour, baking soda, spices, salt and pepper together. Add anise seed. Combine eggs and brown sugar. Add sifted ingredients and mix well. Chill thoroughly. Shape into balls and place on greased baking sheets. Cover and let stand at room temperature several hours. Bake in moderate oven (350° F.) 20-25 minutes. Roll in confectioners' sugar while warm. Makes about 48.

SANTA CLAUS COOKIES

2 cups sifted all-purpose flour
¼ teaspoon salt
1 cup butter or margarine
½ cup confectioners' sugar
2 teaspoons vanilla
1 teaspoon almond extract
½ cup chopped nuts

Sift flour and salt together. Cream butter or margarine, and sugar until light and fluffy. Add vanilla, almond extract and nuts; beat well. Gradually add sifted ingredients and blend well. Shape into small balls and place on ungreased baking sheets. Bake in slow oven (325° F.) about 25 minutes. Makes about 40.

SPRINGERLE

3¾ cups sifted all-purpose flour
¼ teaspoon salt
4 eggs
2 cups sugar
Anise seed

Sift flour and salt together. Beat eggs until thick and lemon colored. Gradually add sugar and continue beating 15 minutes. Fold sifted ingredients into egg mixture. Roll out on lightly floured surface into a rectangle ½" thick. Press springerle board well into dough. Cut cookies. Sprinkle anise seed lightly over ungreased baking sheets. Place cookies on baking sheets. Cover and allow to dry several hours. Bake in moderate oven (375° F.) 5 minutes. Reduce heat, bake in slow oven (300° F.) 25 minutes. Store in airtight container at least 2 weeks before using. Makes about 60.

SPRITZ

1 cup butter
½ cup sugar
1 egg
½ teaspoon salt
½ teaspoon almond extract
2½ cups sifted all-purpose flour

Cream butter and sugar until light and fluffy. Add egg, salt and almond extract; beat well. Gradually blend in flour and mix well. Shape as desired with cookie press. Place on greased baking sheets. Bake in hot oven (400° F.) 8–10 minutes. Makes about 72.

BAR COOKIES

HONDURAS BANANA BARS

½ cup shortening
1 cup sugar
2 eggs, well beaten
½ teaspoon vanilla
1 ¾ cups sifted cake flour
2 teaspoons baking powder
¼ teaspoon salt
1 cup mashed bananas

Cream shortening and sugar together until light and fluffy. Add eggs and vanilla and beat well. Sift flour, baking powder and salt together. Add sifted ingredients alternately with bananas to creamed mixture, beating well after each addition. Turn into greased 9" x 13" pan. Bake in moderate oven (350° F.) 25–30 minutes. Cool and cut into bars. Makes about 24.

CINNAMON CRISPS

1 cup sifted all-purpose flour
1/8 teaspoon salt
¼ teaspoon cinnamon
1/3 cup butter or margarine
½ cup sugar
1 egg, separated
2 tablespoons milk
¼ teaspoon vanilla
3 tablespoons sugar
¼ teaspoon cinnamon
1/3 cup chopped nuts

Sift flour, salt and ¼ teaspoon cinnamon together. Cream butter or margarine, and ½ cup sugar together until light and fluffy. Add egg yolk, milk and vanilla. Beat well. Add sifted ingredients and beat thoroughly. Spread in ungreased 7" x 11" pan. Beat egg white lightly and spread over dough. Combine three tablespoons sugar, ¼ teaspoon cinnamon and nuts; sprinkle over egg white. Bake in moderate oven (350° F.) 25–30 minutes. Cut into bars while warm. Makes about 24.

CHOCOLATE-CHIP HONEY SQUARES

½ cup sifted all-purpose flour
¼ teaspoon baking soda
¼ teaspoon salt
1/3 cup honey
1 egg, well beaten
1 tablespoon melted butter
1 package semi-sweet chocolate pieces
¾ cup chopped nuts
1 teaspoon vanilla

Sift flour, baking soda and salt together. Combine honey and egg; mix well. Add butter, chocolate, nuts and vanilla. Mix well. Add sifted ingredients and beat thoroughly. Turn into greased 8" x 8" pan. Bake in moderate oven (350° F.) 30–35 minutes. Cut into squares. Makes about 24.

COCONUT DREAMS

½ cup shortening
¼ teaspoon salt
½ cup firmly packed brown sugar
1 cup sifted cake flour
1 cup brown sugar, firmly packed
1 teaspoon vanilla
2 eggs
2 tablespoons cake flour

½ teaspoon baking powder
1/8 teaspoon salt
1 cup shredded coconut
½ cup chopped walnuts

Cream shortening, salt and ½ cup brown sugar until light and fluffy. Gradually mix in 1 cup cake flour. Press evenly into 8" x 8" pan. Bake in hot oven (425° F.) 8 minutes. Remove from oven and reduce heat to 350° F. Mix 1 cup brown sugar, vanilla and eggs. Stir in remaining ingredients. Spread mixture over first mixture. Continue baking in moderate oven (350° F.) 15 minutes. Cut into bars while still warm. Makes about 16.

PECAN STICKS

3 eggs, separated
¾ cups sugar
¾ teaspoon vanilla
¼ cup sifted all-purpose flour
¾ cup finely chopped pecans

Beat egg yolks until thick and lemon colored. Gradually beat in sugar. Add vanilla and mix well. Fold in flour and pecans. Beat egg whites until stiff and fold into pecan mixture. Turn into greased 12" x 9" pan. Bake in moderate oven (350° F.) 25–30 minutes. Cut into 4" x 1" bars. Makes about 36.

COCONUT-PUMPKIN SQUARES

2 cups sifted all-purpose flour
1 teaspoon baking powder
¼ teaspoon baking soda
½ teaspoon salt
1 teaspoon cinnamon
¾ teaspoon nutmeg
½ cup shortening
1 cup firmly packed brown sugar
1 egg
¾ cup canned pumpkin
2 tablespoons molasses
½ teaspoon vanilla
½ cup shredded coconut

Sift flour, baking powder, baking soda, salt and spices together. Cream shortening and sugar together until light and fluffy. Add egg, pumpkin, molasses and vanilla. Beat well. Gradually add sifted ingredients and beat well. Blend in coconut. Turn into greased 15" x 10" pan. Bake in moderate oven (350° F.) 25–30 minutes. Makes about 36.

REFRIGERATOR COOKIES

FILBERT COOKIES

1¼ cups sifted all-purpose flour
1/3 cup sugar
¼ teaspoon ginger
½ cup butter or margarine
1 egg white
½ cup filberts

Sift flour, sugar and ginger together. Cut in butter or margarine. Add egg white and mix until dough is smooth. Add filberts and mix well. Shape into a roll about 1½" in diameter. Chill 3 hours. Cut into slices ¼" thick. Place on greased baking sheet. Bake in moderate oven, (350° F.) 12–15 minutes. Makes about 36.

MOLASSES RINGS

½ cup molasses
½ cup shortening
½ cup sugar
1 egg
2½ cups sifted all-purpose flour
¼ teaspoon salt
¼ teaspoon baking soda
1/8 teaspoon allspice
¼ teaspoon nutmeg
½ teaspoon ginger

Combine molasses and shortening. Cook over low heat until shortening melts. Remove from heat and add sugar. Cool. Add egg and beat well. Sift flour, salt, baking soda and spices together; add molasses mixture and mix well. Shape into rolls 2" in diameter. Wrap in waxed paper and chill thoroughly. Cut into slices 1/8" thick and place on greased baking sheets. Bake in moderate oven (350° F.) 12–15 minutes. Makes about 60.

BUTTERSCOTCH COOKIES

½ cups sifted all-purpose flour
1½ teaspoons baking powder
¼ teaspoon salt
½ cup shortening
1¼ cups firmly packed brown sugar
1 egg
½ teaspoon vanilla

Sift flour, baking powder and salt together. Cream shortening and sugar until light and fluffy. Add egg and vanilla and beat well. Gradually add sifted ingredients and mix well. Shape into rolls 2" in diameter and wrap in waxed paper. Chill thoroughly. Cut into slices 1/8" thick. Place on ungreased baking sheets. Bake in hot oven (400° F.) 8–10 minutes. Makes about 50.

BUTTERSCOTCH BITES

1 cup shortening
2 cups firmly packed brown sugar
1 teaspoon vanilla
2 eggs
3½ cups sifted all-purpose flour
½ teaspoon salt
1 teaspoon baking soda
¾ cup chopped nuts

Cream shortening and sugar together until light and fluffy. Add vanilla and beat well. Add eggs and mix well. Sift flour, salt and baking soda together. Add sifted ingredients to creamed mixture and mix well. Add nuts and beat well. Shape into rolls two inches in diameter and wrap in waxed paper. Chill thoroughly. Cut into slices 1/8" thick. Place on ungreased baking sheets. Bake in moderate oven (375° F.) 12 minutes. Makes about 96.

Cakes

APPLESAUCE CAKE

1 cup sugar
1 teaspoon cinnamon
½ teaspoon allspice
¼ teaspoon nutmeg
½ cup shortening
1 egg
1 cup thick applesauce (unsweetened)
1 teaspoon vanilla
2 cups sifted all-purpose flour
½ teaspoon salt
1 teaspoon baking soda
1 teaspoon baking powder
¾ cup chopped raisins
1 cup broken walnuts

Mix sugar and spices; add gradually to shortening, creaming thoroughly. Add egg and beat well. Stir in applesauce and vanilla. Add flour sifted with salt, baking soda, and baking powder; beat smooth. Add raisins and walnuts. Bake in two well-greased 8" layer cake pans in moderate oven (350° F.) about 35 minutes. Makes two 8" layers.

BLACK BLIZZARD CAKE

2 eggs, separated
1 cup sugar
1 cup sour cream
1½ cups sifted cake flour
1 teaspoon baking powder
1 teaspoon baking soda
¼ teaspoon salt
½ teaspoon nutmeg
½ teaspoon cinnamon
1/8 teaspoon allspice
½ cup chopped pecans

Beat egg yolks until thick, add sugar and sour cream. Sift flour, baking powder, baking soda, salt and spices together. Add pecans and mix lightly. Fold flour mixture into egg yolk mixture. Beat egg whites until stiff and fold into batter. Turn batter into waxed paper-lined, greased 8" x 8" pan. Bake in moderate oven (350° F.) about 45 minutes. Serves 6–8.

CLASSIC ANGEL FOOD

1¼ cups sifted cake flour
¾ cup sugar
1½ cups egg whites
1 teaspoon cream of tartar
¼ teaspoon salt
1 cup sugar
1 teaspoon vanilla

Sift flour with ¾ cup sugar 3 times. Beat egg whites with cream of tartar and salt until foamy. Gradually add 1 cup sugar, beating constantly. Continue beating until stiff. Gradually fold in flour-sugar mixture. Fold in vanilla. Pour into ungreased 10" tube pan. Bake in moderate oven (375° F.) 30–35 minutes. Makes one 10" tube cake.

CHEESE CAKE

6-ounce package zwieback
2 tablespoons sugar
½ cup softened butter
½ cup sugar
2 tablespoons flour
¼ teaspoon salt
1 pound cream cheese
2 tablespoons lemon juice
1 teaspoons grated lemon rind
4 eggs separated
1 cup sour cream

Crush zwieback into fine crumbs. With fingers mix crumbs with the 2 tablespoons sugar and softened butter. Reserve ½ cup crumbs. Press remaining crumbs on bottom and a little over halfway up the sides of 9" spring form pan. Combine the ½ cup sugar, flour and salt and blend into cream cheese. Add lemon juice and rind. Beat in egg yolks one at a time. Blend in sour cream. Beat egg whites until stiff but not dry and fold into cheese mixture. Turn into crumb-lined pan. Bake in a slow oven (325° F.) 1 hour and 30 minutes. When cake is done, turn off oven, open door and leave cake in oven until thoroughly cool. Garnish with extra crumbs. Makes one 9" cake.

OLD-FASHIONED CHOCOLATE CAKE

2 cups sifted cake flour
2 teaspoons baking powder
¾ teaspoon baking soda
¼ teaspoon salt
½ cup butter or margarine
1 cup sugar
2 eggs, well beaten
2 squares unsweetened chocolate, melted
½ cup milk
½ cup sour cream
¼ teaspoon vanilla
¼ teaspoon almond extract
½ cup chopped toasted almonds

Sift flour, baking powder, baking soda and salt together. Cream butter or margarine with sugar. Add eggs and chocolate; beat well. Add sifted ingredients, milk and sour cream alternately. Beat well after each addition. Add vanilla and almond extract. Add almonds. Turn into 2 greased 9" layer cake pans. Bake in moderate oven (350° F.) 45–50 minutes. Makes two 9" layers.

CHERRY-COCONUT CAKE

½ cup shortening
1½ cups sugar
2 1/3 cups sifted cake flour
3 teaspoons baking powder
¼ teaspoon salt
¼ cup maraschino cherry liquid
½ cup milk
1 teaspoon vanilla
16 maraschino cherries, cut fine
½ cup chopped nuts
4 egg whites
1 cup shredded coconut

Cream shortening and sugar until fluffy, and light. Sift together flour, baking powder and salt. Combine cherry liquid, milk and vanilla. Add flour mixture in thirds, alternating with milk mixture, to the creamed shortening and sugar, beating smooth after each addition. Fold in cherries and nuts. Beat egg whites until stiff and fold into cake mixture. Fold in coconut. Bake in 2 greased 9" layer cake pans in moderate oven (375° F.) 30–35 minutes. Makes two 9" layers.

CHOCOLATE ANGEL FOOD

¾ cup sifted cake flour
¼ cup cocoa
1¼ cups egg whites
¼ teaspoon salt
1 teaspoon cream of tartar
1¼ cups sifted sugar
1 teaspoon vanilla
¼ teaspoon almond extract

Sift flour and cocoa together 3 times. Beat egg whites and salt until foamy. Add cream of tartar and beat until stiff. Fold in sugar gradually. Fold in vanilla and almond extract. Sift flour over egg-white mixture gradually. Fold in quickly. Turn batter into ungreased 10" tube pan. Cut through batter with spatula. Bake in moderate oven (375° F.) 30–35 minutes. Invert pan and cool. Makes one 10" tube cake.

DENVER RED CHOCOLATE CAKE

(Adapted for ordinary altitudes)

4 cups sifted cake flour
2 teaspoons baking soda
1½ teaspoons salt
1 cup shortening
2½ cups sugar
4 eggs
6 squares unsweetened chocolate, melted
½ cup vinegar
1½ cups milk
2 teaspoons vanilla

Sift flour, baking soda and salt together. Cream shortening with sugar until light and fluffy. Add eggs, 1 at a time, and beat well after each addition. Add chocolate and mix well. Combine vinegar, milk and vanilla. Add milk mixture and sifted ingredients alternately to chocolate mixture; beat well after each addition. Turn into 3 greased 9" layer cake pans. Bake in moderate oven (350° F.) about 30 minutes, or until cake tests done. Makes three 9" layers.

PECAN CHOCOLATE TORTE

1 egg
6 eggs, separated
¾ cup sugar
1 ¾ cups very finely chopped pecans

1 square unsweetened chocolate, grated
½ cup fine dry cake crumbs
1 teaspoon vanilla

Beat egg and egg yolks until lemon colored. Add sugar, pecans, chocolate and crumbs; beat well. Add vanilla. Beat egg whites until stiff; fold into pecan mixture. Turn into 2 well-greased and lightly floured 9" layer cake pans. Bake in moderate oven (350° F.) 20–25 minutes. Cool thoroughly. Fill and frost, as desired. Makes 12 servings.

PECAN DEVIL'S FOOD CAKE

⅓ cup shortening
1¼ cups brown sugar, firmly packed
2 eggs, well beaten
½ cup hot black coffee
2 squares unsweetened chocolate
1½ cups sifted cake flour
1 teaspoon baking soda
1 teaspoon baking powder
½ teaspoon salt
¾ cup finely chopped pecans
½ cup buttermilk
1 teaspoon vanilla

Cream shortening; add sugar gradually, and cream until light and fluffy. Add eggs and beat well. Meanwhile pour coffee over chocolate; stir over low heat until smooth and thick; cool, add to egg mixture, mixing thoroughly. Sift flour, baking soda, baking powder and salt together; add pecans. Combine buttermilk and vanilla, and add alternately with dry ingredients to the chocolate mixture, beating after each addition until smooth. Turn into well-greased and lightly floured 8" x 8" x 2" pan and bake in moderate oven (350° F.) 50–60 minutes. Makes one 8" square cake.

CITRON CAKE

2 cups sifted cake flour
½ teaspoon baking soda
¼ teaspoon nutmeg
¼ teaspoon allspice
¼ teaspoon salt
⅓ cup shortening
1 cup sugar
2 eggs
1 tablespoon grated orange rind
¾ cup orange juice
2 tablespoons chopped citron

Sift flour, baking soda, spices and salt together. Cream shortening with sugar until fluffy. Beat eggs until thick; add to shortening mixture. Add orange rind and beat well. Add sifted ingredients and orange juice alternately, beating thoroughly after each addition. Add citron. Pour into greased 8" x 8" x 2" pan. Bake in moderate oven (350° F.) 50 minutes. Makes one 8"-square cake.

FAVORITE ONE-EGG SQUARE

2 cups sifted cake flour
2½ teaspoons baking powder
¼ teaspoon salt
¼ cup butter or margarine
1 cup sugar
1 egg
1 teaspoon vanilla
¾ cup milk

Sift flour, baking powder and salt together. Cream butter or margarine with sugar. Add egg and vanilla; beat well. Add sifted ingredients and milk alternately, beating well after each addition. Pour into greased 8" x 8" x 2" pans. Bake in moderate oven (350° F.) 50 minutes. Makes one 8"-square cake.

MIDNIGHT FRUIT CAKE

4 pounds seeded raisins, chopped
1 cup citron, chopped
2 cups dried apricots, chopped
1 cup chopped candied pineapple
¼ cup chopped candied lemon rind
¼ cup chopped candied orange rind
½ cup grape juice
½ cup orange juice
2 cups chopped walnuts
2½ cups sifted cake flour
2 cups shortening
1 pound brown sugar
12 eggs
1 cup molasses
1 teaspoon cloves
4 teaspoons allspice
1½ teaspoons mace
½ teaspoon baking soda
½ teaspoon salt
4 squares unsweetened chocolate, melted
2 tablespoons brandy

Combine fruits, grape juice and orange juice. Let stand several hours. Drain; reserve liquid. Combine fruits, walnuts and 1 cup flour; mix lightly. Cream shortening and sugar until fluffy. Add eggs, 1 at a time, to creamed mixture. Beat well after each addition. Add molasses and mix well. Combine remaining 1½ cups flour with spices, baking soda and salt. Add spice mixture alternately with grape-juice mixture and fruit mixture to egg mixture. Beat well after each addition. Add chocolate and brandy. Mix well. Pour into greased waxed paper-lined 7" x 3" loaf pans. Steam 2 hours. Bake in slow oven (300° F.) about 1½ hours. Cool slightly and remove paper. Makes about 7 loaves.

HOLIDAY FRUIT CAKE

4 cups sifted cake flour
1 teaspoon mace
¼ teaspoon nutmeg
2 teaspoons cinnamon
½ teaspoon baking soda
6 cups currants
4 cups raisins
1 pound citron, sliced
½ cup candied orange rind
½ cup chopped candied cherries
1 cup blanched almonds, slivered
1 cup chopped pecans
2 cups shortening
2 cups brown sugar, firmly packed
9 eggs, separated
¾ cup cold coffee
¼ cup rum or brandy

Sift flour, spices and baking soda together. Add fruits and nuts; mix lightly. Cream shortening with sugar until light. Beat egg yolks until thick. Beat egg whites until stiff. Add egg yolks and egg whites to sugar mixture; mix lightly. Add fruit mixture alternately with coffee and rum or brandy. Pour into 4 greased wax paper-lined 9" x 5" x 3" pans (or bake 1 or 2 at a time, keeping remaining batter in bowl). Bake in slow oven (275° F.) 1½-2 hours, or until top of cake looks dry. Makes about four 2-pound cakes.

YANKEE DOODLE FRUIT CAKE

5½ cups sifted cake flour
2½ teaspoons baking powder
¼ teaspoon mace
1 cup shortening
2 cups brown sugar, firmly packed
3 eggs, well beaten
1 teaspoon vanilla

3¼ cups raisins
½ cup sliced candied orange rind
¼ cup sliced candied cherries
¼ cup sliced candied pineapple
1 cup chopped pecans
1 cup cranberry juice

Sift flour, baking powder and mace together. Cream shortening with sugar until fluffy. Add eggs and beat well. Add vanilla, fruits and pecans; mix well. Add sifted ingredients and cranberry juice alternately. Beat well after each addition. Turn into greased, lined 10" tube pan. Bake in slow oven (300° F.) 2–2½ hours. Makes one 10" tube cake.

ALEPPO HONEY CAKE

1 cup molasses
2 cups honey
¾ cup sugar
½ teaspoon nutmeg
1½ teaspoons ginger
3 tablespoons grated lemon rind
4½ cups sifted cake flour
4½ teaspoons baking powder
¼ teaspoon salt
¾ cup milk
½ cup chopped crystallized ginger
½ cup chopped pistachio nuts

Combine molasses, honey, sugar, spices and lemon rind. Sift flour with baking powder and salt. Add sifted ingredients and milk alternately to molasses mixture, beating well after each addition. Add crystallized ginger and nuts; mix well; pour into 2 greased 8" x 8" x 2" pans. Bake in moderate oven (350° F.) for 1 hour. Makes two 8"-square cakes.

JELLY CAKE

2 cups sifted cake flour
1½ teaspoons baking powder
1/8 teaspoon salt
2/3 cup shortening
1¼ cups sugar
1 teaspoon vanilla
¼ teaspoon almond flavoring
3 eggs, separated
½ cup milk
¾ cup raspberry jam
Confectioners' sugar

Sift flour, baking powder and salt together. Cream shortening with the 1¼ cups sugar until light and fluffy. Add vanilla and almond flavoring; mix well. Beat egg yolks until thick and add to sugar mixture; beat well. Gradually add sifted ingredients and milk alternately; beat well after each addition. Beat egg whites until stiff and fold into batter. Turn into 2 greased 9" layer cake pans. Bake in moderate oven (350° F.) about 25 minutes. Cool thoroughly. Spread jam between layers. Sprinkle confectioners' sugar over top. Makes one 9" layer cake.

LORD BALTIMORE CAKE

2½ cups sifted cake flour
½ teaspoon salt
3 teaspoons baking powder
¾ cup shortening
1¼ cups sugar
8 egg yolks
¾ cup milk
½ teaspoon almond extract
½ teaspoon grated orange rind

Sift flour, salt and baking powder together. Cream shortening and sugar until light. Beat egg yolks until thick. Add to shortening mixture and beat thoroughly. Add sifted ingredients alternately with milk. Beat well after each addition. Add almond extract and orange rind; beat well. Pour into 3 greased 8" layer cake pans. Bake in moderate oven (375° F.) about 20 minutes. Fill and frost with Lord Baltimore Filling and Frosting (page 166). Makes three 8" layers.

VERMONT MAPLE CAKE

1/3 cup shortening
½ cup sugar
¾ cup maple syrup
2¼ cups sifted cake flour
3 teaspoons baking powder
¼ teaspoon salt
½ cup milk
3 egg whites
1 teaspoon lemon extract

Cream shortening with sugar until light and fluffy. Add syrup and beat well. Sift flour, baking powder and salt together. Add sifted ingredients alternately with milk to syrup mixture, beating well after each addition. Beat egg whites until stiff and fold into batter. Add lemon extract. Turn into

2 greased 9" layer cake pans. Bake in moderate oven (350° F.) 25–30 minutes. Makes two 9" layers.

DRIED PRUNE-APRICOT UPSIDE-DOWN CAKE

1¼ cups sifted cake flour
1½ teaspoons baking powder
¼ teaspoon salt
½ cup granulated sugar
1 egg, well beaten
½ cup milk
½ teaspoon almond extract
¼ cup melted shortening
3 tablespoons butter or margarine
¼ cup firmly packed brown sugar
8 canned apricot halves, well-drained
8 cooked prunes, well-drained
½ cup shredded coconut, toasted

Sift flour, baking powder, salt and granulated sugar. Combine egg, milk and almond extract. Gradually add flour mixture. Mix well after each addition. Stir in shortening; beat vigorously 1 minute. Melt butter or margarine in 8" x 8" pan. Add brown sugar and stir until sugar is dissolved. Arrange apricot halves and prunes in sugar mixture. Pour batter over fruits. Bake in moderate oven (350° F.) 40–50 minutes. Cool slightly and turn out of pan. Top with coconut. Makes one 8"-square cake.

RASPBERRY JELLY ROLL

1 cup sifted cake flour
¼ teaspoon salt
5 eggs, separated
1 cup sugar
2 tablespoons orange juice
Confectioners' sugar
1 cup raspberry jelly

Sift flour with salt. Beat egg whites until almost stiff. Add ½ cup sugar gradually, beating constantly until very stiff. Beat egg yolks until thick; add remaining ½ cup sugar gradually, beating constantly, until thick. Add orange juice. Fold egg-yolk mixture into egg whites. Fold flour mixture gradually into egg mixture. Line 11" x 16" pan with waxed paper; grease paper. Turn batter into pan. Bake in moderate oven (350° F.) about 15 minutes. Turn out on towel sprinkled with confectioners' sugar. Remove paper and trim crusts. Roll up and cool. Unroll; spread with jelly and roll. Makes 1 jelly roll.

STATE OF MAINE FUDGE CAKE

1 cup shortening
2 cups sugar
4 eggs, separated
1 cup grated raw potato
2½ cups sifted cake flour
¼ teaspoon salt
3 teaspoons baking powder
1 teaspoon cinnamon
¾ cup chopped pecans
½ cup milk
2 squares unsweetened chocolate, melted
1 tablespoon grated lemon rind

Cream shortening with sugar until light and fluffy. Add egg yolks and beat well. Add potato and beat. Sift flour with salt, baking powder and cinnamon. Add pecans to sifted ingredients and mix lightly. Add nut mixture and milk alternately to creamed mixture, beating well after each addition. Add chocolate and lemon rind. Beat egg whites until stiff and fold into chocolate mixture. Turn into greased 13" x 9" x 2" pan. Bake in moderate oven (350° F.) for about 1 hour. Makes 1 loaf.

NEW ENGLAND GINGERBREAD

2 cups sifted all-purpose flour
1 teaspoon baking soda
¼ teaspoon salt
1¼ teaspoons ginger
½ teaspoon allspice
¼ teaspoon nutmeg
½ cup firmly packed light brown sugar
2 eggs, beaten
½ cup molasses
1 cup buttermilk
½ cup shortening, melted

Sift dry ingredients together. Combine eggs, molasses, buttermilk and shortening. Gradually add to flour mixture; beat well. Turn into greased 8" x 8" pan. Bake in moderate oven (350° F.) 35–40 minutes. Serves 6.

MARASCHINO WALNUT CAKE

2 cups sifted cake flour
¼ teaspoon salt
2½ teaspoons baking powder
½ cup shortening
1¼ cups sugar
2 eggs, separated
1/3 cup maraschino syrup (drained from cherries)
1/3 cup milk
½ teaspoon lemon juice
1 5-ounce bottle maraschino cherries
½ cup chopped walnuts

Sift flour, salt, baking powder. Cream shortening and sugar, stir in egg yolks. Add liquids and dry ingredients, alternately, to creamed mixture. Fold in stiffly beaten egg whites. Divide batter into 2 bowls. Add chopped maraschino cherries (floured) to half of batter and chopped walnuts (floured) to other half. Bake in two greased 8" x 8" x 2" pans in moderate oven (375° F.) about 25 minutes. Makes two 8"-square layers.

BRAZIL NUT CAKE

½ cup shortening
1 cup sugar
2 egg yolks
2 cups sifted cake flour
1 teaspoon baking soda
¼ teaspoon salt
¼ teaspoon ginger
½ teaspoon nutmeg
¾ cup ground Brazil nuts
1 cup buttermilk

Cream shortening with sugar until light and fluffy. Add egg yolks and beat well. Sift flour with baking soda, salt, ginger and nutmeg. Add Brazil nuts and mix lightly. Add nut mixture and buttermilk alternately to creamed mixture, beating well after each addition. Turn into greased 8" x 8" x 2" pan. Bake in moderate oven (350° F.) about 45 minutes. Makes one 8"-square cake.

SPECIAL NUT TORTE

2½ cups very finely chopped or grated Cashew nuts or walnuts
1½ cups sugar
¼ teaspoon salt
8 eggs, separated
1¼ teaspoons vanilla
½ teaspoon almond extract

Combine nuts, sugar and salt. Beat egg yolks until thick; add nut mixture and mix well. Beat egg whites until stiff; fold into nut mixture. Fold in vanilla and almond extract. Turn into 3 well-greased 9" layer cake pans. Bake in slow oven (325° F.) 30–35 minutes. Cool thoroughly. Fill and frost with whipped cream, raspberry jam, or as desired. Makes 12 servings.

OLD-TIME PORK CAKE

1 cup hot coffee
1 cup brown sugar, firmly packed
1 egg, beaten
1 teaspoon baking soda
½ cup molasses
½ pound fat salt pork, ground fine
½ pound golden raisins
¾ cup currants
½ cup nuts, chopped
1 teaspoon cinnamon
½ teaspoon allspice
½ teaspoon cloves
¼ teaspoon nutmeg
3 cups sifted all-purpose flour

Combine coffee, sugar, egg, baking soda and molasses. Blend well. Stir in pork. Combine remaining ingredients, except flour, and add to coffee mixture. Sift in flour. Mix well. Pour into 2 greased and floured 9" x 5" loaf pans, and bake in moderate oven (350° F.) 1 hour. Wrap in heavy waxed paper. Place in air-tight container for 1 week. Slice and serve. Makes 2 loaves.

CLASSIC POUND CAKE

1 cup butter
1 cup sugar
5 eggs, separated
2 cups sifted cake flour
½ teaspoon nutmeg
¼ teaspoon salt
1 teaspoon vanilla

Cream butter with sugar until very light and fluffy. Beat egg yolks until thick and lemon colored. Add egg yolks to butter mixture and beat well. Sift flour with nutmeg and salt. Add sifted ingredients gradually to sugar mixture, beating well after each addition. Beat until batter is smooth. Beat egg whites until stiff and fold into batter. Fold in vanilla. Turn into greased 9" x 5" x 3" pan. Bake in slow oven (325° F.) for about 1 hour. Makes one 9" loaf.

ELECTION DAY CAKE

1½ cups warm, not hot, water (lukewarm for compressed yeast)
2 teaspoons sugar
2 packages active dry yeast, or 2 cakes compressed yeast
4½ cups sifted all-purpose flour
¾ cup butter or margarine
1 cup sugar
2 eggs
1 teaspoon salt
1½ teaspoons cinnamon
¼ teaspoon cloves
1 teaspoon grated orange rind
½ cup candied orange peel
½ teaspoon nutmeg
1½ cups raisins
½ cup chopped pecans

Measure water into a mixing bowl (warm, not hot, for active dry yeast; lukewarm for compressed). Add and stir in 2 teaspoons sugar. Sprinkle or crumble in yeast; stir until dissolved. Add 1½ cups of the flour and beat well. Cover with a cloth and let rise in a warm place, free from draft, until very bubbly, about 30 minutes. Cream butter or margarine with 1 cup sugar. Add and beat in eggs. Combine with bubbly yeast mixture. Sift together salt, spices and remaining 3 cups flour, and add to yeast mixture. Beat until smooth. Add and stir in fruits and nuts. Turn into a greased, lightly floured 10" tube pan or into 2 well-greased loaf pans (9" x 5" x 3") or two well-greased 1½-quart casseroles. Cover with a cloth. Let rise in a warm place, free from draft, until doubled in bulk, about 1½ hours. Bake tube cake in a moderate oven (375° F.) for 1 hour; bake loaves or casseroles in a moderate oven (350° F.) 60–70 minutes. Cool cake in pans 5 minutes. Turn out on cake rack. Cool.

MOCHA LAYER CAKE

2 squares unsweetened chocolate melted
1 cup boiling coffee
½ cup salad oil
2 cups sugar
¼ teaspoon salt
2 cups sifted all-purpose flour
1½ teaspoons baking soda
½ cup buttermilk
2 eggs, beaten

Combine chocolate, coffee and oil. Add remaining ingredients. Beat 2 minutes. Pour batter into 2 greased 9" layer cake pans. Bake in moderate oven (350° F.) 30-35 minutes. Makes two 9" layers.

BABKA

¾ cup milk
1 package active dry yeast, or 1 cake
   compressed yeast
¼ cup warm, not hot, water (lukewarm for
   compressed yeast)
¼ cup butter or margarine
½ cup sugar
1 teaspoon salt
½ teaspoon ground cardamon
2 egg yolks
2½ cups sifted all-purpose flour
½ cup raisins
¼ cup chopped candied cherries
¼ cup chopped nuts
Soft butter or margarine
Fine dry bread crumbs

Scald milk; cool to lukewarm. Sprinkle or crumble yeast into water (warm, not hot, water for active dry yeast; lukewarm water for compressed yeast), stir until dissolved. Cream butter or margarine. Mix in sugar, salt, cardamon and egg yolks. Beat until light. Stir yeast into lukewarm milk; add alternately with sifted flour to sugar-egg yolk mixture. Beat until smooth. Add fruits and nuts. Turn out on floured board and knead until light and springy. Place in greased bowl and grease top of dough. Cover and let stand in warm place until double in bulk. Punch down. Rub butter or margarine in a 1-quart mold, dust with bread crumbs. Place dough in crumb lined pan. Grease top of dough. Cover, let rise in warm place until double in bulk. Bake in moderate oven (350° F.) 40 minutes. Makes 1 cake.

SPICE CAKE

2½ cups sifted cake flour
2½ teaspoons baking powder
¼ teaspoon salt
½ teaspoon cinnamon
½ teaspoon nutmeg
½ teaspoon cloves
½ cup shortening
1 cup sugar
2 eggs
1/3 cup molasses
¾ cup milk

Sift flour, baking powder, salt and spices together. Cream shortening and sugar thoroughly, and add eggs one at a time, beating thoroughly after each addition. Blend in molasses and add sifted ingredients alternately with milk. Beat well. Pour into 2 greased 9"layer cake pans. Bake in moderate oven (375° F.) for 25 minutes. Makes two 9" layers.

WALNUT SPICE CAKE

½ cup shortening
1 cup granulated sugar
1 egg, beaten
3 cups sifted cake flour
1½ teaspoons baking soda
1 teaspoon allspice
¾ teaspoon cloves
1½ teaspoons cinnamon
½ teaspoon nutmeg
½ teaspoon salt
1 cup buttermilk
½ cup seedless raisins
½ cup chopped walnuts

Cream shortening; add sugar gradually, creaming well. Add egg and beat. Sift together 2¾ cups flour, baking soda, allspice, cloves, cinnamon, nutmeg and salt, and add alternately in thirds with buttermilk to sugar mixture. Add raisins and walnuts dredged with remaining ¼ cup of flour, and mix. Bake in 10" greased tube pan in moderate oven (350° F.) 50-60 minutes. Makes one 10" tube cake.

TUTTI-FRUTTI HONEY CAKE

2 cups sifted cake flour
2 teaspoons baking powder
¼ teaspoon salt
2/3 cup butter or margarine
½ cup sugar
½ cup honey
3 eggs
¼ cup milk
1 cup candied fruits
1 teaspoon vanilla

Sift flour, baking powder and salt together. Cream butter or margarine, sugar and honey until light and fluffy. Add £ of the dry ingredients and blend until smooth. Beat egg whites until stiff, then fold into batter. Add remaining dry ingredients and milk alternately. Add fruits and vanilla. Turn into greased 9" x 5" x 3" pan. Bake in slow oven (325° F.) about 1 hour and 25 minutes. Makes 1 loaf.

SEMINOLE ORANGE CAKE

½ cup shortening
1 cup sugar
2 eggs, well beaten
2 cups sifted cake flour
3 teaspoons baking powder
½ teaspoon salt
¾ cup milk
2/3 cup candied orange peel
¼ teaspoon lemon extract

Cream shortening with sugar until light and fluffy. Add eggs and beat well. Sift flour with baking powder and salt. Add sifted ingredients and milk, alternately, to creamed mixture, beating well after each addition. Fold in orange peel and lemon extract. Turn into 2 greased 8" layer cake pans. Bake in moderate oven (375° F.) 25-30 minutes. Makes two 8" layers.

ORANGE-COCONUT CAKE

4 eggs, separated
1½ cups sugar
1 cup butter
1 teaspoon salt
2 tablespoons grated orange rind
1¼ teaspoons orange extract
3 cups sifted cake flour
3 teaspoons baking powder
1¼ cups milk
1 cup shredded coconut

Beat egg whites until stiff. Cream sugar, butter, salt, rind and orange extract Add egg yolks and beat. Sift flour with baking powder and add, alternately, with milk. Fold egg whites into mixture; fold in coconut. Turn into 3 greased 8" layer cake pans. Bake in moderate oven (350° F.) 25-30 minutes. Makes three 8" layers.

Frostings & Fillings

FILLINGS

APPLESAUCE-DATE FILLING

1 cup thick applesauce
½ cup chopped dates
¼ teaspoon cinnamon
1/8 teaspoon nutmeg

Combine all ingredients and mix welL Makes about 1½ cups.

LORD BALTIMORE FILLING AND FROSTING

1 recipe Seven-Minute Frosting
¼ cup chopped figs
¼ cup raisins
¼ cup chopped candied cherries
¼ cup chopped pecans
¼ teaspoon orange extract

To 1/3 cup of the Seven-Minute Frosting, add remaining ingredients. Spread between Lord Baltimore cake layers. Frost top and sides of cake with remaining frosting.

NUT CREAM FILLING

2 tablespoons sugar
1 tablespoon cornstarch
1/8 teaspoon salt
1 egg yolk, beaten
1 cup sour cream
½ teaspoon grated lemon rind
½ cup chopped walnuts or almonds

Combine sugar, cornstarch, salt and egg yolk. Add sour cream and cook over very low heat, stirring constantly, until mixture coats spoon. Stir in lemon rind and nuts. Cool thoroughly. Makes about 1½ cups.

MISSION ORANGE FILLING

1 tablespoon all-purpose flour
¾ cup sugar
1/8 teaspoon salt
½ cup water
3 egg yolks, well beaten
2/3 cup orange juice
½ teaspoon lemon extract
1 tablespoon orange rind

Combine flour, sugar, salt and water. Add egg yolks and mix well. Add remaining ingredients and cook over low heat, stirring constantly, until thickened. Cool thoroughly.

CUSTARD FILLING

1/3 cup sugar
3 tablespoons cornstarch
¼ teaspoon salt
2 egg yolks
2 cups milk, scalded
2 tablespoons butter
2 teaspoons rum

Combine sugar, cornstarch and salt. Add egg yolks and beat well. Add a little milk slowly, mix and return mixture to remaining hot milk. Cook over boiling water, stirring constantly until mixture thickens. Add butter; cool. Add rum. Makes about 2½ cups.

DATE-CREAM CHEESE FILLING

2 8-ounce packages cream cheese
3 tablespoons light cream
¾ cup chopped dates
½ cup chopped pecans
1/8 teaspoon salt
¼ teaspoon vanilla

Cream cheese with cream until light and fluffy. Add remaining ingredients and mix well.

PINEAPPLE-FIG FILLING

2 cups dried figs
1 cup crushed pineapple
3 cups pineapple juice
¼ teaspoon salt
2 cups sugar
½ teaspoon vanilla

Rinse figs in hot water and drain. Cut figs into thin strips. Combine with pineapple and juice; cook 10 minutes. Add salt and sugar. Cook, stirring occasionally, until figs are tender (about 15 minutes). Cool. Add vanilla. Makes about 5 cups.

JANICE'S PINEAPPLE FILLING

½ cup sifted all-purpose flour
1 cup sugar
⅛ teaspoon salt
2 eggs
2 cups scalded milk
½ teaspoon lemon extract
½ teaspoon grated lemon rind
½ teaspoon grated orange rind
1½ cups canned crushed pineapple

Combine flour, sugar, salt and eggs. Add milk and stir until smooth. Cook over very low heat, stirring constantly, until thickened. Cool thoroughly. Add remaining ingredients and mix well. Makes about 4 cups.

BROWN BUTTER FILLING

½ cup butter
¼ cup cocoa
⅛ teaspoon cinnamon
2 egg whites
2 cups confectioners' sugar
1 teaspoon vanilla

Melt butter; add cocoa and cinnamon; mix well. Beat whites until stiff; fold in sugar. Fold cocoa mixture into egg-white mixture. Add vanilla and mix lightly. Makes about 3 cups.

PEANUT FILLING

½ cup peanut butter
¼ cup orange juice
¼ cup honey
¼ cup chopped peanuts
1 teaspoon grated orange rind

Combine all ingredients and mix well. Makes about 1¼ cups.

FROSTINGS

RASPBERRY FROSTING

1 teaspoon unflavored gelatin
3 tablespoons cold water
1 cup sugar
¼ cup hot water
2 egg whites
1 cup red raspberries

Soften gelatin in cold water. Combine sugar and hot water. Cook over low heat to soft-ball stage (236° F. on candy thermometer). Add gelatin and stir until dissolved. Beat egg whites until stiff. Gradually add gelatin mixture, beating constantly. Cook over boiling water, stirring occasionally, until very thick. Remove from heat. Stir until cool. Fold in raspberries. Makes about 2¼ cups.

RUM MOCHA FROSTING

5 squares unsweetened chocolate
½ cup butter
3½ cups sifted confectioners' sugar
⅛ teaspoon salt
2 tablespoons rum
2 tablespoons coffee

Melt chocolate; add butter and beat well. Add remaining ingredients and beat until light and fluffy. Makes about 4½ cups.

SNOW FROSTING

1 cup heavy cream
¼ teaspoon vanilla
¼ teaspoon lemon extract
¼ cup confectioners' sugar
1½ cups grated coconut

Beat cream until stiff. Fold in remaining ingredients. Makes about 3 cups.

ORANGE BLOSSOM FROSTING

2 egg whites
¾ cup sugar
⅓ cup light corn syrup
2 tablespoons orange juice
¼ teaspoon cream of tartar
⅛ teaspoon salt
2 teaspoons grated lemon rind

Combine all ingredients in top of double boiler. Place over boiling water. Beat with rotary beater until mixture stands in stiff peaks. Remove from heat. Beat until slightly cooled. Cool thoroughly. Makes about 2 cups.

PINEAPPLE-CHEESE FROSTING

1 8-ounce package cream cheese
2 tablespoons butter
3 cups sifted confectioners' sugar
1 tablespoon drained crushed pineapple
3 tablespoons pineapple juice
1 teaspoon lemon juice

Cream cheese with butter until light. Add remaining ingredients and beat until fluffy. Makes about 4 cups.

IN-THE-OVEN FROSTING

1 egg white
¼ teaspoon baking powder
¾ cup firmly packed brown sugar
½ cup chopped pecans

Beat egg white until frothy. Add baking powder and beat until stiff. Gradually add sugar. Beat well. Spread over 8" x 8" cake and top with chopped nuts. Bake in moderate oven (350° F.) about 10 minutes. Makes about 1½ cups.

SIMPLE BUTTER FROSTING

¾ cup butter
4 cups confectioners' sugar
2 egg whites
⅛ teaspoon salt
1 teaspoon vanilla

Cream butter until soft. Add 2 cups of the sugar and beat well. Add egg whites and blend. Add salt and remaining sugar. Beat until light and fluffy. Add vanilla and mix well. Makes about 5 cups.

BUTTERSCOTCH FROSTING

1 cup firmly packed brown sugar
⅓ cup butter
⅛ teaspoon salt
¼ cup milk
1½ cups sifted confectioners' sugar

Combine brown sugar, butter and salt. Cook over low heat until mixture boils, stirring constantly. Add milk and cook, stirring constantly, three minutes. Remove from heat and cool thoroughly. Add confectioners' sugar and beat until well blended. Makes about 2½ cups.

VERMONT CARAMEL FROSTING

3 cups sifted confectioners' sugar
1 cup firmly packed brown sugar
⅓ cup hot water
½ cup butter
½ teaspoon vanilla
½ teaspoon maple flavoring

Combine sugars and water. Cream butter until soft. Add sugar mixture and beat until light and fluffy. Add vanilla and maple flavoring; beat well. Makes about 4 cups.

VELVET CHOCOLATE FROSTING

1 egg yolk, beaten
1 cup sugar
¼ cup light cream
⅛ teaspoon salt
2½ squares unsweetened chocolate
1 tablespoon butter
1 teaspoon vanilla

Combine egg yolk, sugar, cream, salt and chocolate. Cook over hot water until thickened, stirring occasionally. Remove from heat. Add butter and vanilla. Beat until thick. Makes about 1½ cups.

JERSEY STRAWBERRY FROSTING

1 cup fresh strawberries
2 egg whites
1/8 teaspoon salt
1 teaspoon lemon juice
1/4 teaspoon cream of tartar
1/2 cup sugar

Force berries through sieve. Beat egg whites with salt, lemon juice and cream of tartar until foamy. Gradually add sugar, beating constantly. Continue beating until stiff. Fold in berries. Makes about 2 1/4 cups.

CHOCOLATE CREAM FROSTING

1 square unsweetened chocolate
2 tablespoons milk
1/3 cup sugar
1 egg
1 cup heavy cream, whipped
1/2 teaspoon vanilla
1/2 cup shredded coconut

Melt chocolate over hot water. Add milk and sugar; mix well. Cool. Add egg and beat well. Fold cream into chocolate mixture. Fold in vanilla and coconut. Fill and frost cake. Chill thoroughly. Makes about 2 cups.

CHOCOLATE PUFF FROSTING

1/2 cup butter
2 squares unsweetened chocolate, melted
2 1/2 cups confectioners' sugar
1 egg, beaten
1 teaspoon vanilla
1/8 teaspoon salt
1 cup chopped walnuts
1 cup shredded coconut

Cream butter until soft. Add chocolate and mix well. Add remaining ingredients and beat until light and fluffy. Makes about 4 1/2 cups.

CHOCOLATE PECAN FROSTING

1/4 pound sweet chocolate
1/2 cup chopped pecans
1 cup heavy cream, whipped

Melt chocolate over hot water. Add nuts and mix well; cool. Fold in cream. Makes about 2 cups.

COFFEE FROSTING

1/4 cup butter
1 1/2 cups sifted confectioners' sugar
1/4 cup strong coffee
1/8 teaspoon salt

Combine all ingredients and beat until light and fluffy. Makes about 2 cups.

Candy

CARAMEL APPLES

1 cup sugar
¾ cup dark corn syrup
1 cup light cream
1½ tablespoons butter or margarine
½ teaspoon vanilla
6 medium-sized red apples
¾ cup chopped nuts

Combine sugar, syrup, cream, and butter or margarine. Cook over low heat to hard-ball stage (260° F. on candy thermometer). Remove from heat and add vanilla. Meanwhile stick wooden skewers into stem ends of apples. Dip apples into sugar mixture and roll in nuts. Cool thoroughly. Makes 6.

CANDY-COATED BRAZIL NUTS

1½ cups sugar
¼ cup orange juice
1 teaspoon grated orange rind
¼ cup water
1½ cups Brazil nuts

Combine sugar, orange juice, rind and water. Cook over low heat, stirring until sugar melts. Cook over low heat to softball stage (236° F. on candy thermometer). Remove from heat and add Brazil nuts. Stir until creamy. Turn out on waxed paper. Makes about 2½ cups.

CARIBBEAN CONFECTION

3 cups gingersnap crumbs
1 cup chopped almonds
1½ cups confectioners' sugar
¼ cup honey
¼ cup cocoa
2½ tablespoons melted butter or margarine
¼ cup rum
Powdered sugar

Combine crumbs, almonds, confectioners' sugar, honey, cocoa, butter or margarine, and rum. Mix well and shape into 1" balls. Roll in powdered sugar. Makes about 48.

STUFFED DATES

1 cup pitted dates
½ cup marshmallow halves (approx.)
½ cup pecans (approx.)
Granulated sugar

Stuff dates with marshmallows and pecans. Roll in sugar. Makes about 24.

DIVINITY

3 cups sugar
1 cup light corn syrup
½ cup water
1 teaspoon vinegar
2 egg whites, stiffly beaten
1 teaspoon vanilla
1 cup chopped walnuts

Combine sugar, syrup, water and vinegar. Cover and cook over low heat 5 minutes. Cook, uncovered, to hard-ball stage (265° F. on candy thermometer). Cool slightly. Pour gradually over egg whites. Beat until stiff. Cool, stirring occasionally, until mixture reaches 100° F. Add vanilla and nuts. Drop by teaspoonfuls onto waxed paper. Makes about 60.

CHOCOLATE ALMOND CANDY

2 cups sugar
1 cup light cream
2 tablespoons butter or margarine
¼ cup cocoa
¾ cup chopped almonds
3 tablespoons marshmallow cream
½ teaspoon almond extract
10 marshmallows, quartered

Combine sugar, cream, butter or margarine, and cocoa. Cook over low heat to soft-ball stage (236° F. on candy thermometer). Remove from heat; add almonds, marshmallow cream and almond extract. Beat until mixture begins to thicken. Arrange marshmallows on greased baking sheet. Pour chocolate mixture over marshmallows. Cool thoroughly. Cut into pieces. Makes about 24.

CHOCOLATE CARAMELS

1 square unsweetened chocolate
1 cup sugar
1 cup light corn syrup
1/8 teaspoon salt
3 tablespoons butter or margarine
1 cup light cream
1 teaspoon vanilla
1/2 cup chopped nuts

Melt chocolate; add sugar, syrup and salt. Bring to boil, stirring constantly. Add butter or margarine. Gradually add cream so that mixture does not stop boiling. Cook, stirring constantly, until mixture reaches firm-ball stage (242° F. on candy thermometer). Add vanilla and nuts. Pour into greased shallow pan. Do not scrape sides of pan. Cool thoroughly. Makes about 1 pound.

CHOCOLATE COCONUT ALMONDS

1 6-ounce package semi-sweet chocolate
   morsels
2½ cups blanched almonds
1 cup shredded coconut

Melt chocolate; cool to lukewarm. Dip almonds in chocolate and roll in coconut. Makes about 4 cups.

COCOA FUDGE

2 cups sugar
½ cup cocoa
1 cup light cream
2 tablespoons butter or margarine
1 teaspoon vanilla
¾ cup chopped nuts

Combine sugar, cocoa and cream. Cook over low heat, stirring until sugar dissolves. Cook until mixture reaches softball stage (236° F. on candy thermometer). Add butter or margarine, and vanilla. Cool to lukewarm. Beat until mixture holds shape. Add nuts. Turn into greased shallow pan. Cut into squares. Makes about 24.

FUDGE ROLL

2 squares unsweetened chocolate
2 cups sugar
¼ cup light corn syrup
½ cup light cream
1 tablespoon butter or margarine
½ teaspoon vanilla

¾ cup chopped nuts
½ cup shredded coconut

Melt chocolate; add sugar, syrup, cream, and butter or margarine. Cook over low heat, stirring until sugar dissolves. Cook until mixture reaches soft-ball stage (234° F. on candy thermometer). Cool to lukewarm. Add vanilla, nuts and coconut. Beat until mixture holds shape. Shape into a roll and cool thoroughly. Slice. Makes about 24.

QUICK FUDGE

2 6-ounce packages semi-sweet chocolate
   morsels
2/3 cup sweetened condensed milk
½ teaspoon vanilla

Melt semi-sweet chocolate morsels over hot water. Remove from heat; stir in milk and vanilla. Mix well. Turn into greased shallow pan. Let stand several hours. Makes about 1¼ pounds.

BLACK WALNUT FUDGE

1 tablespoon instant coffee
1 cup boiling water
3 cups firmly packed brown sugar
1½ tablespoons butter
1 teaspoon vanilla
1 cup chopped black walnuts

Combine coffee and water; stir to dissolve coffee. Add sugar and cook over low heat, stirring constantly, until mixture reaches soft-ball stage (236° F. on candy thermometer). Add butter and cool to lukewarm. Beat until creamy. Add vanilla and walnuts. Mix well. Turn into greased shallow pan and cool. Cut into squares. Makes about 36.

CANDIED GRAPEFRUIT PEEL

2 large grapefruit
1 cup sugar
½ cup water
3 tablespoons light corn syrup
Granulated sugar

Remove skins from grapefruits in quarters. Cook, covered, in boiling salted water 20 minutes. Drain and cover with fresh water. Cook 30 minutes. Cool and cut into thin strips. Combine 1 cup sugar, water and syrup. Heat to boiling point; add grapefruit peel. Cook over low heat until liquid is absorbed. Cool and separate strips. Roll in granulated sugar and dry. Makes about 2 cups.

NOUGAT SQUARES

1 cup sugar
1/3 cup light corn syrup
1/3 cup honey
1/4 cup water
1/8 teaspoon salt
2 egg whites
1/2 teaspoon vanilla
3/4 cup chopped walnuts

Combine sugar, corn syrup, honey and water. Cook over low heat to hard-ball stage (260° F. on candy thermometer). Combine salt and egg whites. Beat until stiff. Gradually add sugar mixture, beating constantly. Add vanilla and beat until mixture is thickened. Add nuts. Cook over hot water until mixture dries, stirring constantly. Turn into greased shallow pans. Cover with pan or board. Press with heavy weight at least 12 hours. Cut into squares and wrap in waxed paper. Makes about 36.

NUT MINTS

1/4 cup sweetened condensed milk
1 1/4 cups confectioners' sugar
1/2 teaspoon mint extract
2/3 cup pecans (approx.)

Combine milk and sugar; mix well. Add mint extract. Shape into balls 1/2" in diameter. Top with pecans. Makes about 36.

MARZIPAN

2 egg whites
1 cup almond paste
1 teaspoon vanilla
1 cup confectioners' sugar

Beat egg whites and almond paste until well blended. Add vanilla and sugar; mix well. Let stand 24 hours. Form into fruit shapes, or other shapes, as desired. Makes about 1 pound.

MOCHA ALMOND BALLS

1/4 pound unsweetened chocolate, grated
1/4 cup confectioners' sugar
1/3 cup almond paste
2 tablespoons coffee
1 teaspoon butter or margarine
1/2 teaspoon vanilla
1/4 cup cocoa
1 teaspoon nutmeg

Combine chocolate, sugar, almond paste, coffee, butter or margarine, and vanilla; mix until smooth. Shape into 1/2" balls. Combine cocoa and nutmeg. Roll balls in cocoa mixture. Makes about 24.

SUGARED PEANUTS

1 1/2 cups sugar
1/4 cup light corn syrup
1/2 cup water
1/2 teaspoon vanilla
2 cups shelled peanuts

Combine sugar, syrup and water. Cook over low heat to firm-ball stage (242° F. on candy thermometer). Remove from heat and add vanilla. Stir until creamy. Add peanuts and mix well. Turn out on waxed paper. Cool and break into pieces. Makes about 24.

PECAN CREAMS

3 cups firmly packed brown sugar
1 cup evaporated milk
1 teaspoon vanilla
1 tablespoon butter or margarine
1 1/2 cups chopped pecans

Combine sugar and milk. Cook over low heat stirring until sugar melts. Cook until mixture reaches soft-ball stage (234° F. on candy thermometer). Cool to lukewarm. Add remaining ingredients. Beat until creamy. Drop by spoonfuls onto waxed paper. Makes about 48.

CLASSIC PENUCHE

3 cups firmly packed brown sugar
1 cup milk
1 1/2 tablespoons butter or margarine
1 teaspoon vanilla
1/8 teaspoon salt
3/4 cup chopped walnuts

Combine sugar and milk. Cook over low heat, stirring constantly, until mixture reaches soft-ball stage (236° F. on candy thermometer). Remove from heat; add butter or margarine, and salt. Cool. Beat until mixture will hold shape. Add walnuts. Turn into greased shallow pan. Cut into squares. Makes about 24.

CORN SYRUP POPCORN BALLS

1 cup sugar
¼ cup light corn syrup
1 cup water
1/8 teaspoon salt
1 teaspoon vanilla
3 quarts popped corn

Combine sugar, syrup and water. Cook over low heat, stirring until sugar melts. Cook over low heat until mixture reaches soft-ball stage (236° F. on candy thermometer). Remove from heat; add salt and vanilla. Cool. Pour syrup mixture over popped corn and mix lightly. Shape into balls. Makes about 24.

APRICOT TURKISH DELIGHT

3 cups sugar
¼ teaspoon salt
2 envelopes unflavored gelatin
1 cup water
1 cup cold water
¼ cup apricot nectar
2 tablespoons lemon juice
½ cup chopped pistachio nuts
½ cup confectioners' sugar

In a saucepan combine the 3 cups sugar, salt and gelatin. Add water, bring to boil and simmer 20 minutes. Remove from heat and add apricot nectar and lemon juice. Chill until slightly thickened. Stir in nuts. Turn into 8" x 4" pan that has been rinsed in cold water. Chill until firm. Turn out of pan onto board lightly covered with confectioners' sugar. Cut into cubes. Roll in confectioners' sugar. Makes about 50 ¾" cubes.

PRALINES

1 cup firmly packed brown sugar
1 cup granulated sugar
½ cup light cream
2 tablespoons butter or margarine
¾ cup pecans

Combine sugars and cream. Cook over low heat, stirring until sugar melts. Cook until mixture spins a thread (228° F. on candy thermometer). Add butter or margarine, and pecans. Cook until mixture reaches soft-ball stage (236° F. on candy thermometer). Cool. Beat until mixture begins to thicken. Drop by spoonfuls onto greased baking sheets. Cool thoroughly. Makes about 12.

MAPLE POPCORN

4 quarts popped corn
2 cups granulated sugar
2 cups maple syrup
1 teaspoon vinegar
2 tablespoons butter
1 cup chopped peanuts

Combine sugar, syrup and vinegar and cook over low heat, stirring until sugar dissolves. Cook to 275° F. on candy thermometer. Remove from heat; add butter and stir until melted. Add peanuts and pour over popcorn; blend well.

WALNUT ROLL

2 cups granulated sugar
1 cup firmly packed brown sugar
½ cup light corn syrup
1 cup light cream
1 teaspoon vanilla
1¼ cups chopped walnuts

Combine sugars, syrup and cream. Cook over low heat, stirring constantly until sugar dissolves. Cook over low heat to soft-ball stage (236° F. on candy thermometer). Remove from heat and cool until mixture reaches 110° F. Add vanilla. Beat until mixture holds shape. Cool and knead until firm. Shape into rolls 1½" in diameter. Roll in walnuts. Chill until firm and cut into slices ½" thick. Makes about 24.

MOLASSES TAFFY

4 cups molasses
1 cup firmly packed brown sugar
½ cup water
3 tablespoons butter or margarine
½ teaspoon baking soda

Combine molasses, sugar and water. Cook over low heat until mixture reaches soft-crack stage (272° F. on candy thermometer). Remove from heat; add butter or margarine, and baking soda. Turn into shallow pan. Let stand until cool enough to handle. Gather into a ball and pull until firm. Cut into pieces. Makes about 48.

OLD-FASHIONED TAFFY

2 cups sugar
½ cup light corn syrup
½ cup water
1¼ teaspoons vanilla

Combine sugar, syrup and water. Cook over low heat to soft-crack stage (272° F. on candy thermometer). Remove from heat and add vanilla. Turn out on greased baking sheet. When mixture is cool enough to handle, pull until firm. Cut into pieces. Makes about 24.

ENGLISH NUT TOFFEE

2½ cups sugar
¼ teaspoon salt
½ cup water
1¼ cups butter or margarine
1 cup chopped nuts

Combine sugar, salt, water, and butter or margarine. Heat to boiling point. Add nuts. Cook, stirring constantly, to soft-crack stage (285° F. on candy thermometer). Pour into greased shallow pan. Cool thoroughly and break into pieces. Makes about 36.

Jams, Jellies, Relishes

JAMS, PRESERVES, CONSERVES

SPICED BLUEBERRY JAM

2 quarts blueberries
½ cup lemon juice
1 teaspoon cinnamon
1 teaspoon nutmeg
½ teaspoon allspice
2 cups sugar

Crush berries and combine with lemon juice and spices; simmer 30 minutes. Add sugar and simmer until thickened, stirring occasionally. Pour into hot sterilized jars and seal. Makes about 2 pints.

GUAVA JAM

4 cups sugar
1 cup water
5½ pounds guavas
¼ cup grated lemon rind

Combine sugar and 1 cup water and cook over low heat to 238° F. Cut guavas in half and remove stones; cook in small amount of water until tender. Put through sieve. Strain and add to sugar mixture. Cook until thickened. Add lemon rind. Pour into hot sterilized jars and seal. Makes about 6 6-ounce glasses.

PAPAYA-LIME JAM

6 cups papaya pulp
1/3 cup lime juice
2 tablespoons pineapple juice
5 cups sugar

Press papaya through coarse sieve. Cook over medium heat until thickened. Add remaining ingredients and cook until thickened, stirring frequently. Pour into hot sterilized jars and seal. Makes about 5 pints.

PEACH CONSERVE

4 pounds peaches
2 oranges, peeled and chopped
Rind of 1 orange, sliced
3 pounds (6¾ cups) sugar
1 cup broken walnuts

Cut peaches into ½" cubes. Mix peaches, oranges, orange rind and sugar. Cook, stirring occasionally, until mixture is thick. Remove from heat and add nuts. Turn into hot sterilized jars and seal. Makes 8–10 6-ounce glasses.

HAWAIIAN PEACH JAM

1 pound dried peaches
1 fresh pineapple
Sugar
½ tablespoon grated lemon rind
1 tablespoon grated lime rind
1 tablespoon grated orange rind

Soak peaches in water overnight. Pare and core pineapple. Drain peaches. Put peaches and pineapple through food chopper. Reserve juice. Measure fruit and juice into a saucepan. Add ¾ cup sugar for each cup peach mixture. Stir over low heat until sugar is dissolved. Add lemon, lime and orange rinds. Heat to boiling point. Cook over low heat 25–35 minutes, stirring occasionally. Pour into hot sterilized jars and seal. Makes about 3 pints.

QUINCE NECTAR

7 cups peeled, cored and ground quinces
6 cups pared, cored and ground apples
2 oranges, ground
6 cups sugar

Put fruits in a saucepan and add enough water to cover. Heat to boiling, cover and simmer 15 minutes. Add sugar and cook over low heat until dissolved, stirring constantly. Pour into hot sterilized jars and seal. Makes about 8 pints.

RED RASPBERRY CONSERVE

5 cups red raspberries
2 cups currants
4½ cups sugar
¼ cup orange juice

Wash and drain raspberries. Crush currants. Cook currants over low heat until juice runs. Add raspberries and heat to boiling. Add sugar and orange juice; cook over medium heat until thickened. Pour into hot sterilized jars and seal. Makes about 6 pints.

GOOSEBERRY JAM

4½ cups gooseberries
4 cups sugar
1 tablespoon cinnamon

Wash and drain berries. Mash and heat to boiling point, stirring constantly. Add sugar and stir until sugar is dissolved. Cook over low heat 20 minutes, stirring frequently. Add cinnamon. Pour into hot sterilized jars and seal. Makes about 6 6-ounce glasses.

STRAWBERRY JAM

3 cups crushed strawberries
5 cups sugar
1 package powdered pectin
1 cup water

Mix strawberries and sugar and let stand 20 minutes, stirring occasionally. Dissolve pectin in water; bring to a boil and boil 1 minute. Add to fruit-sugar mixture and stir 2 minutes. Spoon into hot sterilized jars to about ½ inch of top; cover and let stand until jellied (24–48 hours). Seal with hot paraffin and a metal lid or heavy aluminum foil. Freeze or refrigerate. Jam keeps in refrigerator a few months and in freezer 1 year. Makes 9 6-ounce jars.

TANGERINE CONSERVE

4½ cups ground carrots
2 tangerines, ground
1 lemon, ground
4 cups sugar

Cook carrots in small amount of salted boiling water until all water has evaporated. Add tangerines, lemon and sugar. Cook over low heat, stirring occasionally, until thickened. Pour into hot sterilized jars and seal. Makes about 4 pints.

SPICED TOMATO PRESERVES

6 pounds green tomatoes
2 pounds red tomatoes
5 pounds granulated sugar
1 teaspoon whole cloves
1 3-inch stick cinnamon
4 lemons, sliced

Scald tomatoes; peel and cut into quarters. Add sugar, spices and lemons. Heat to boiling point. Cook over low heat until thickened. Pour into hot sterilized jars and seal. Makes about 8 pints.

DAMASCUS FIG PRESERVES

3½ pounds ripe black figs
Water
¾ cup vinegar
1 tablespoon orange juice
3 cups sugar
1½ teaspoons whole cloves
1 cinnamon stick

Stem figs. Cover with water. Heat to boiling point. Simmer 20 minutes. Drain. Combine vinegar, orange juice, sugar and spices. Heat to boiling. Cook until syrup spins a fine thread. Add figs and cook 10 minutes. Remove spices. Turn into hot sterilized jars and seal. Makes about 6 pints.

GREEN GRAPE CONSERVE

1 orange
2 lemons
1 lime
1½ cups water
3 cups sugar
3 cups cut seeded green grapes
1 tablespoon white raisins

Chop orange, lemons and lime. Add water and cook, covered, 10 minutes. Add sugar, grapes and raisins. Cook, uncovered, until thickened. Pour into hot sterilized jars and seal. Makes about 4 pints.

RHUBARB-ORANGE JAM

4 pounds rhubarb
4 pounds sugar
2 tablespoons grated orange rind
1½ cups orange juice
½ teaspoon nutmeg
1 teaspoon allspice

Wash rhubarb and cut into 1" pieces. Add sugar and let stand several hours. Add remaining ingredients. Heat to boiling point. Simmer until thickened, stirring frequently. Pour into hot sterilized glasses and seal. Makes about 4 pints.

JELLIES

GRAPE JELLY

5 pounds Concord grapes
¼ cup lemon juice
¼ cup water
7 cups sugar
½ cup commercial liquid pectin

Wash and stem grapes. Crush grapes and add lemon juice and water. Cook, covered, over low heat 15 minutes. Drip grape mixture through jelly bag. Measure 4 cups juice. Combine grape juice and sugar. Cook over high heat until mixture boils. Add pectin, stirring constantly. Heat to boiling point. Cook 1 minute, stirring constantly. Remove from heat and skim. Pour into hot sterilized glasses. Cover with paraffin. Makes about 10 6-ounce glasses.

LEMON-MINT JELLY

¾ cup lemon juice
¾ cup water
½ cup mint leaves
Green food coloring
3 cups sugar
½ cup commercial liquid pectin

Combine lemon juice, water and mint leaves. Add enough food coloring to tint mixture a light green. Add sugar and mix well. Cook over high heat until mixture boils. Add pectin, stirring constantly. Heat to boiling point and cook 30 seconds, stirring constantly. Strain and pour into hot sterilized glasses. Cool thoroughly and cover with paraffin. Makes about 4 8-ounce glasses.

PINEAPPLE-ORANGE JELLY

1½ cups unsweetened pineapple juice
1½ cups orange juice
¼ cup grated orange rind
2 tablespoons grated lemon rind
6 cups sugar
1 cup commercial liquid pectin

Combine pineapple juice, orange juice, orange rind, lemon rind and sugar. Cook over high heat until mixture boils. Add pectin, stirring constantly. Heat to boiling point. Cook 1 minute, stirring constantly. Strain and pour into hot sterilized glasses. Cover with paraffin. Makes about 12 6-ounce glasses.

RHUBARB-RASPBERRY JELLY

1 pound rhubarb
2 quarts red raspberries
8 cups sugar
1 cup commercial liquid pectin

Grind rhubarb. Crush raspberries. Drip rhubarb and raspberries through jelly bag. Measure 3 ½ cups juice. Add sugar and mix well. Cook over high heat until mixture boils. Add pectin, stirring constantly. Heat to boiling point and cook 30 seconds, stirring constantly. Remove from heat and skim. Pour into hot sterilized glasses. Cover with paraffin. Makes about 9 8-ounce glasses.

BLACK RASPBERRY JELLY

3 quarts black raspberries
7 cups sugar
2 tablespoons lemon juice
1 cup commercial liquid pectin

Crush raspberries and drip through jelly bag. Measure 4 cups juice. Combine raspberry juice, sugar and lemon juice. Cook over high heat until mixture boils. Add pectin, stirring constantly. Remove from heat and skim. Pour into hot sterilized glasses. Cover with paraffin. Makes about 10 8-ounce glasses.

BUTTERS AND MARMALADES

TROPICAL MARMALADE

1 pineapple
1 grapefruit
2 limes
Water
Sugar
2 tablespoons grated orange rind

Pare and core pineapple and chop. Cut grapefruit and limes in fourths lengthwise. Slice very thin crosswise and remove seeds. Measure fruit including juice and add 1½ cups water for each cup fruit. Let stand several hours. Simmer, covered, over low heat about 2 hours or until tender. Measure and add an equal amount of sugar. Add orange rind. Cook over medium heat until mixture sheets when dropped from spoon. Pour into hot sterilized glasses and seal. Makes about 9 6-ounce glasses.

WATERMELON MARMALADE

4 cups water
4 cups thinly sliced watermelon rind, 1/8"
   thick and ¾" long
4½ cups sugar
¾ cup orange juice
Rind from 2 oranges, coarsely ground
1 cup raisins

Pour water over watermelon rind and soak 24 hours. Add sugar, orange juice, orange rind and raisins. Cook, stirring frequently, until syrup sheets from spoon. Pour into hot sterilized jars and seal. Makes about 2 pints.

COUNTRY-STYLE APPLE BUTTER

10 pounds apples
Cider
Sugar
1 tablespoon allspice
1 teaspoon nutmeg
1 tablespoon cloves

Pare, core and slice apples. Measure apples and add an equal amount of cider. Cook over low heat until tender. Press through sieve. For each cup of pulp, add ½ cup sugar. Add remaining ingredients and cook over low heat until thickened. Turn into hot sterilized jars and seal. Makes about 12 pints.

CARROT-RAISIN MARMALADE

3 oranges
4 cups water
1 cup coarsely grated carrots
¼ cup lemon juice
4 cups sugar
1 cup raisins

Peel oranges. Cut peel in very thin strips and cook in water until tender. Add carrots and boil 10 minutes. Cut oranges into very small pieces and add to carrot mixture. Add other ingredients. Boil, stirring frequently, until syrup sheets from spoon. Pour into hot sterilized jars and seal. Makes 2½ pints.

ORANGE MARMALADE

7 large oranges
Water
Sugar
1 tablespoon lime juice
2 tablespoons lemon juice
1 tablespoon grated lemon rind

Wash oranges and cut in fourths lengthwise. Slice very thin crosswise, remove seeds. Measure fruit including juice and add 1½ cups water for each cup fruit and let stand 24 hours. Simmer covered over low heat about 2 hours or until tender. Measure fruit; add 1 cup sugar for each cup fruit. Add lime juice, lemon juice and lemon rind; cook until mixture sheets when dropped from spoon. Pour into hot sterilized glasses and seal. Makes about 8 6-ounce glasses.

PEACH BUTTER

4 cups peach puree
½ cup lemon juice
1 tablespoon grated lemon rind
2 cups sugar

Combine all ingredients. Cook over low heat, stirring constantly, until sugar melts. Cook until mixture is thickened, stirring frequently. Pour into clean hot sterilized glasses. Cover with paraffin. Makes about 5 8-ounce glasses.

PRUNE BUTTER

Wash prunes and cook in a small amount of water until soft. Rub through a colander, then through a fine wire strainer. If pulp is quite juicy, boil until thick. Add 1 cup sugar for each 2 cups pulp. If a tart butter is desired, use less sugar. Cook slowly until butter is the desired thickness. Stir in cinnamon, allspice, and cloves to taste. Pour boiling hot butter into hot sterilized jars. Cover with paraffin.

RELISHES AND PICKLES

DUTCH PICKLED CHERRIES

5 quarts sour cherries
Vinegar
¼ cup grated lemon rind
Sugar

Remove pits from cherries, cover with vinegar and let stand 24 hours. Add lemon rind. Drain; put in layers in hot sterilized jars, sprinkling each layer with 2 teaspoons sugar. Seal. Makes about 6 quarts.

PICKLED CARROTS

1 cup vinegar
1 cup water
1 cup sugar
½ teaspoon salt
2 quarts hot diced cooked carrots

Boil vinegar, water, sugar and salt 2 minutes and pour over carrots. Let stand several hours. Seal in hot sterilized jars. Makes about 2 quarts.

CATSUP

2½ quarts (15 to 17 medium-sized) sliced tomatoes
1 cup chopped onions
3" piece stick cinnamon
1 large garlic clove, chopped
1 teaspoon whole cloves
1 cup cider vinegar
½ cup sugar
½ teaspoon ground ginger

1¼ teaspoons salt
1 teaspoon paprika
Dash cayenne pepper

Simmer together tomatoes and onion for 30 minutes; press through sieve. Put cinnamon, garlic and cloves loosely in clean, thin, white cloth; tie top tightly; add to vinegar and simmer 30 minutes. Remove spices. Boil tomatoes rapidly until ½ original volume. Stir frequently. Add vinegar, sugar, ginger, salt, paprika and cayenne pepper to tomato mixture. Boil rapidly, stirring constantly, about 10 minutes or until slightly thickened. Pour into hot sterilized jars and seal. Makes about 2 pints.

SPICED RED CABBAGE

4 quarts shredded red cabbage
½ cup salt
6 cups vinegar
1 cup sugar
1 cup chopped celery
½ teaspoon pepper
1 teaspoon mustard seed
½ teaspoon allspice
½ teaspoon nutmeg

Sprinkle cabbage with salt. Let stand overnight. Drain. Combine remaining ingredients. Boil 5 minutes and pour over cabbage. Turn into hot sterilized jars and seal. Makes about 4 quarts.

CHILI SAUCE

4 quarts peeled and chopped tomatoes
1¾ cups chopped sweet red pepper
2½ cups chopped onions
½ teaspoon Tabasco
1 tablespoon mustard seed
1 teaspoon whole cloves
1 teaspoon ginger
1 teaspoon nutmeg
2 3" pieces stick cinnamon
1 cup firmly packed brown sugar
3 cups vinegar
2 tablespoons salt

Combine tomatoes, sweet pepper, chopped onions and Tabasco. Add mustard seed, cloves, ginger, nutmeg and cinnamon. Boil slowly about 2 hours, stirring often. Add sugar, vinegar and salt. Cook, stirring constantly, 5 minutes or until desired thickness. Turn into hot sterilized jars. Seal. Makes about 3 quarts.

TOMATO-APPLE CHUTNEY

3 quarts (18 to 20 medium-sized) chopped tomatoes
3 quarts (12 to 15 medium-sized) chopped apples
1½ cups chopped green pepper
3 cups chopped onions
2 cups seedless raisins
4 teaspoons salt
4 cups firmly packed brown sugar
4 cups cider vinegar
½ cup preserved ginger
1/3 cup whole mixed pickle spices

Combine tomatoes, apples, green pepper, onions, raisins, salt, sugar, vinegar and ginger. Put spices loosely in clean, thin, white cloth; tie top tightly; add to tomato mixture. Bring to a boil; simmer 1½ hours; stir frequently. Remove spices. Pack chutney into hot sterilized jars and seal. Makes about 3 quarts.

CORN RELISH

15 medium-sized ears of corn
2½ cups diced sweet red peppers
2 cups diced green peppers
4 cups chopped celery
1 cup sliced onions
1 cup sugar
4 cups vinegar
2 tablespoons salt
2 teaspoons celery seed
2 tablespoons dry mustard
¼ cup all-purpose flour
½ cup water

Remove husks and silks from corn. Place in boiling water. Simmer 10 minutes. Drain; cut corn from cob. Combine red peppers, green peppers, celery, onions, sugar, vinegar, salt and celery seed. Boil 15 minutes. Mix mustard and flour; blend with water. Add with corn to pepper mixture. Stir and simmer 5 minutes. Turn into hot sterilized jars and seal. Makes about 7 pints.

CUCUMBER CRISPS

10 pounds medium-sized cucumbers
1 cup salt
2¼ quarts vinegar
½ cup lemon juice
3 cups sugar
1/3 cup mixed pickling spices

Wash and cut cucumbers into slices ¼ inch thick. Combine cucumbers and salt. Let stand several hours. Drain. Rinse in cold water. Combine vinegar, lemon juice, sugar and spices. Boil 1 minute. Add cucumbers and simmer 5 minutes. Turn into hot sterilized jars and seal. Makes about 12 pints.

TANGY CUCUMBER SAUCE

1 quart ground cucumbers
1 tablespoon salt
½ cup grated onions
1 cup vinegar
1 cup lemon juice
½ teaspoon black pepper
½ teaspoon cayenne
½ teaspoon ground cloves
½ teaspoon dry mustard
¼ cup brown sugar, firmly packed

Mix cucumbers and salt thoroughly. Let stand 30 minutes. Drain. Combine cucumbers and onions. Combine vinegar, lemon juice, spices and sugar. Heat to boiling point. Simmer 5 minutes. Add vegetables and remaining ingredients. Heat to boiling; simmer 5 minutes. Seal in hot sterilized jars. Makes about 3 pints.

SPICED CURRANTS

2 quarts currants
1 cup lemon juice
2 cups sugar
1 teaspoon allspice
¼ teaspoon cloves
½ teaspoon nutmeg

Stem and wash currants. Combine lemon juice, sugar and spices. Heat to boiling point. Cook over high heat about 5 minutes. Add currants and cook over low heat until thickened. Turn into hot sterilized jars and seal. Makes about 5 pints.

DUTCH RED EGGS

2½ cups small beets
¼ cup brown sugar, firmly packed
1 cup lemon juice
½ teaspoon salt
4 cloves
6 hard-cooked eggs

Cook beets until tender. Drain and peel. Combine sugar, lemon juice, salt and cloves; pour over beets and cook over low heat 10 minutes. Add eggs; chill. Makes 1½ pints.

CAPE COD KETCHUP

2½ pounds cranberries
Vinegar
2½ cups sugar
1 tablespoon cinnamon
1 teaspoon nutmeg
1¼ teaspoons ground cloves
¼ teaspoon powdered ginger
¼ teaspoon paprika

Wash cranberries; cover with vinegar. Heat to boiling point. Cook until berries are tender. Press through sieve. Add remaining ingredients. Cook over low heat until thickened. Turn into hot sterilized jars. Makes about 6 pints.

PICKLED PEACHES

8 pounds medium-sized peaches
2½ tablespoons whole cloves
8 2" pieces stick cinnamon
2 pounds sugar
1 quart cider vinegar
¼ cup grated lemon rind

Wash and pare peaches. Put cloves and cinnamon loosely in clean, thin, white cloth and tie top tightly. Cook together spices, sugar and vinegar 10 minutes. Add peaches and lemon rind; cook until tender. Let stand several hours. Remove spices. Drain syrup from peaches; boil syrup until thickened. Pack peaches in hot sterilized jars. Pour syrup over peaches. Seal. Makes about 6 pints.

RED AND GREEN RELISH

4½ cups finely chopped onions
2 cups finely chopped sweet red peppers
2 cups finely chopped green peppers
1 cup sugar
1 quart vinegar
1 tablespoon salt

Combine all ingredients and heat to boiling point. Cook until slightly thickened. Pour into hot sterilized jars and seal. Makes about 8 pints.

PICCALILLI

4 cups chopped green tomatoes
2 medium-sized sweet red peppers, chopped
2 medium-sized green peppers, chopped
3 large mild onions, chopped
1 small head cabbage, chopped
½ cup salt
3 cups vinegar
1 pound (2 cups firmly packed) brown sugar
2 tablespoons mixed pickle spices

Combine vegetables; mix with salt. Let stand overnight. Drain and press in clean, thin, white cloth to remove all liquid possible. Combine vinegar and sugar. Place spices loosely in thin, white cloth; tie top tightly. Add to vinegar mixture; bring to boil. Add vegetables and simmer about 30 minutes. Remove spice bag. Pack into hot sterilized jars and seal. Makes about 4 pints.

SPICED PRUNES

1 pound prunes, cooked
1 cup lemon juice
1 cup sugar
1 cup water
1 teaspoon nutmeg
1 teaspoon cinnamon

Combine prunes, lemon juice, sugar, water and spices. Heat to boiling point and cook 1 minute. Turn into hot sterilized jars and seal. Makes about 2 pints.

WATERMELON PICKLE

4 pounds prepared thick watermelon rind
Limewater made with 2 quarts of cold water and 1 tablespoon of lime (calcium oxide, purchased from drugstore)
2½ tablespoons whole allspice
1 tablespoon ginger root, chopped
2 tablespoons whole cloves
10 2" pieces stick cinnamon
1 quart cider vinegar
1 quart water
4 pounds sugar

Select thick rind from firm, not overripe melon. To prepare, trim off green skin and pink flesh. Weigh 4 pounds of remaining portion and cut in 1" pieces. Soak 1 hour in limewater. Drain, cover with fresh water, and cook 1½ hours, or until tender. Add more water as needed. Drain. Put spices loosely in a clean, thin, white cloth; tie top tightly. Bring to boiling spices, vinegar, 1 quart water and sugar. Add watermelon rind and simmer 2 hours. Remove spice bag. Pack rind in hot sterilized jars. Fill jars to top with hot syrup and seal. Makes about 6 pints.

RED PEAR RELISH

2½ cups chopped tomatoes
2½ cups diced pears
½ cup chopped green pepper
½ cup chopped onions
1 cup sugar
½ cup vinegar
1 teaspoon salt
½ teaspoon ginger
½ teaspoon dry mustard
¼ cup chopped canned pimiento

Combine tomatoes, pears, green pepper, onions, sugar, vinegar, salt, ginger and mustard. Cook over low heat 1 hour, stirring occasionally. Add pimiento. Turn into hot sterilized jars and seal. Makes about 2 pints.

SPICY PICKLED PEARS

7 pounds pears
3½ pounds (6¾ cups) sugar
4 cups vinegar
6 3" sticks cinnamon

Peel pears. Combine remaining ingredients; heat to boiling point. Add pears and cook, over low heat, until pears are tender. Remove pears. Continue cooking syrup until reduced ½ in volume. Pack pears into hot sterilized jars. Pour syrup over pears and seal. Makes about 9 pints.

TOMATO-PEPPER RELISH

2 quarts ripe tomatoes
1½ cups chopped onions
1 cup sugar
½ cup salt
2 green peppers, chopped
1 cup diced carrots
1 tablespoon prepared mustard
2 cups white vinegar
¼ cup horseradish

Peel tomatoes and chop; drain. Add remaining ingredients. Pour into hot sterilized jars and seal. Makes about 3 quarts.

RED TOMATO SPREAD

2 pounds tart apples, pared and sliced
5 pounds tomatoes, peeled and chopped
1 cup vinegar
6 cups sugar
1 teaspoon mace
1 teaspoon whole cloves
1 teaspoon nutmeg
½ teaspoon allspice

Combine apples, tomatoes, vinegar and sugar. Add spices. Simmer about 3½ hours, until thickened. Turn into hot sterilized jars and seal. Makes about 12 pints.

Index

Poultry, 57

Stuffings, 65

Meat, 68

Beef, 68

Fruit, 108

Salads, 112

Fruit Salads, 112

Gelatin and Frozen Salads, 112

Meat, Fish, and Cheese Salads, 114

Vegetable Salads, 115

Salad Dressings, 121

Uncooked, 121

Pie, 137

Cookies, 146

Rolled Cookies, 146

Drop Cookies, 148

Milton Keynes UK
Ingram Content Group UK Ltd.
UKHW050839220124
436466UK00013B/660

9 798869 031624